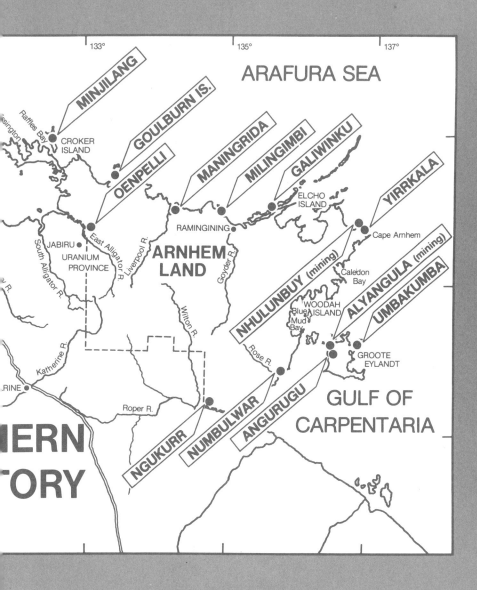

133° 135° 137°

ARAFURA SEA

MINJILANG

GOULBURN IS.

OENPELLI

MANINGRIDA

MILINGIMBI

GALIWINKU

YIRRKALA

NHULUNBUY (mining)

ALYANGULA (mining)

UMBAKUMBA

NGUKURR

NUMBULWAR

ANGURUGU

Raffles Bay

CROKER
ISLAND

ssington

ELCHO
ISLAND

RAMINGINING

Cape Arnhem

JABIRU

URANIUM
PROVINCE

ARNHEM
LAND

East Alligator R.

Liverpool R.

Goyder R.

South Alligator R.

Caledon
Bay

WOODAH
ISLAND

Blue
Mud
Bay

Witton R.

Rose R.

GROOTE
EYLANDT

Katherine R.

RINE

Roper R.

GULF OF
CARPENTARIA

ERN
TORY

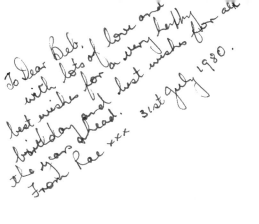

To Dear Bob,
with lots of love and
best wishes for a very healthy
birthday and best wishes for all
the years ahead.
From Rae xxx 31st July 1980.

The
ABORIGINES
of ARNHEM
LAND

The
ABORIGINES
of ARNHEM
LAND

Keith Cole

RIGBY

National Library of Australia
Cataloguing-in-Publication entry

Cole, Edmund Keith, 1919–
    The Aborigines of Arnhem Land.
    Index
    Bibliography
    ISBN 0 7270 1041 7
    1. Aborigines, Australian – Northern Territory –
    Arnhem Land. 1. Title.

301.451'991'094'29[5]

RIGBY LIMITED • ADELAIDE • SYDNEY
MELBOURNE • BRISBANE • PERTH
First published 1979
Copyright © 1979 Keith Cole
All rights reserved
Designed and typeset in Australia
Printed in Singapore by
Kyodo-Shing Loong Printing Industries Pte. Ltd.

Dedicated to the memory of
Reverend Lazarus Lamilami M.B.E.

Contents

List of Illustrations

ix

Preface

I have written this book to give the thoughtful reader a general overview of the Aborigines of remote Arnhem Land. It is not a specialised study of their history and anthropology. Such a work would need to be more detailed, more technical, and much longer, and would perhaps require a number of volumes. Instead I have tried to highlight some of the main issues in a fairly simple and straightforward way. I hope that this will enable average white Australians to learn something of the background, contemporary state, and hopes and aspirations of these black Australians, who have lived in this part of the country for more than twenty thousand years.

As the book is for the general reader, I have not used footnotes. However, to help those who may wish to study further some of the topics mentioned, I have included a select chapter bibliography as well as a general reading list.

The Arnhem Land Aborigines have helped generously in providing information for this book. I have tried wherever possible to let them speak for themselves by using direct quotations. I have sometimes identified the speakers. More frequently I have not identified them, in order to avoid embarrassment.

My late colleague and personal friend over a number of years, the Reverend Lazarus Lamilami, was of the greatest help. He generously gave me of his time, wisdom and insights into many aspects of the culture of his people. We spent many hours together in the recording studio at the College as he spoke of his own experiences and those of his people. His sudden death in Darwin Hospital on 21 September 1977 came as a great shock to us, and to his many friends throughout Australia. I count it a privilege to dedicate this book to his memory. Before his death Lazarus had written an outstanding autobiography called *Lamilami Speaks*. Professor Ronald Berndt of the Department of Anthropology, University of Western Australia, initiated and encouraged the preparation of this work. I had no need to quote from this book as Lazarus had given me much more material than I needed. He had also very kindly given me permission to quote anything he said.

The passing of Lazarus Lamilami has taken from us an Aboriginal who, more than almost anyone else, had the capacity for friendship and for bridging black and white cultures. He would often say, 'We must walk together, hand in hand'; and he practised what he preached.

I have tried to let non-Aborigines also speak for themselves, by using direct speech wherever possible. The similar technique of quoting from documents enables the reader to be involved in a more personal way. I have also given some personal anecdotes and experiences derived from more than ten years' association with Arnhem Land Aborigines. Further information can be found in the books I have written on the Roper River Mission (Ngukurr), Oenpelli and Groote Eylandt, and about some of the missionaries who have worked in these places.

I am grateful to the people who kindly read and commented on different chapters of manuscript. Such people include Mr Justice Forster, Senator Ted Robertson, Mr Laurie Kirkman S.M., Mr Tom Pauling S.M., Dr Soong, Dr Basil Sansom, Professor H.W.S. Philp, and Messrs Peter Spillett, Ian Pitman, Peter Carroll, Ted Milliken, Ray Wilkie, David Raff and Reg Bond. Members of the Northern Land Council were also helpful. They made some valuable suggestions, though I remain fully responsible for the thoughts expressed in the book.

I thank most sincerely my secretary, Mrs Joyce Gullick, for the many hours which she spent in typing and retyping the manuscript; and Merle, my wife, for the many suggestions she made, for the preparation of the index, and for reading the proofs.

Keith Cole
Nungalinya College, Darwin

1
This is our country

'This is our country', an Aboriginal of Arnhem Land said to me one day. 'We love our country. We do not want to live anywhere else. This is where our ancestors lived. We don't want to live in Darwin because there is much trouble there. We want to live in our own country.

'We don't live on our own land', he continued. 'We now live where missions started. But many of us are going back to our land. We want to build our own houses and live there. The Government has now given us back our land. We have different names for our own land but you Balanda call it Arnhem Land.'

Many Aborigines of Arnhem Land are saying words like these nowadays. They might not all say them the same way but they all mean much the same thing. They are feeling a sense of liberation and of freedom. They have fought for their land and they have won. There is a new spirit abroad in Arnhem Land.

Arnhem Land was left to Aborigines because white men thought that the region was economically useless. Pastoralists had tried to settle there during the late nineteenth and early twentieth centuries, but their attempts had proved to be abortive. They failed because they did not come to grips with the extreme climatic variations of the wet and the dry seasons. They were foiled by the persistence of the small, decimated Aboriginal groups, who were determined to preserve this last bit of their country in a last-ditch stand.

When the pastoralists moved out the missionaries moved in 'to smooth the pillow of a dying race'. They toiled with the most primitive facilities and under the most appalling conditions to bring Christianity and civilisation to these outcast people. Because

1

of mission care and that uncanny ability which had enabled them to maintain their existence in a harsh environment for thousands of years, the Aborigines did not die. They lived. They not only lived, but they began to multiply. They began their struggle to recover their land and their identity.

Arnhem Land was proclaimed an Aboriginal Reserve in 1931 in order to protect the Aborigines from the harmful effects of white 'civilisation'. They were able to live without outside interference. Nomadic family groups soon began to drift into mission compounds and to camp there. From time to time they visited the other Top End towns, where many of them dissipated themselves with the white man's vices. Aborigines now became a protected people, unable to look after themselves.

World War II brought Darwin and Arnhem Land into focus as Australia's northern gateway and Australia's front line of defence against the Japanese invaders. The existence of an outside world, and the challenge to aggressive white Australians by equally aggressive Asiatic people became a reality for the Arnhem Land Aborigines. They became hewers of wood and drawers of water for the armed services. They tracked and found missing allied airmen and captured Japanese air-crew. They were brought out of their protected seclusion into the wider experiences of technology and machines. They tasted a little of a new life-style and began to clamour for more.

The aftermath of World War II saw the emergence of the Third World of Africa and Asia. Non-whites in most countries of the world gained their independence. A new sentiment was abroad among the nations. Australian Aborigines and their treatment by colonial administrators and settlers came under international scrutiny. The aroused conscience of white Australians and Governments demanded positive action. Money began to pour into desperately poor Aboriginal missions. The age of welfare which was to last two decades had begun. The protected Aborigines became a dependent people, second-rate citizens relying on the handouts of white men.

Anthropologists, linguists, school teachers, social workers, medical specialists, dietitians and dentists now joined with bureaucrats, missionaries, builders, mechanics and clerks in the hurly-burly race for the souls and bodies of Aboriginal people, and perhaps for a career and prestige for themselves. Almost all of these welfare agents were motivated by a policy of assimilation. 'Make the Aborigines the same as us, and we will have no racial problem in this lucky country of white Australia', was what they said. 'We formerly came to grips with the "yellow peril" outside Australia by the White Australia policy. Now we will solve the racial question within our own country by absorbing the small black minority in the large white majority. We will then have one race, with one culture and one civilisation.' This was another kind of white Australia policy, more insidious than the first.

To the chagrin of white Australians, black Australians refused to become 'like one of us'. They accepted and demanded many of the benefits of white civilisation in the form of limited education, housing, medical facilities, and training allowances. But they were Aborigines and they were determined to stay Aborigines. They wore white man's clothing, travelled in his aeroplanes, and bought his broken-down motor cars. They had transistors and ate food bought from the store and supermarket. But they still wanted to keep their kinship system, even though this increasingly came under threat. They continued to sing the age-old totem songs of their ancestors, who gave them their land and the food which, in earlier days, they had derived from it. They became a people 'hanging in the middle way', between the old and the new.

In the 1970s a new way forward for Aboriginal advancement is being sought through Government, and church policies of 'self-determination' and 'self-management'. Aborigines themselves are being encouraged to determine the nature and pace of their own development within the legal, social and economic restraints of Australian society. The granting of land rights, bilingual education and Aboriginal administration of their own communities by incorporated town councils are parts of this new policy. Aborigines are also being assisted to return to their homelands, their ancestral country. This decentralising move is helping to remove the frustrations and tensions which Aborigines experience in having to live with disparate neighbours in artificial communities which grew up during the welfare era of the 1950s and 1960s.

Only time will tell whether these new policies of self-determination and self-management will remove from the Aborigines the sense of inferiority and dependence on welfare handouts, and make them independent and self-reliant. Only after some years have passed will it be possible to see whether they have recovered a true sense of dignity, taking their rightful place, in their own way, with their culture, in the wider life of Australia. But there are indications that they are being successful.

Granting of freehold title in perpetuity to Aboriginal communities in Arnhem Land in 1976 is basic to self-determination and integration.

3

In former years Aborigines derived their food from the land. They were one with nature. Their singing or dreaming spoke of the way in which their totem ancestors, part human and part some other phenomenon of nature, came to their country, providing them with food and water, and establishing their people there. Their dancing enacted the exploits of these great culture heroes. The land was part of their soul.

When Arnhem Land Aborigines were shot and poisoned by the pastoralists in white man's inexorable march in search of new pastures in the early days, they retaliated with spears in their desperate bid to save their lives and keep their land. In the early years of white intrusion, their feeble, inarticulate cry was, 'Give us back our land, for if you take away our land, you take away our soul'. Only the dramatic tropical variations of climate and the rugged, impenetrable mountain ranges saved them and saved for them Arnhem Land, their land.

In the dependent years of the welfare era the Aborigines became wards of the Government. They were told that the land on which they had lived for thousands of years did not belong to them but to the Government. 'The land does not belong to the Aborigines but the Aborigines belong to the land', Judge Blackburn said. This time a stronger, but despairing cry of this troubled people went up, 'Give us back our land'.

A new threat to the land came with the discovery of rich deposits of manganese, bauxite, uranium and other minerals in Arnhem Land and the establishment of two large mining towns in this once despised country. Prospectors bucketted in four-wheel drive vehicles throughout the length and breadth of their country. Huge bulldozers ripped the heart out of the sacred sites. Most of the country came under some form of prospector's or mining lease. Now their cry went up with increased vigour and with a new belligerent tone, 'Give us back our land'. Only then were they given title to the land, the land on which they had lived since the Dreamtime.

Much has to be done in implementing the new Land Rights Act. Problems relating to delineation of areas, ownership, the form of title, entry permits, and the use of waters adjoining Aboriginal land still have to be worked out. The constitutional validity of assigning large areas of the country to one specific group of Australians is open to legal challenge. Many white people are talking of discrimination favouring Aborigines, and of the establishment of an apartheid situation. Yet despite all these things Aborigines have been given back their land. They hold legal title to it communally and in perpetuity. The threat of land alienation has gone. Within the tensions of a multi-racial society and in the face of growing opposition in other parts of the nation, they now have the responsibility for the care and development of Arnhem Land. As they constantly say with pride and deep feeling, 'This is our country'.

2
Arnhem Land
is a beautiful place

Arnhem Land is a very beautiful place. It enchants the visitor
and captivates the residents. The western escarpment has a timeless and unspoiled grandeur. The rolling sand-dunes of the eastern
coast have a solitary splendour. The inland forests are like an
evergreen heart. The serpentine rivers teem with fish. The swamplands are the home of myriads of water birds. Rocky outcrops are
the haunt of rare and timid animals. Long, white, sandy beaches
gleam in the tropical sun. Arnhem Land is a northern paradise.

Arnhem Land fills the eastern half of the broad peninsula of
the Northern Territory between the Gulf of Carpentaria in the east
and the Joseph Bonaparte Gulf in the west. The Arafura Sea laps
the northern coast, while the stately Roper River forms the southern
boundary. The Gulf of Carpentaria lies to the east, and the Alligator
Rivers form its western boundaries.

The east-west distance from Cape Arnhem to the East Alligator
River is about 350 km, and north-south from Elcho Island to the
Roper River is 300 km. The whole area, including the offshore
islands, is 95 828 square kilometres.

Part of the fascination of Arnhem Land lies in its inaccessibility.
The swampy coastal plains and the rugged interior plateau provide
natural barriers. The two major roads are on the perimeter and
do not penetrate the interior. The new Arnhem Highway to the
'uranium province' gives easy access to Oenpelli in western Arnhem
Land during the dry season. The new highway to the Roper Bar
Police Station in southern Arnhem Land enables speedy travel to
Ngukurr, the former Roper River Mission. But even these roads
are impassable during the wet season. Air travel, therefore, is the

only reliable means of access to these remote and isolated communities.

Aborigines formerly went walkabout throughout Arnhem Land on foot. Nowadays, they go walkabout only by vehicle and by air, and their age-old custom of walking has almost vanished. Not infrequently they travel to corroborees in chartered aircraft or by vehicle. On arrival they remove their Western-style clothes, paint themselves with ochre, and perform their ancient singing and dancing. After the ceremonies they bathe, don their Western clothes, and ride or fly away in their vehicles or aeroplanes, to resume their Western-type jobs.

Arnhem Land takes its name from the Dutch vessel, *Arnhem,* which had been exploring the western side of Cape York Peninsula with the *Pera* in 1623. These two ships had been sent by the Governor of Amboina to explore 'Nova Guinea', following the 1605 and 1606 explorations of Willem Jansz in the *Duyfken*. In April 1623, the *Arnhem* under the command of Willem Joosten van Colster deserted the *Pera* in the Gulf of Carpentaria, and made her way back to the Netherlands East Indies. During his return journey Colster discovered the north-eastern coast of Arnhem Land, which he originally named Speutsland after the governor who had sent them out. The whole area was subsequently renamed Arnhem Land in honour of the *Arnhem*, which, in turn, had been named after the large town in Holland.

The climate of Arnhem Land is tropical as the region is situated between 12° and 15° South. There are two distinct seasons, the Wet and the Dry. The Wet extends from December to March and the Dry from May to October. April and November are the transitional months. In April the 'knock-em-down' rains flatten the tall spear grass, marking the end of the Wet. November is the build-up for the Wet, when the hot, sticky, humid conditions make life distinctly unpleasant. This month is called the 'suicide month', with very good reason.

During the Wet, the warm, moist, north-west monsoon comes rolling in from over the Timor Sea. The accompanying monsoonal trough and the organised convection system produce thunderstorms and heavy rain. This is the time of the tropical cyclones similar to, though not normally as violent as, Cyclone Tracy, which devastated Darwin on Christmas Eve 1974. Such cyclones spawn over warm tropical waters and move into coastal areas of the Northern Territory or skirt the Territory coast and move away down the West Australian coast. They bring high winds and intensive rain over the whole of Arnhem Land, often causing damage to the coastal communities.

7

In earlier years Aborigines sought refuge in the higher ground of the plateau during the Wet, living in caves, which they adorned with numerous paintings.

During the Dry, the cool, dry, south-east winds blow from the centre of the continent, bringing fine, pleasant, sunny days. Hardly any rain falls during these months, and the region experiences very dry conditions towards the end of the six months' season. Water evaporation during this time is high, rising from an estimated mean of 100 mm in February to 260 mm in October. The dry season enabled Aborigines to go 'walkabout' with ease, to engage in hunting and food gathering in their traditional areas, and to participate in corroborees.

The difference in rainfall between the wet and dry seasons is most marked. In the Arnhem Land communities, an average of 836 mm falls between December and March, while only 23 mm falls in the Dry between May and October. The north coastal region facing the Arafura Sea has an annual average of 1232 mm in contrast to 729 mm at Roper River on the southern boundary.

Arnhem Land sustains high temperatures throughout the year. The mean maximum temperatures of the main centres range from 30.4°C on the north coast to 34.2°C in the south at Roper River. The other inland centre of Oenpelli has the high reading of 33.9°C. The mean minimum temperature ranges from 19.7°C on Groote Eylandt in the south-east in the Gulf of Carpentaria, to 24.0°C on Croker and Goulburn Islands in the north-west. Because the low temperature range is high, Aborigines formerly wore no clothing. Today Aborigines and Europeans normally wear only the bare essentials.

The Aborigines of Arnhem Land adapted themselves to their environment in a remarkable way. They hunted, fished and gathered food in different places, depending on the two seasons of the year. They maintained themselves as small nomadic family groups, in direct contrast to the pastoral and agricultural enterprises undertaken by the white man in the nineteenth and twentieth centuries which ended disastrously. The Aborigines learned to come to terms with their environment in a way which white men so far have failed to do.

The plains and plateaux of Arnhem Land have a unique beauty and fascination. The plains consist of the lowlands, the flood plains and the tidal flats. The massive Spencer Ranges in the west and the Mitchell and Parsons Ranges in the east form the backbone of the area. The north-eastern coast is marked by sand-dunes formed by the constant south-easterly winds of the Dry and by hills and low ranges coming right down to the sea. The hills and plateaux of the entire region have a comparatively low elevation, ranging from 50 to 250 m.

Geologists call the massive sandstone outcrop of the Arnhem Land plateau the 'Kombolgie formation'. This vast area is criss-crossed with deep gorges, while the surfaces are usually bare. Shallow sandy soils in the crevices frequently support heathlike shrubs and spinifex. Sandstone woodland and tall open forest occur in the deeper, wider valleys.

The plateau escarpment provides a rugged splendour of great scenic beauty. Viewed from the grassy, lowland plains, this vast rock mass stretches out as far as the eye can see. The colours of the sandstone, gleaming through the sparse, green vegetation, vary throughout the day from light brown in the mornings to rich orange and gold in the late afternoons. Numerous crevices, gorges, caves, bluffs, massive boulders and columns of rock etched by wind and rain into geometrical patterns are clearly visible. During the Wet countless streams tumble through narrow gorges and box canyons, and come cascading over rocky scarps with a thundering roar. Most of these streams in the plateau cease flowing in the Dry, and become series of rock pools with sandy beaches.

The presence of water, the shelter afforded by numerous caves and the relative abundance of food nearby provided, until recent times, an attractive environment for Aborigines, especially during the wet season. As a result a large number of caves, particularly those in western Arnhem Land, contain Aboriginal stone implements, bones, and galleries of cave paintings. Many of these have been investigated by archaeologists and anthropologists and the paintings photographed.

The lowland areas consist of undulating plains with areas of rocky hills and alluviated drainage lines along the main streams and rivers. Occasional isolated hillocks, frequently capped with laterite, stand out in bold relief. Two such sandstone pillars on the north-western Arnhem Land plains, Tor Rock and Nimbuwah, are like silent sentinels standing watch over the surrounding undulating plains. It is not surprising that Aborigines of the area not only use these two striking rock-formations as identification markers, but also tell numerous totemic stories associated with them.

The soils of the lowland areas vary from shallow to deep, sandy to clay, and stony to gravelly. Consequently the vegetation is variable, from eucalypt woodlands and open forest stands, to savannah grasslands, scrub and estuarine sedges. Parts of these

9

lowlands, in the west around Oenpelli, in the north-east by the old Florida station on the Goyder, and in the south-east about Ngukurr on the Roper, are suitable for cattle-raising and beef-production.

The floodplains of Arnhem Land are large sections of the northern and eastern coastal areas which are inundated with fresh water during the Wet. During these months the whole area becomes one vast, waterlogged mass, with only the tops of tall trees and the fragmentary outline of mangrove-fringed rivers faintly visible. These conditions make overland travel impossible, and are hazardous for horses and cattle.

The complete change in the appearance of the countryside when waterlogged, and the absence of accustomed landmarks, some-times make visible navigation of light aircraft difficult during the driving rains of the north-west monsoon. On several occasions the pilot has said somewhat ruefully to me as we have been heaving and lurching in the plane, weaving our way through corridors of the huge cumulus clouds as they come rolling in from the Timor Sea, 'I'm afraid we are lost for the time being'. We always eventually discovered where we were, but only after considerable difficulty and the easing of the storms.

The soils of the flood-plains are mostly impermeable clays, and the vegetation is varied. Plains which are flooded up to nine months of the year have an herbaceous swamp vegetation, and those flooded for only six months are broad sedgelands. Some permanently wet areas carry stands of paperbark with bracing roots systems, and permanent lagoons are often fringed with tall pandanus and fresh-water mangroves.

Buffaloes, imported from Timor in the early nineteenth century, flourish in the flood-plains, grazing and severely damaging the herbaceous swamps and grasslands. Many species of aquatic birds congregate in huge numbers in the swamp areas, and are an important tourist attraction. One such place is the swampland of the Marrakai Plains near the Adelaide River on the Arnhem Highway, only eighty kilometres from Darwin. Here visitors can see all kinds of aquatic birds, and herds of buffalo grazing on the wide plains.

The north coast of Arnhem Land lapped by the Arafura Sea is subjected to tidal flooding. During the Wet the rivers disgorge tons of grey mud kilometres out into the sea, which stand out in marked contrast to the surrounding green of the shallow waters of the region. Long sections of mangrove vegetation occur on the coastal and riverine fringe with samphire and sedge communities on the slightly higher flats. Stunted non-eucalypt woodland grows on the sand-dunes. The saltwater mangrove is important for the marine ecosystem.

Arnhem Land's tropical rainfall during the summer wet season causes a large number of streams and rivers to flow across the lowland plains from the central plateaux. During the winter months the streams drain into marshes or become a string of billabongs and water-holes. The larger rivers, having numerous tributaries in the heart of the ranges, continue to flow all the year round. Rivers such as the East Alligator, Liverpool, Blyth, Goyder, Rose and Roper are tidal for many kilometres upstream, and can be used by shallow-draught boats. In the early days supplies were brought up the East Alligator River for Oenpelli, which is completely isolated during the Wet. During the construction of the Overland Telegraph Line in 1871 and 1872, materials and stores were brought about 150 kilometres up the Roper River to Leichhardt's Crossing at Roper Bar.

The flora of Arnhem Land is extraordinary diverse, even though this may not be apparent at first sight. A visitor may gain the impression that nothing grows except monotonous forests of tall, slender, stringybark trees, forming a canopy over smaller shrubs and grasses. This is not so, for a wide variety of trees and plants grows in the area. Moreover, the immediate and incorrect conclusion that this kind of bush could not maintain human life does injustice to the ability of Arnhem Land Aborigines to obtain a great deal of food, 'bush tucker' as they call it, from the land.

It is certainly a fact that large areas of Arnhem Land are covered by open forests which are dominated by stringybarks, and woollybuts. The stringybarks grow to a height of about twenty metres, and have straight, slender trunks from 20 cm to 45 cm thick. The woollybuts are characterised by rough bark from the base up to about three metres, giving a woolly appearance at the lower part of the trunk.

The open forest understorey varies considerably depending on the type of soil. Where soils are sandy some stands of cypress pine occur. Timber from these trees is white-ant resistant, and was used extensively for building by early missionaries. Other smaller trees include the billy-goat plum, bloodwood, box, the fan or sand palm, with its slender trunk and fan leaves, and the tree-fern-like cycad, whose female plants grow fruits called 'burrawong' on the stems just below the fronds, and whose male grows an orange, oval cone, 12 cm to 20 cm long. After a fire has swept through the bush, the cycad sends out brilliant green leaves which stand in striking contrast to the charred fern-like trunk and the surrounding blackened understorey. Different species of acacia or wattles with their characteristic sweet-smelling yellow flowers are often present, together with annual grasses such as the waving golden spear grass and several sorghum species.

Open forests give way to woodlands which are characterised by a wider variety of shorter trees. Here many different eucalypts occur, including bloodwoods and boxes. The understorey is similar to that of the tall open forest, but with more grass. These woodlands usually occur on sloping portions of the lowland. In sandstone areas different eucalypts occur with lower trees such as *Owenia xanthostemon* and *Erythrophloeum*.

Where soils are shallower, the medium-height smooth white-bark and the scaly reddish-grey bark gums are dominant, with understoreys of *Xanthostemon*, a small tree growing to a height of seven metres with yellow flowers in dense heads, and *Calytrix* or turkey bush, a striking shrub with pink, star-like flowers. Different types of grevillea with their pleasant sprays of golden, pink, red and mauve spidery flowers frequently occur.

Two types of pandanus palm are found throughout the region. *Pandanus basedowii* usually occurs in crevices and bases of sandstone rocks, growing three to five metres high with prop roots clawing the base of the tree to the rocks; and *Pandanus spiralis*, the screw palm, growing to a height of about ten metres, without prop roots and with a spirally marked trunk, occurs frequently on seepage slopes, margins of drainage channels, banks of small watercourses and the edges of coastal plains.

The shallow soils and sand among the cracks and crevices of the rugged sandstone hills and plateau afford suitable habitats for only the most sclerophyllous vegetation. Large tussocks of the grass dominate the sparse region. Hard-leafed grevillea, certain species of acacia, and *Solanum* occur. Where sands are deeper, *Calytrix*, *Pentalostigma*, hibiscus and acacia are present. On even deeper sands stunted trees are found growing within the interstices of the rocks, including the stately Kentia palm. In similar places several species of gardenia with their sweetly-scented flowers occur, together with sand palms, and the yellow-flowering *Cochlospermum*, a species of small fig tree.

The black soil coastal plains near the estuaries of the major rivers flood during the Wet and become waterlogged for several months. Here tall forests of paperbarks grow to a height of up to fifteen metres. These paperbarks are sometimes characterised by arched root stems, the bark being used by Aborigines for many different purposes. Several species of grass grow thickly on the plains when they dry out. Water-lilies and many kinds of sedges are common in and bordering the lagoons. Pandanus palms and the small freshwater mangrove tree also occur around the edges of these flood plains and along small freshwater streams.

Savannah and grassland occur on flats in lowland areas and parts of the flood plain which are flooded for only short periods. These are mixed areas with patches of low trees and grassland. Eucalypts and non-eucalypts are common and perennial grasses are prominent.

Mangrove forests occur along tidal rivers and in patches along the sea coasts. Stands of the small hibiscus are sometimes associated with the higher areas of mangrove forests. Large, spreading she-oaks or casuarinas are frequently found on sand-dunes and beach fronts together with spinifex grass.

Rain forests occur in different parts of Arnhem Land. They range in height from five to fifteen metres and occur in coastal areas or in broken terrain on the sandstone plateau. Many of the trees have yet to be named, but the deciduous kapok tree is sometimes present.

The flora of Arnhem Land is therefore very varied, and many of the fruits, nuts, and roots were eaten by Aborigines, and many of the trees, barks, leaves and flowers were used for a large number of purposes. Nothing is more enchanting than to go walkabout through these tall forests, or open woodlands and savannahs, smell the bush, hear the birds, see the animals and become aware how close you are to nature. Miriads of insects, however, make camping out at night-time uncomfortable if the camper is not well prepared with nets and insect-repellents.

The extensive and varied vegetation supports a wide variety of interesting and rare wildlife. The open forests and woodland abound with many kinds of fauna whose species are fairly widespread and well known. The swamplands, rain forests, mangroves and sandstone escarpments have an outstanding number of birds. The swamplands are of importance for frogs and reptiles. The escarpments have special importance for all groups of animals and contain some rare species. Arnhem Land is a naturalist's paradise.

Kangaroos are always a delight to watch either grazing, or eating leaves with their front paws, or bounding off through the bush. Those found in Arnhem Land include the antilopine kangaroo or wallaroo, the euro, the black wallaroo and species of rock wallaby. These intriguing animals are herbivorous. They have greatly enlarged hind feet and powerful tails which enable them to move with characteristic hopping motion at fairly high speeds.

Wallaroo have a rich red colour, with white on the chest and inside the arms. They are not to be confused with the great red kangaroos of Central Australia. They are found in open forests and billabongs throughout Arnhem Land.

The Alligator River euro is found in the rocky habitats of the Alligator Rivers and is less common than the wallaroo. It is a shy animal and well adapted to its arid environment. The euro is often associated with the northern black wallaroo. This handsome, rusty-black hill kangaroo is quite common on the steep slopes of the escarpments and ranges of western Arnhem Land.

The agile wallaby needs little introduction to dwellers in the Top End. It shelters in the daytime in fringes of rain and paperbark forests, large pandanus clumps and riverbank vegetation, and emerges at dusk to graze in woodlands and the open coastal plains. Its Roman nose, black-tipped ears, sandy coat with pale hip-stripe and cheek-stripe make it easily distinguishable.

Rock wallabies of different species are found in sandstone country on the mainland and also on Groote Eylandt. They are small, delicate animals, emerging from crevices and caves at dusk and feeding on nearby shrubs and grasses. Like other members of the kangaroo family, wallabies are highly prized for food by Aborigines, and are still eaten by them when they have been hunted.

Other animals occurring fairly commonly in Arnhem Land include the echidna or spiny ant-eater, various species of marsupial mice, the northern native cat, the northern short-nosed bandicoot, several species of possum and the sugar glider. A number of different kinds of bats and flying foxes are common in various open localities as well as caves on the escarpments. All these animals were, and still are, food for Aborigines. In earlier days these animals were an essential part of their diet; nowadays they are hunted and eaten to supplement food from the store.

Animals which have been introduced to Arnhem Land are the dingo, which is found in all habitats; the feral or wild cat, which, fortunately for bird-life, is fairly rare; the feral horse, again not common; feral pigs, which are quite numerous and found in areas associated with flood plains; feral cattle, which roam in small groups in various places, including eastern Arnhem Land, and are the legacy of earlier pastoral enterprises; feral buffalo, which were introduced for the early settlements on the Coburg Peninsula. The buffalo like the wild pigs are very numerous in most areas, but are found in the greatest concentrations on the flood plains. They cause great destruction to the vegetation and moist communities such as rain forests, and paperbark forests by their grazing, trampling and wallowing.

The dugong or sea-cow is still highly prized by the Aborigines and hunted by them in the estuaries and coasts of Arnhem Land. These aquatic mammals are from 2.5 to 3 metres long and weigh from 300 to 350 kg. They have the appearance of a small whale, and their meat is not unlike beef, although more fatty and salty.

The large green turtle and the pitted-shelled or pig-nosed turtle are also highly prized by Aborigines. The green turtle is found in all Arnhem Land waters and grows to a weight of about 380 kg. They lay up to 200 eggs in seven layings at about fortnightly intervals on beaches, and these are greatly sought after by Aborigines. Turtle shells are used extensively by non-Aborigines.

Estuarine or salt-water crocodiles are very numerous in the rivers and on the Arnhem Land coasts. They grow to a length of eight metres and are extremely dangerous to men and animals. They were so numerous when seen for the first time by the explorer P.P. King in 1818 that he erroneously named the three main rivers of western Arnhem Land, the West, South and East Alligator Rivers. The smaller freshwater or Johnston's crocodile grows to a length of about three metres, and is found in many freshwater streams, billabongs and lagoons. It is very timid, feeds on frogs, fish and insects, and is not harmful to man.

Other reptiles occurring in Arnhem Land and sought after by Aborigines include various kinds of goannas and lizards. A wide range of geckoes exist, including the house gecko, whose barking sound at night time as it catches small insects on the walls and ceilings of houses is a delight. The large number of snakes which are found in Arnhem Land include carpet snakes, black-headed, water and olive pythons, water and tree snakes, the death (or deaf) adder, the northern coral snake, the whip snake, the king brown and the taipan.

The bird-life of Arnhem Land is varied and magnificent. Sea birds include the large white-breasted, grey sea-eagle, frigate birds, brown, red-footed and masked boobies, tropic-birds, noddies, ospreys, silver gulls and terns. Birds of the sea-shore or its environs include the brahminy kite, the pied and sooty oyster-catcher, various kinds of dotterels, sandpipers, godwits, stints, tattlers and plovers. On the mangrove fringes of rivers the chestnut rail, black-tailed and brown whistlers, broad-billed flycatchers, yellow silver eye, mangrove heron, little kingfisher, large billed warblers are common. The oriental cuckoo is an Asian migrant in summer months.

The swamplands are the main refuge for incredibly large numbers of magpie (pied) and pigmy geese, and many species of pelicans, cormorants, herons, egrets, ibis, spoonbills, ducks, and teals. Numbers of darter, black bittern and jabiru stork are to be seen. Other swampland birds include the mangrove heron, water, sea and wading birds. The swamplands are important watering grounds for migratory Asiatic waders. Fortunately areas inside and adjoining the Arnhem Land Reserve are being proclaimed wild-life sanctuaries.

The coastal plains are the habitats for kites, hawks, buzzards, quail, pigeons, brolga and scrub fowl. On the plains and in woodlands, galahs, cuckoos, cuckoo-shrikes, the pheasant coucal, red-tailed and sulphur-crested cockatoos, corellas, lorikeets, owls, nightjars, the tawny frogmouth, the blue-winged kookaburra, with its unfinished laugh, bee-eaters, doves, babblers, warblers, larks, wrens, flycatchers, fantails, honey-eaters, whistlers, robins, finches, orioles, bower birds, butcher birds and spangled drongo are all to be seen. Migratory birds such as whimbrels and pratincoles from Asia arrive and depart seasonally.

Other birds found in plains or in woodlands are the emu, whistling kite, brown goshawk, collared sparrowhawk, little eagle and wedge-tailed eagle, black, peregrine, little and grey falcon and the kestrel.

The sandstone rain forest birds include the black-banded pigeon, white-lined honey eater and the sandstone friar-bird. In other rain forests the crested hawk, scrub fowl, little shrike-thrush, yellow fig-bird, little kingfisher, black butcher bird and the brilliantly plumaged rainbow pitta occur.

A very large number and extremely wide variety of insects are found in Arnhem Land. That many of these insect fauna are of the biting, stinging and blood-sucking kind is soon very evident to any traveller camping in the region. Human nocturnal activity is severely limited, for flies and sandfly bites can make life miserable for even the most enthusiastic naturalist.

Insects have an important role in the total ecology of the area because of the part they play in the various food chains, recycling processes and in the overall ecological network. Many species are dependent on the continued existence of the larger water-holes, permanently moist forest areas and permanent spring-fed streams. Should these be changed or modified dramatically, then the whole environment could be affected. An important feature of former Aboriginal life-style was that it in no way upset the balance of nature.

Thousands of species of insects such as dragonflies, moths, butterflies, flies, blowflies, beetles, wasps, grasshoppers, mantis, ticks, mites, midges, ants and many others have been classified, and yet more have still to be named. Three kinds of native bee are found and their honey is highly prized as a food by Aborigines, who call it 'sugar bag'. The bees usually nest in tree holes. Walkabout on foot with Aborigines is held up when they see a hole in a live or dead tree. They climb the tree or cut it down to obtain this coveted prize. The thin honey varies in flavour with the surrounding bush flowers.

Termites, commonly called white ants, are well represented in Arnhem Land. They live in colonies numbering several million, and build mounds which are dotted throughout the whole of the forest and woodland areas. Many of these mounds are up to five metres in height and their colour and texture reflect the undersoil, which has been brought to the surface by these incredible insects. The narrow magnetic or medianal termite mounds probably face north-south to minimise the direct sun, rather than for the supposed reason of facing the magnetic north.

Termites are a hazard to buildings, shrubs and trees, and agricultural projects. A number of early missionary buildings in Arnhem Land quickly disintegrated when not constructed of cypress pine. Early attempts at gardening often failed because plant roots were eaten by white ants. Many books and records were destroyed almost overnight when these insects were given the chance.

Over seventy species of blood-sucking insects have been listed, including the anopheles mosquito, which is a potential malaria vector or carrier. Malaria was common in Darwin and in the Roper River area in early days. Modern techniques of spraying and draining have eliminated this scourge. Mosquitoes (and there are still millions of them) are of nuisance value only.

Many kinds of tropical fish abound in the seas and inlets of the Arnhem Land coast. The various species include barracuda, tuna, mackerel, queenfish, marlin and sailfish. Nowadays Aborigines troll for these fish in aluminium boats with outboard motors, whereas formerly they caught them by spearing from dug-out canoes. One of the joys of living and working the Top End is to go out with Aborigines, trolling for large fish. Cord handlines are normally used, as nylon lines would slice the hands to pieces. Even with cord lines I have frequently had to grab a leather glove or wind cloth or canvas around my hands to land fighting fish that frequently come shooting out of the water to a height of about three metres when hooked.

17

Other sea fish and salt-water fish caught off reefs and beaches include batfish, bream, catfish, cod, coral trout, flathead, golden snapper, grunters, herring, javelin, jewfish, mangrove jack, moon-fish, mullet, pike, red emperor, salmon, sweet lip, swordfish, threadfin, trevally, trumpeter and whiting. Sharks of different kinds are common, and horrible to watch thrashing around in shallow water, catching and eating cornered fish. Rays, eels, crabs, cray-fish, prawns, jellyfish, including the deadly sea wasp, bêche-de-mer (trepang), shells, molluscs and other aquatic life associated with coral, reefs and beaches abound.

Estuarine fish such as the succulent silver barramundi or giant perch are to be found in great numbers in both salt and freshwater. Freshwater aquatic fauna have to contend with the change in the quality of water between the wet and the dry seasons. During the Wet, surface waters flow quicker and do not have such a high proportion of dissolved solids. In the Dry the rivers change drama-tically from rapid flowing to gently flowing and still water. Lagoons, billabongs and rivers team with numerous freshwater fishes in-cluding perch, of which family the silver barramundi is a member, bass, bream, catfish, grunter, herring, long tom, mullet and a large number of smaller species of aquarium type.

Almost all Arnhem Land Aboriginal men formerly fished in the rivers, streams, billabongs and coastal waters with their barbed fish spears. All aquatic life formed an important part of their diet. Even today, when they purchase most of their food from the local store, they try to supplement their diet with fish foods. Fishing by both men and women, either from high-powered boats, or from the beach or rocks, would be the most-used form of hunting which has survived from the early days.

This then, was the world of the Aborigines of tropical Arnhem Land. They knew almost every boulder and every tree in their traditional homeland. They had a profound knowledge of the animals, the insects, the birds and the fish. They knew the times and the seasons when the trees and shrubs would blossom and seed, when marine life would migrate, and where animals were to be found. The night sky had a particular fascination for them. Life in nature was at one with their life. From nature they derived their whole being, both material and spiritual. The land was their life in this beautiful part of the Top End.

3
We came from the North

The Reverend Lazarus Lamilami, a respected Maung elder, said that his people have a story of how Aborigines became black. 'This is what I used to hear from my great-grandfather, that is, my mother's father's father when he and his sister were alive. He used to tell me how we became black. He said to me, "You see the sun up here. It rises in the east and sets in the west." And he said, "We are in the centre of this place. That is our country, and we have the sun right up here (overhead). That is why we are black. The people over there in the west where the sun is not hot are white. The people in the east where it is not too hot for them are white. But we are black."'

Lamilami also told how his great-grandfather said that they had come originally from the north. 'We people were not here (in Australia) all the time. Our great-great-great-great and so on grandfathers, our ancestors, have never been here at the first. I used to hear this from way far back. We came from the north outside Australia. We don't know where we came from. It might have been Manggadjara, that is, the place of the Macassans. It might have been Manggadjara or it might have been Yandu, India.'

Lamilami added, 'I really think that we came from Yandu or something like that and our people travelled down from there. We said this before any white man came. Other old men in other parts of Arnhem Land thought that way. That we came from Manggadjara or we might have come down from Yandu.'

This view is shared by most anthropologists. They say that the Australian Aborigines probably originated in Asia. Their ancestors were probably Kolarians and Dravidians, the aboriginal inhabitants

19

of India, and Veddahs of Ceylon. These early people are usually called the Indian Australoids. Fossil remains from Solo and Wadjak in Java have a possible link with early skeletal remains of Australian Aborigines which also supports this view. Links with the Ainu, the aborigines of Japan, appear to be more tenuous.

The ancestors of Australian Aborigines probably migrated southwards over land bridges through South China, the Philippines, Borneo, Celebes and New Guinea and then to north western Australia, Arnhem Land, and Cape York Peninsula. If they came during late Pleistocene times, that is, before the 12000 - 10000 BC, then ocean levels would have been lower, and more land bridges would have been in existence than at present. The land bridges, however, did not link Australia with Timor, so they would have had to come through New Guinea.

Anthropologists also differ about the number of migrations to Australia which the Indian Australoids made. Some maintain that there was only one major migration and that consequently Aborigines of mainland Australia are of one basic stock. The Tasmanian Aborigines were of a different stock, because they were small in stature, dark in colour and had curly or woolly hair.

Other anthropologists say that two successive waves of people came to Australia during the late Ice Age. The first wave known as the 'Murrayians' migrated as far as Tasmania. The Murrayians in turn were invaded by the 'Carpentarians', who confined them to the south-east in the region of the Murray. There were also the 'Barrineans' in North Queensland, which they say have negrito affinities. These theories are necessarily highly conjectural.

Available contemporary evidence favours the view that the Aborigines of the mainland are homogenous and that the Tasmanoids are of different stock.

Opinions also differ regarding the date of arrival of Aborigines in Australia. The more popular view dates their migration during the Pleistocene Era. This view is supported by radiocarbon dating of artefacts found at Keilor in Victoria c30000 BC; Malangangerr near Oenpelli in Arnhem Land c21000 BC; and Nawamoyn also near Oenpelli, c19500 BC. Radiocarbon dating, however, is not infallible. Also no skeletal remains have been found to support this very early dating.

An alternative view places the date of their arrival after the Ice Age. Exponents of this view claim that Keilor and Talgai skulls cannot be dated conclusively earlier than about 9000 BC. Their culture pattern also fits better into the Mesolithic or post-glacial age. If this is so, then they must have come great distances.

Whatever the actual date of their arrival, there seems little doubt that Australian Aborigines originated in Asia. Most probably they entered Australia through north-western Australia, Arnhem Land or Cape York Peninsula, bringing with them the dingo. They then spread eastwards, southwards through the centre and down the south-west. They may have continued to migrate to Tasmania, although present evidence supports the view that the Tasmanian Aborigines originated from Melanesians who drifted there.

Although prehistorians differ regarding their date and place of origin they agree, almost without exception, that Australian Aborigines are true members of the race, Homo sapiens. They are not primitive or sub-human, but are true representatives of modern man. They possess all the characteristics and capabilities of contemporary humans.

Aboriginal archaeology focuses attention on Arnhem Land. Following her investigation of rock shelters near Oenpelli in Western Arnhem Land, Dr Carmel White concluded that Aborigines used hafted edge-ground axes at the Malangangerr and Nawamoyn caves between 21000 — 19500 BC. If her theories are correct, then these people would have been in the area 19000 years before the Kakadu (Gagadju), who are known to have been there with a similar culture for the last 3000 years. The Arnhemlanders would then have almost the longest known ancestry of all Australian Aborigines.

Arnhem Land Aborigines have very pleasant physical character-istics and attractive personalities. The young women have dark flowing hair, white teeth, gentle brown eyes and well formed figures. They were highly sought after in the early settlement days by itinerant Asiatics and white men, who greatly coveted what they called 'black velvet'. The young men are lithe, slender-hipped and quick moving. Their brown bodies glisten and shine in the sun when they bathe. The volatile faces of both men and women shine with pleasure or become black in quick, sullen anger. The middle aged become more stolid. The women move around slowly with many offspring of their own and those of their children. The older men and women have a quiet dignity and great wisdom. To be invited to sit on their rough blanket in the shade of a tree and to talk with them is a great privilege.

The men vary in height much as do European men, the range being between 152 and 190 cm. The women are from 7.5 to 10 cm shorter. Young men and women are usually of slender build, having long heads, and faces, narrow shoulders, slim trunks, thin legs and arms, and long, thin hands and feet.

Their skin varies in colour from dark brown bordering on black to light brown. Newly-born babies are a pinkish yellow all over, which gradually becomes brown during their first few weeks. The black skin pigmentation does not penetrate the dense skin of the hands and the soles of the feet. Albinos — those lacking skin pigmentation — are occasionally seen.

Arnhemlanders have dark brown to black hair, sometimes with tawny or reddish streaks in it. The hair is usually of a fairly fine texture, straight, wavy or curly, but with no appearance of being woolly or frizzy like that of Bantu peoples of Africa. Baldness is uncommon, but their hair usually changes to grey and white from about forty-five years of age. In former days men usually cut off their wives' hair, which they plaited into belts. Many men grow beards, which formerly were often shaped like those of the Macassans.

They usually do not have very hairy bodies. Primary hair on the trunks and limbs is not as thick as that on Europeans. Secondary hair under the armpits and pubic hair is present, and like primary hair, is from medium-brown to black in colour.

Almost all Arnhem Land Aborigines have soft brown eyes with fine, long and deeply curled eyelashes. Their eyes are usually fairly deep set beneath heavy eyebrow ridges and retreating foreheads. In former days they were noted for their excellent teeth. Unfortunately changed diet of damper and tea, and a large intake of sugar including lollies, have played havoc with their teeth. Many comparatively young people now have lost many, if not all, of their teeth. Unlike their counterparts in Central Australia, Arnhemlanders tend to have fairly thin lips, high cheek bones and broad noses and fairly large jaws.

Women have smaller bodies than men, but in much the same proportion. They have smoother body contours and wider hips. Their firm, pear-shaped breasts in adolescence usually become slack and pendulous in later life because of frequent pregnancies and suckling children for two or three years each. Young children tend to be pot-bellied and have a distinct lumbar curve, which usually straightens as the child gets older.

Well-fed indolence of the present welfare age, food foraging in the community's supermarket instead of in the bush, sitting under the trees instead of walking and hunting, and a radically different diet have all contributed to a change in the physical well-being of the Aborigines of Arnhem Land. Walking is limited to a short trip to the community's hospital for free hand-outs of medicine. Formerly lithe, wiry, muscular men and women are becoming prematurely obese with attendant physical disabilities.

The blood groupings of Aborigines throughout Australia are generally A and O, which are also the normal groupings of Europeans. Group B, which is characteristic of Asians, is sometimes present, but is found almost exclusively in Arnhem Land and Cape York Peninsula. This strain is thought to be due to Macassan (Indonesian) visitors in the west and New Guineans and Melanesian influences in the east. The Rh-negative group has not been found among Aborigines. Thus Aboriginal blood is almost identical with European blood, although some divergences in white cell formations have been found among Aborigines.

Formerly the average reading of blood pressures of Arnhem Land Aborigines was very much lower than that of Europeans of the same age in the same environment. Today, their more sedentary life-style, different diet, high consumption of alcohol, work pressures, community and racial tensions have increased their overall blood pressure. It is still lower on average than that of the white man.

Girls tend to become pregnant while still young. In former days, girls were promised to older men at birth. They often would be brought to the husband's camp when five or six years of age and grow up there. They might be taken by the man at puberty or before and have children at a very early age. In general Aboriginal women had less trouble in childbirth in the bush because of their advanced muscular development. Nowadays, babies are born in mission or community hospitals, or in Darwin if the mother has complications.

Modern scientific investigation does not substantiate the frequent claim that the sense of sight, hearing and smell of Aborigines surpass those of other races. The astonishing abilities to track and observe, to hear woodland and animal sounds, and to identify different smells derive from skills which were aquired over many years of basic training in hunting and food gathering and of walking through the bush. These skills are fast disappearing with changing life-styles, and visual and aural weaknesses through disease are becoming apparent.

In mental ability Arnhem Land Aborigines seem comparable with any other race. The usual variations of brain size exist, (though the size of the brain has been demonstrated to be no guide to intellectual capacity). Intelligence testing over a period of time with better understanding of environmental circumstances suggests the same basic variations as among any other young people. In other words Aborigines intellectually are neither inferior nor superior to any other race.

Generally speaking Aborigines were and are temperamentally different from white Australians. They are less conscious of time; they set less value on ownership of things; among themselves they are co-operative rather than competitive; they have a high regard for old people; they strive for anonymity; they understood concrete terms rather than abstract concepts. Many of these traits are changing through continued contacts with white culture. Compulsive time-observance accompanies Western work patterns. Money earned and goods purchased are now not shared so readily. Sport and opportunities for individual achievement tend to break down co-operative effort and personal anonymity. Educated young people frequently despise the non-educated elders. Yet despite these tendencies, an unpredictable ambivalence between old and new ways is adopted by many Aborigines today.

In general, then, Aboriginal man of Arnhem Land has his own specific physiological and psychological characteristics. But as a person he is no different from other human beings. His former life-style was determined by the world around him. He had the outstanding ability to exist in the face of a harsh and hostile environment. His social organisation, religion and art were the produce of living that way. But as a man he was and is no different from anyone else.

Aborigines of Arnhem Land, however, were different from other Australian Aborigines because they had a more intensive contact with the outside world. They stood at the frontiers of their country's shores. Maritime visitors may have visited them over the centuries. Stories and songs from bygone days speak of the brown-skinned Bajini or Baiini, who came from western lands. Who they were and where they came from is not known. The Chinese probably did. Annual visits for at least two hundred years by the Macassans from Sulawesi in modern Indonesia are well known, and their influence was considerable.

Anthropologists estimate that about 300 000 Aborigines were living in Australia when white settlement commenced in 1788. They think that there were then approximately 500 tribes, each consisting of about 600 persons. Tribal territories seem to have been more populous in the well-watered coastal areas. Many of those tribes have now died out as a result of killing by white settlers, or from disease or intermarriage. The Aboriginal population was decreasing so rapidly at the beginning of the twentieth century, that missions looked on their work as helping them to die out with dignity.

The complete destruction of Aborigines was halted through the efforts of missions and then later by governments, under a rigid policy of protection. As a result the population is not decreasing but increasing. There are now 6680 Arnhemlanders whereas in the 1930s it was estimated that there were fewer than 4000. In 1977 a quarter of the Territory's population of 102000 were Aborigines. (See Table 1.)

Arnhem Land tribes are made up of family groups and clans. The family groups hunted and foraged for food within the strict confines of their own country. The boundaries of their country were landmarks such as rocks, waterholes, trees and other physical features. These were given to them by their ancestral totemic heroes, whose journeys have been remembered down the centuries by ritual and song.

The family band or bands formed the clan. Clans were linked by language, marriages, ceremonies and ritual exchanges. Except in eastern Arnhem Land, groups of clans could be termed tribes, which had a basic language structure with a variety of dialects.

The Aborigines of eastern Arnhem Land are often referred to as the Murngin or Wulamba. Lamilami, who came from western Arnhem Land said, 'We call all the eastern Arnhem Land people Malarrk. These are the people who practise circumcision. That is the meaning of the word because they have been circumcised. They call us Daulingu, that means uncircumcised'. The various Aboriginal groups in eastern Arnhem Land are differentiated by language and kinship rather than by tribes.

During the welfare era the former nomadic clans settled on missions and settlements. The eleven communities which have come into existence are quite artificial. Each community has an average population of 600, with representatives of eight to ten tribes or clans. The number of clans is greater in the larger communities. This great diversity of small, different groups often makes local co-operation and joint effort difficult. The divergence between the clans has always been a great source of friction. During the past few years clans and tribes have been encouraged to move back to their own country and set up their homeland communities.

Lamilami spoke of the difficulty regarding marriage across moiety and language divisions. 'When a Maung marries an Iwadja girl, we could hear each other's language but she would speak Iwadja. The children would hear two languages, but the first language they must learn is the father's language, not the mother's language. Take the example of my children. They all learned my language and can all speak Maung. But my wife is completely different. She is Marrgu and comes from Croker Island. I don't

25

even understand what she is saying, but she speaks my language. And my children don't understand Marrgu, but they speak my language. Most of the time she speaks Iwadja and that's how the children can speak Iwadja.

'This is so all around. They can learn their mother's language but their main language is the language of their father. My father was a Maung but my mother was a Walang, and I never knew Walang until I grew up to be a man. Then I started to pick up words. But when I was a boy I just learned Maung and spoke to my mother in Maung.'

Aboriginal languages in Australia bear no known affinity to any other world languages. This is probably due to the isolation of Aborigines from other peoples for thousands of years. A great diversity, moreover, exists within Aboriginal languages themselves. This is due to the large variety of tribes and groups which became established over the very wide geographical area of Australia over a long period of time. Despite this great diversity, however, the languages are part of one family and have a common ancestry.

Over eighty languages and dialects are spoken in Arnhem Land. Of these the main ones are Gunwinjgu, spoken in western Arnhem Land at Oenpelli and its environs; Nunggubuyu spoken at Numbulwar in south-eastern Arnhem Land; Anindilyaugwa used at Groote Eylandt; and Gupapuynu Djinang and Djimba spoken by the Murngic people of north-eastern Arnhem Land.

The absence of an Aboriginal lingua franca for the whole area where so many languages are used is unfortunate. For this reason basic English is the normal language of communication. While the knowledge and use of English has obvious advantages for Aborigines, it has severe limitations when used by a large number of them. So often Aborigines and non-Aborigines have thought that they have been understanding each other when they have not.

Fortunately, an increasing number of non-Aborigines are starting to learn several of the more widely-used languages. But even then more than a knowledge of the language is required. Paralinguistic features such as the tone of the voice, facial expression, body posture and the experiences which the speaker and listener have previously shared are vital for meaningful interpersonal communication.

An understanding of Aboriginal social behaviour is also necessary for full comprehension. For example, often Aborigines consider 'thank you' to be superfluous if the non-Aboriginal has agreed to provide the service or whatever. It is not discourteous for him not to express what he may feel in this way. He sometimes will not explain why he is late or has not kept an appointment. He assumes that you understand that he would be there under normal circumstances, and does not have to explain his absence. He often becomes embarrassed or evasive when questions are too direct or are considered by him to be improper. These are but a few of many examples which indicate the complexity of meaningful communications between Aborigines and non-Aborigines.

Aboriginal Australians have been here for thousands of years. During that time their special physical characteristics have formed and they have developed their distinctive language and life-styles. During the past two centuries dominant, aggressive white culture has placed them under great threat. They almost died out. But they now remain and will increasingly have an important role to play in the country which formerly belonged to them.

4
Living and loving

The Aborigines of Arnhem Land hunted, gathered and foraged for their food. They had no flocks or herds. They did not plant crops or harvest grain. The natural world around them supplied all that they needed. It is not surprising, then, that they speared for food the cattle introduced by the pastoralists. They were amazed to see white men cultivate crops, when their cultural heroes from time immemorial had provided their food from the bush and from the sea. As they often say, 'Our ancestors gave us our food'.

The Aborigines were totally dependent on the world around them, and so they had a special relationship to that world. They saw themselves as one with nature. Their ancestral totems linked them with nature and with each other. The totem heroes had natural as well as human attributes, and joined nature to them and them to nature. A close relationship with the natural world formed the basis of their religious beliefs and practice.

Though dependent on nature, Aborigines did not disturb its delicate balance. Regular burning of the grass and woodlands during the Dry encouraged new and vigorous growth in the Wet. Their walkabout from place to place ensured the conservation of natural resources. Different foods gathered at different times of the year did not adversely exploit nature. Frequently lily stems were replaced when the roots were removed so that they could continue to grow. Grasses and yams were occasionally planted. The firestick and the digging-stick did not harm the environment, for how otherwise could their users have survived for so many thousands of years?

Availability of food depended on a seasonal cycle. As different foods grew and ripened at different times of the year, so the Aborigines moved from place to place. When food was exhausted in one place they would move on to another. They were nomads of the northland, hunting and gathering different foods in different places as it was available. They would move only within the limits of their own 'country' unless food was scarce. If they had to hunt in the territory of another group, then they would ask that group's permission to do so. Sometimes other groups or clans would invite them to come and share with them when food in their country was plentiful.

Hunting and food gathering occupied much of the Aborigines' time. Life was not easy. They could only keep a few kinds of food, and then only for a day or two. Each new day required its quota of food. At the same time they were not rushed. They were not under pressure. The food was there but they continually had to go and get it.

Coastal Aborigines usually camped on the beach during the dry season. Each family built its own rough bark shelter or wind-break. Here they cooked, ate, talked and slept. Sometimes during the heat of the middle of the day they sat around or slept under nearby trees. The common, if incongruous, sight of itinerant Aborigines sitting or camping under trees in Darwin and other towns reflects these age-old habits.

Aborigines living inland during the Dry made shelters of branches and bark, each shelter being a few metres from the next. Families would camp by their own shelters. Where mosquitoes were bad they would sometimes build elevated platforms, about two metres from the ground. A smoky fire, tended by the women on the ground, would keep the mosquitoes away from the men sleeping above. When food became scarce or the camp became dirty, they would move off to another place.

Everyone moved to higher ground during the Wet, when the plains were awash. Some lived in caves. Others built long, low, bark huts and lived there. They would hunt and gather food near these refuges. During the dreary hours of rainy days they would cover the walls and roofs of caves and bark huts with sketches, drawings and designs. Modern bark paintings originated this way, although body painting was an additional influence. While some rock paintings were of little significance, others painted in sacred places were of great religious importance.

Women were the main food-gatherers. Their food-gathering in the bush was more predictable than the hunting activities of the men. The women spent long hours collecting a wide variety of wild fruits, nuts and grasses, diving and wading for lily roots, or digging for yams and other edible roots. They also caught small animals, crabs and fish, and were in constant search for 'sugar bag' or wild honey, eggs and birds.

The women used a variety of implements and containers when hunting. They had hardwood digging-sticks, sticks to kill animals or knock down fruit, wooden and paperbark containers and string and pandanus-leaf baskets. They were assisted in their work by dogs, which were invariably part of their life. The women now use billy-cans, tins, calico bags, plastic containers, nylon fishing lines, metal hooks and metal digging rods when they go looking for 'bush tucker'. (This usually takes place at weekends.)

A typical day in the life of Aboriginal women before the coming of the white man was probably something like this. They would get up when it was light and forage around the fire for the remains of the kangaroo meat or yams left from the night before. About an hour or so later they would set off at a leisurely pace with the children and dogs to a prearranged place. While walking they would be on the lookout for wild honey, fruits or berries, or any small animals.

At their selected place they would make a fire and have a rest. Depending on their numbers and the time of year, some would then dig for yams while others dived for lily roots. Sometimes they would walk along the edges of the streams or beach catching crabs and small fish. From time to time throughout the morning they would return to the fire, sit down and eat part of what they had gathered. At noon they would probably lie down with their children and sleep.

During the afternoon they would collect more food, which they would carry in their dilly bags or on pieces of paperbark. Then they would set off for the camp, where they would gather wood and make a fire. If they had seeds, they would grind them into flour and make a small damper. They would start cooking the yams and smaller animals in the ashes, as they awaited the return of the men from their hunting.

The men were the hunters of large animals and the fishermen. They supplemented the staple vegetable foods gathered by the women and the children. They would not give up easily, even if they were unable to catch anything for hours. I have sometimes seen men become more and more anxious as the day wore on and they had caught only a few fish. Their concern was not hunger, as they had plenty of other food. It may have been pride or fear of the taunts of their wives and kinswomen if they returned home with little but the story of 'the one who got away'. Their concern probably sprang from the deeply ingrained urge of the hunter to persevere until he is successful.

The men hunted for kangaroos, wallabies, emus, possums, goannas and snakes. They caught these by spearing, by clubbing or by ingenious snares and traps. Spears were usually thrown by means of woomeras or spear throwers. Boomerangs were used only in the open country in south-eastern Arnhem Land. Nowadays the hunting of smaller animals is usually accompanied by yelling and shouting and plenty of laughter and fun.

For fishing in rivers and the open sea, the men used long-rafts and paperbark canoes. They quickly changed over to dugout canoes when these were introduced by the Macassans. Some Arnhemlanders went back with them to Macassar to learn how to make them. The men had fishing spears with three to five ironwood prongs, and ironwood harpoons for catching turtle and dugong. Metal prongs and harpoons were used later. They also used fishing nets, fishing lines with bone hooks, and pandanus harpoon ropes.

Lamilami said that when men went out hunting in western Arnhem Land 'they carried their spears and woomeras, stone axes, shells or their stone flints which they used as knives. They had different kinds of hunting spears with heads carved from ironwood. They also had several kinds of fishing spears. These had three, four or five ironwood prongs. The wooden prongs were changed to metal when the Macassans came.'

As far as can be determined, a typical day in the life of an Arnhem Land Aboriginal man followed this pattern. After picking through the remains of the previous evening meal for a scratch breakfast, they would set off with their hunting or fishing implements. They would look out for wild honey, nuts and fruit as they went through the bush. They then fished by billabongs, streams and rivers, off rocks, or in the open sea from canoes. If they caught a turtle or dugong they would usually immediately take it back to camp and make preparations for cooking it. Sometimes they would cook it on the beach, summoning their families later. Similarly when the men caught a kangaroo or wallaby, they would return immediately with it to the camp to cook it. Different members of the family had their appointed pieces of meat or fish. The evenings would be spent in eating, singing and dancing, often to the accompaniment of the didjeridu.

Both men and women acquired extraordinary skills in tracking and hunting. They could, and still can, immediately identify the tracks of birds, animals and humans. They are quick to observe the faintest signs of birds or animals in broken twigs, disturbed stones or faint indentations in the ground.

I remember on one occasion wanting some crabs for bait. A sixteen-year old girl was deputed to find them for me. After looking intently at the sand, she would point and say, 'There.' Sure enough, after scooping up some sand, a crab would emerge. As it made its sideways scramble to the sea, she arrested its movements by skilfully throwing a handful of sand onto it. She then leisurely caught the crab and popped it into a plastic bag which she pulled from her bosom. I had my bait in no time! Yet, try as I could, I was unable to see anything on the surface of the sand which indicated the presence of a crab beneath.

I was recently on the beach at Croker Island looking for somebody. My enquiry from an old man as to his whereabouts elicited a lot of information as to where he was and what he had been carrying from a quick glance at his almost indistinguishable footprints. Aborigines in one community know the footprints of all others living there. They have footprint rather than fingerprint identification!

The men spent much of their time making tools and weapons, fishing gear and ceremonial objects from stone, wood, bark and fibres. Hafted stone axes were quite efficient, before being superseded by steel products. They fixed flint and hardwood heads to their spears and hunting implements until these were superseded by iron from the Macassans. The shovel-nosed spears used in fighting were deadly weapons.

Both men and women cleverly made rope and string from rubbed hibiscus or pandanus strips. The men used the rope for their harpoons and the women wove baskets and dilly bags from the string. They shaped wooden coolamons for carrying babies and food. Paperbark was a handy wrapper and used for a variety of purposes. Stringybark was basic for the construction of canoes and shelters.

Contrary to the popular belief that the small, black, stingless bee is the only one of its species in Arnhem Land, Lamilami speaks of three. He said, 'There are three different kinds of bees. A large white and yellow one bites and gives a sting. This was a natural one and was there before the white man came. There was another smaller one which is more or less white. Then there are the little black ones. The little black and white ones do not bite you. To get the honey they would cut down the tree with their stone axes, or else they would climb up and cut a hole where the bees had their hives. They would usually eat the honey there. Sometimes they put it into a basket made out of cabbage palm and that was the main thing in which to carry food or even water.'

Sometimes honey placed in the basket was later mixed with water and drunk as a beverage. At no time was it allowed to ferment. Aborigines had no form of alcohol or intoxicating liquor before the coming of the Macassans. The bees' wax was placed into a basket and was often used when making implements.

Speaking of non-vegetable foods Lazarus said, 'We ate all different kinds of birds and animals and fish. We could not eat some fish because they were poisonous. We did not eat frogs. Some of the fish we ate were trevally, parrot fish, white and red snappers, rock cod, groper, mackerel, and kingfish. We ate little sharks, not big ones. In eastern Arnhem Land they eat the big sharks. We ate dugong, turtles, stingrays and eels. We only ate small sawfish; the big ones tasted a bit different. I know most people throughout Arnhem Land ate these things.'

The use of fire and how to make it was of great importance for Aborigines. Lamilami said, 'We kept our fires going all the time if we stayed in one place. If we were travelling or going out hunting we would have to carry fire. Either we would take two sticks which we rubbed together to get fire or we had one stick about a foot long from a certain tree. We would break the point off put it in the fire and light it up. We could carry this for days and with our hands as it burnt very slowly. We also had special sticks to make fire with. We would hold one on the ground with our foot and rub the other with our hands. We had no trouble making fire this way.'

Arnhem Land Aborigines smoked a kind of tobacco. They made this by rubbing leaves of a special bush in their hands, and smoking them in a shell or crab claw. The Macassans introduced them to the tobacco as we know it today.

The normal diet of the traditional Arnhem Land Aboriginal was therefore well-balanced with the 'bush tucker' of the women and the fish and game provided by the men. This food was readily available even though people had constantly to go out and get it. Few ever went hungry. There were no known cases of malnutrition. Cannibalism was occasionally practised, but for ritual rather than for dietary reasons. Aborigines quickly abandoned their traditional hunting and food gathering when Europeans introduced them to flour, sugar, tea, tobacco and alcohol. These new foods became their staple diet. The resulting deteriorating health and widespread malnutrition led the authorities to provide communal feeding during the 1950s and 1960s.

Most Arnhem Land Aborigines today have large amounts of money to spend from their award wages and social security cheques. They can choose what foods and other goods they want from the community stores or large supermarkets. The choice is theirs, so educational programs are essential. Tinned meat and processed foods are readily available and are very popular. So are the takeaway foodshops in Darwin for the itinerants. Most of the cooking is still done on the open fire outside their houses or humpies, so stewed or barbecued meat is often the main meal. They supplement these foods with 'bush tucker' obtained from weekend walkabouts and fishing. Existing dietary problems and protein malnutrition are still evident because of the misuse of money on alcohol and gambling.

In former days Aborigines exchanged gifts and had a simple form of trade. They sometimes gave gifts to relatives who helped build a big item, such as a canoe. A complex system of exchanging gifts took place in connection with marriage, before and after the girl went to the family of her husband. Sometimes gifts were given and exchanged in settlement of some grievance, to prevent blood feuds. More formal trade and gift exchange was connected with ceremonies. On these occasions goods brought from different places such as spears, bailer shells, baskets, stone implements and ochre were traded. Trade of this nature was widespread throughout Australia.

The physical environment and the basic economy of the Arnhem Land Aborigines determined their social structure and organisation. They were nomads, hunting and gathering food on their land. The basic unit was the family group, consisting of the man, his wives and children, and sometimes several old men and women. Sometimes there were additional relatives. Groups of families formed clans, all of whom could trace a common ancestry. Each clan had its own totemic ancestors who gave them their land. A clan or group of clans formed a tribe, speaking a common language and occupying a recognised area of country. The tribe was a territorial and linguistic unit, of less political and economic importance than the clans.

The moiety system was and is also a feature of Aboriginal social organisation. A moiety means a half. The moieties are the two natural parts of each tribe or clan, and are basic to marriage and kinship. Once a person is born into a moiety he or she is there forever. A person must marry into the opposite moiety, the man and woman thus becoming one. Thus casual liaisons or even marriage with non-Aborigines pose serious problems.

The two moieties in north-eastern Arnhem Land are called dua and yiritdja. Elsewhere they are just called Moiety 1 and Moiety 2, as on Groote Eylandt. In western Arnhem Land there is a complex moiety-phratry system. All nature also falls into the two moiety divisions, so that everything has its rightful place and is complete in the universe.

An example of the relatively uncomplicated kinship system is seen among the Warnindilyaugwa, the tribe at present occupying Groote Eylandt. Moiety 1 consists of four clans, the Wurrawilya, Jaragba, Wurragwaugwa and the Bara-Wurrabadalamba. Moiety 2 also has four clans: the Mamarika and Amagula (classed as one), the Bara Bara, the Wurramara, and the Wurramarrba. Each of the eight clans has smaller family groups, some large and some small. Totem stories indicate that the clans came originally from the mainland, and settled on Bickerton Island and Groote Eylandt. They all now live on Groote, and are loosely joined together with the linguistic tribal name of the Warnindilyaugwa.

Kinship is therefore an integral part of the social organisation of the Arnhem Land Aborigines and controls the relationship of individuals with each other. Everyone ultimately has to be related. The relationship has to be ascertained so that one person can determine his behaviour towards any other person. If you know what to call a person, then you know how to behave towards that person.

On one occasion an old man from Mornington Island was staying at our College. The other students came from Arnhem Land or from Centralia. The old man, with the help of the younger men and a large blackboard, spent several hours working out who the others were and where they fitted in to the overall social organisation of Aboriginal people. The genealogical intricacies which were shared were as fascinating as they were complex. In the end he was able to establish who the others were, where they fitted in, how he should address them, and whom he should avoid. Normal relationships were then established to the satisfaction of all.

In western Arnhem Land the Gunwinjgu and the Maung have a moiety-phratry organisation. No moiety name is used among the Maung, but the two phratries have two divisions. Each phratry is not a unit as on Groote Eylandt. Its members come together only at ceremonial times. But its members call each other by the usual kinship names.

Ideally a Gunwinjgu man should marry his mother's brother's daughter's son's daughter, or his mother's brother's daughter's daughter's daughter, or his mother's mother's brother's daughter's daughter. But there are also many variations of these, and divergences between the tribes in Arnhem Land. The endless variations and combinations seem tedious and irrelevant to the non-Aboriginal. For the Aboriginal they are fundamental. No one working among Aboriginal people can begin to understand them unless he has a clear understanding of their kinship system, and is then able to appreciate how everyone relates to everyone else.

Tribes in western Arnhem Land are matrilineal, that is they trace their descent through their mothers. In eastern Arnhem Land land owning groups are patrilineal, membership in the clan deriving from the father.

In north-eastern Arnhem Land the major units are the *mala* or clans, and the *mada*, a linguistic unit in addition to the two moieties. Every person by birth belongs to a specific *mada-mala* combination. As in western Arnhem Land, Aborigines in this area are exogamous, that is they must marry someone of the opposite moiety outside the clan.

Because of the kinship system, relationships between people are expressed in broad terms. These are not confusing to anyone except the non-Aboriginal. Father's brothers are called fathers, mother's brothers are called uncles, father's sisters are called aunties and mother's sisters are called mothers. These classificatory titles bind the whole group into a composite whole.

Marriage has been, and still is, the basic institution among the Aborigines of Arnhem Land. A few possibilities among many of possible combinations for marriage have been mentioned. Marriage is a group matter, and in former times babies were discussed and swapped even before birth. Every girl was expected to marry, and girls needed the place in society which marriage gives to them.

Anthropologists differ regarding Aboriginal understanding of the cause of pregnancy. Some insist that Aborigines understood that this resulted from intercourse. Others say that their informants state that pregnancy is the result of the entry of the totem spirit into the womb of the woman. It seems that many Aborigines held to both views. They understood to some extent the results of physical union. This is more than evident in the love songs and great myths of the past. At the same time they held that their totem spirit entered the woman so that the child was truly a child of the totem.

Some men say that they have been out fishing, and they have been aware of a special feeling of happiness. They say that feeling is so strong that they are convinced that the ancestral spirit is entering the womb of their wife. Others say that they have a special dream and later tell their wife, 'The spirit is now in you'. Some women state that when they realise that they are pregnant the place where they realised it assumes a totemic value, at least for them.

A pregnant woman had to observe certain taboos, especially regarding food. In north-eastern Arnhem Land the father also had to observe certain sexual taboos until the child was born, thus heightening his desire for the child, and for the mother. Pregnant women also often wore charms to guard against evil spirits.

Aboriginal women normally had less difficulty in child-bearing than their non-Aboriginal counterparts. This was due to their well-toned muscles from hunting and food gathering. Complications often occurred with the first child, however, especially as the mother was usually very young. Deformed children and one of each pair of twins were usually killed. Nowadays most Aboriginal women are encouraged to have their babies in hospital or with the help of nursing sisters or trained midwives. The homeland move ment sometimes makes this difficult, although the Aerial Medical Service usually flies out any with complications. Aboriginal infant mortality rates are now scrutinised by international bodies. The situation today is so different from the plaintive cry of the little mite born not many decades ago, under a pandanus tree, with no one to help the mother, and few to care if it lived or died.

A baby was always born into the company of the members of the wider family. His own mother or his other 'mothers' would breast-feed him. He would be fondled and petted by sisters and aunts and grandparents. He would rarely be alone, becoming totally dependent on the wider group for his material and psychological support. He was not just 'one of the family'. He was part of the larger family who were always with him. They in turn were part of the wider family of the totem ancestor.

The dependence of children on others is a continuing problem for Aborigines living at boarding schools away from their families, unless they have some of their relatives with them. The situation is always difficult, even when married families live away from home together for a period of time. Some cope. Others become extremely homesick and depressed. They still need the support of the wider group.

Aboriginal children were pampered as they grew up, and were rarely disciplined by European standards. Mothers and fathers were not expected to correct them. That was the responsibility of the uncles. Thus parents have been very permissive, and children in their early years have rarely been controlled. Following initiation, however, the boy's life became regulated by the one placed in charge of him, and he increasingly came under group pressure. Aboriginal customs have made western-type education of teenagers very difficult. In many cases it just breaks down. Conversely the breakdown of the older social norms, especially relating to discipline, has had a devastating effect on young people, who now tend to do what they like. There is now a wide generation gap between the partly educated young and the uneducated old.

As children grew up they learned to sing and to dance, to swim and to hunt, to fish and to find bush food. They would learn the names of the birds and animals and how to track them. They would soon know when trees bore good fruit and which were poisonous. They would play with their brothers and sisters in the camp, and sometimes go out, with their fathers if they were boys, and with their mothers if they were girls. Life for the children was free and easy, and so different from the restrictions of school and its formalised educational patterns.

As children grew older their responsibilities became greater. They were under increased restrictions regarding whom they could speak to and what they could do. Initiation was the first major ceremony for the boys. It took place when the boys were between eight and twelve years old, depending on the area where they lived.

In north-eastern Arnhem Land initiation took the form of preparation and circumcision. Circumcision is not now practised by many groups in western Arnhem Land. Many of the elders insist, however, that they had circumcision in earlier generations but that the rite was abandoned when a great proportion of the boys died soon after circumcision.

Through initiation the boy was 'born again' into the spiritual life of the clan. He had a sponsor who taught him many of the stories of the past. He told him how he should live and what was the 'law' (which was not dissimilar in many respects to the Ten Commandments). He was instructed in his responsibilities as a member of the tribe, and trained to know what things he could do, what things he could not do, to whom he could speak and to whom he could not speak. After initiation he was considered an adult and a full member of the clan. He was theoretically able to marry, although normally there would be no 'promises' available at that time. He would have to wait in practice, possibly for a long time, before he could marry. He could, however, engage in sexual activities within certain limits.

In some areas of north-eastern Arnhem Land subincision as well as circumcision is practised. This is a fairly modern innovation, having been introduced along with the *kunapipi* ceremony. Some Aborigines say that *kunapipi* means subincisure, or the womb of the great fertility mother. The penis symbolises the Rainbow or Lightning Snake, the incision is the uterus. With subincision both male and female organs are present, representing the two elements of fertilisation.

Initiation rituals for girls took place when they reached puberty. They were not as elaborate or as formal as those for the boys, but were still of significance for the girl and for the whole community. After the ceremonies she went to the camp of her promised husband, and lived there until he took her. Sometimes she was carried off by force by her 'promise' and his friends, all of whom had access to her. The introduction of the *kunapipi* ceremony into Arnhem Land was usually accompanied by ceremonial defloration of a girl as soon as she menstruated, and ceremonial coitus by a number of men.

Sexual acts in the camp were observed by children from very early age. As sexual activity was part of life and of nature this was not hidden. Children as well as adults became known as camp gossips concerning almost everything that was going on. They also experimented among themselves with sex at an early age. Frequently girls had full sexual experience at an early age. This frank and open approach to sex is probably the reason why there were few reports of sexual abnormality and homosexuality.

Certain taboos were observed by menstruating women in most tribes. In many areas care had to be taken not to attract the attention of the Rainbow Serpent, who had a particular liking for blood. They had to be careful not to stand too close to the fire or to go near a billabong, in case he might attack and swallow them.

When the young girl went to the camp of her promised husband, she would join the camp routine of hunting and foraging. She would live with the other wives, and be available to the man when he wanted her. A young girl who had just reached the age of puberty was normally considered to be most desirable. She often therefore had precedence in the attentions of the husband, and was the subject of jealousy among the other wives. The marriage was sealed when the girl gave birth to her first child. She would then be accepted as a full member of the family.

Polygyny, or the practice of a man having more than one wife, was widespread throughout Arnhem Land. The grand old man Wonggu in eastern Arnhem Land had twenty-two wives. Extra wives meant prestige, more hands to gather basic bush food, more sexual variety, and more children to care in old age. Polygyny also meant that a number of young men had to wait many years until women were available for them. This led to numerous elopements, fighting, feuding, 'payback', and frequently possession of a wife by another man. The cost for such a conquest normally was a number of fights and some spear wounds for the man, and severe beating for the woman. Love knows no bounds!

Polygyny was seriously frowned upon or even banned by many early missionaries. They adopted this attitude, not only from a Christian moral stance, but also because of the consequent fighting and feuding, which could disrupt a camp for many days. Many young men just did not have the chance of having a wife in a foreseeable future. Often the missionaries had to intervene in fights, with the real possibility of being speared or killed in the process.

Despite the missionaries' good intentions, many older pro-mission Aborigines point to their interference in marriage arrangements as the main matter by which missionaries caused harm. They were unaware of the implications of the complex kinship system, and caused, or could have caused, untold damage to traditional tribal organisation.

By non-Aboriginal standards Aborigines engaged in widespread sexual activity before and after marriage. But then Aboriginal marriage was not the same as Christian marriage, and society was communal rather than individualistic. Highly erotic love-songs from all parts of Arnhem Land indicate the wide variety of liaisons which took place. Men and women frequently had access to their classificatory wives and husbands. A man could lend out his wife without her consent. Young men often had married women as sweethearts because of polygyny. Such widespread sexual licence in non-Aboriginal eyes was usually controlled within the possible range that kinship allowed, but not beyond it.

Normal kinship taboos relating to sexual partners were in some cases relaxed during some ceremonies. The significance of the ceremony was of greater importance than even the strict rules governing kinship. During these ceremonies or at special parts in them, men had access to any woman who was available for ritual coitus.

Aboriginal sexuality as among any other people in the world was a source of physical gratification. The love songs and many of the exploits of the great totem heroes make this clear. But ceremonial sexual acts went beyond pleasure. Through these acts the participants were linked with the great nature cycles. Environmental change depended on these ceremonies and the way they were performed. Human sex acts insured the recycling and continued fertility of the whole of the natural world.

Wider sexual experience did not mean that Aboriginal men and women did not love one another. The reverse was and is true, and examples from the past indicate this. Old people of the present, who formerly were and sometimes still are polygamous, usually speak with deep love and affection for their spouses, either dead or alive.

The life of the man from initiation to old age was continued learning. He was introduced to new rituals and new ceremonies. He gained more knowledge of the law and its ramifications. Sometimes each new stage in discovery was marked by the addition of chest cicatrixes. These were deep gashes cut across the chest just below the nipples, performed with flint or sharp stones. The operation was extremely painful.

New information and privileges meant new restrictions and responsibilities. Only when he was grey headed was the Aboriginal man considered to be the one who knew the law. He was the authority for the clan. It has always been a pleasure to sit with the old men and listen to their measured and dignified words of wisdom.

Old men and women were cared for by the younger members of the family. They had their special rights to food, and special portions of it. The men often spent much time dreaming of the past and sing softly to themselves snatches of the songs of their ancestors. Often they would pass the time whittling away at spears or artifacts. The old women were usually the great and powerful talkers who ruled the whole camp with the force of their personalities and the sharpness of their tongues.

When death came the whole family and clan went into deep mourning. The dead person's name could not be mentioned. Complex mortuary ceremonies were held to assist the spirit back to its final resting place. The person had died, but the spirit returned to the eternal dreaming of the ancestor.

5
Myth and ritual

Arnhem Land Aboriginal religion is concerned with the mystery of the natural world. Aborigines believe that the ancestral heroes or totems emerged out of the distant past. The totems gave them their land and laid the foundations for their social organisation. The exploits of these remarkable beings are vividly told in myth and in song. Their deeds were re-enacted in ritual and ceremony. The performance of these religious rites ensured continued participation in the eternal life of creation.

Aborigines call the distant past of the creative period the 'dreamtime', the 'eternal dreamtime', or 'dreaming'. These words do not do justice to the Aboriginal concept. Even when they themselves use 'dreaming' and 'dreamtime' in the vernacular and in English, the words have deeper significance than the vernacular or the English conveys. In using these terms Aborigines are trying to convey in non-philosophical terms the idea of a timeless world and an eternal life of the spirit of the people. All life is part of an endless continuum.

Lamilami, with his good understanding of English says that he has difficulty with the use of the word dreaming. He said, 'The first time when I heard this word dreaming I was confused. I asked myself, "What is this dreaming? Is it something like when we go to sleep and dream? Or is it something else?"'

He continued, 'I understand that people mean this when they talk about the dreamtime. I would say that the Aboriginal did not get the dreamtime, but someone gave this to him. It was someone a long time ago. Dreamtime seems to me to be something that the Aborigines look back and they can see what their ancestors have passed on to them. They say "This is my dreaming, that is, that which my ancestors passed on to me. That is my story."'

Lamilami then spoke about his own story. He is a Maung of western Arnhem Land, where the line of descent is matrilineal. 'Take my mother's land and her country. She used to say, "My dreaming is the big rock that stands out of the water". This is called Mandjulug. At low tides during the day you can see this rock but at night time you cannot see this rock. It is too dark. Sometimes you might see it when it is moonlight. At moonlight you can sometimes see at low tide some figures which a long time ago they say these are the figures of a people. Mandjulaku. They were the mermaids.'

Lamilami also spoke of Namumuiag, which he called the creator. This word is also used in Maung for 'dreaming' or 'dreamtime.' 'We do not know who Namumuiag is. That is just a name. He was the one who gave us this land. He made those trees. He made the islands. He made the water. He made the grass and the animals. Namumuiag is just like the creator God of the Bible. Namumuiag made the heavens. He made the Milky Way. He made the stars. He made the moon and he made the sun. He made the sea. He made everything. He gave our ancestors their totems. Sometimes they say about a rock or a tree or something like that, "O, the brolga made that," or "the crocodile made that," or sometimes they say, "an eagle made that." But Namumuiag made the brolga. He made the crocodile. He made the eagle.

The link between the dreamtime and the present are the totems. Totems join man to the natural objects around him. Through them man and nature are brought into one social and ceremonial whole. They determine Aboriginal social groups and mythologies. They inspire the rituals and dances through which they are joined to the past. They are the subjects of traditional religious bark and rock painting.

These great heroes of the past are considered human but the life force they embodied was not limited to human appearance. They were sometimes thought of as birds, animals, rocks, fish, insects, trees, winds or as any other manifestation of nature. As humans or non-humans they emerged out of the mists of the great creation period of long ago. They are the ones who formed the clans, who provide the spirit of all their members and who give them their food through nature around them. Ceremonies maintain the vital life-giving link with them and through them the whole world of nature in which they live.

Miss Judith Stokes, who has spent many years as linguist on

Groote Eylandt, speaks of totems in this way. 'Supposing you came to Groote Eylandt, how would you find out what a person regarded as his totem? It certainly would be wiser not to use the English word, but to ask about his song or his story. The word for story is *alawudawarra*. A man might answer, "I sing about Yandarrnga because that is my alawudawarra".

'"Yandarrnga" is the Aboriginal name for the rocky outcrop which catches your eye as you fly over Groote Eylandt. It is only about six hundred feet high, but is conspicuous because of the general flatness of the rest of the island.

'When the Aborigines who own Yandarrnga as a totem catch a glimpse of it in the distance, they recall all the associations of their clan. They think of how long ago, Yandarrnga lived on the mainland but came across to Groote Eylandt, stopping along the way until he found a suitable place to settle. Yandarrnga's story explains the migration of their clan.

'There is no prohibition concerning killing and eating totemic creatures, except concerning two connected with the mainland. These are scrub hen and a type of duck. Only certain people in a particular relationship are allowed to eat either the flesh or the eggs.

'The clan/totemic system not only links the clans of the Groote Eylandt people, but can help them to inter-relate with mainland tribes. As well as asking, "What is your song, or story?" one may ask, "What is your mother?" This is the way a man finds "brothers" in strange territory far from home, men who will accept him immediately, look after him, and provide the link through which he relates to every member of the tribe. The terms "mother" and "brother" have a much wider meaning for Aborigines than for Europeans. "Mother" is used for all one's actual mother's sisters, and can be used even to refer to certain female relations in a different generation level. A man says "Shark-ray is my mother", and another man from a different tribe replies, "You are my brother (because we have a common totem mother)", or "You are my uncle", or whatever the particular relationship may be. He himself calls Shark-ray by a kinship term, and so he calls anyone owning Shark-ray as a totem by exactly the same term.

'The totemic system provides the basis for a very close relationship between Aborigines, certain members of the animal world, and the land they share. This relationship is still important in spite of community living today. In the past it was vitally important. People in small scattered groups were not cut off and rootless. No man need feel lost in himself, isolated or helpless. Each one had a defined place in a much wider circle than his everyday contacts permitted. This gave the feeling of identity and security that he needed. He could be a lone hunter in the bush but not lonely. He belonged, he was important. Existence was meaningful. All he knew and believed came from his ancestors, rooted in the past and in the world around that still sustained him as it had sustained them from day to day.

'Preoccupation with future, which could not be provided for, could not be manipulated or foreseen, would have spelt intolerable insecurity. Preoccupation with the past and the present spelt stability and permanence.'

In some cases totemism is more important for kinship rather than for land. This is frequently the case in western Arnhem Land, where the descent is matrilineal. Lamilami said, 'My totem comes from my mother not from my father. This is different from some other places in Arnhem Land. Walang, Maung, Yiwadja and Gunwinggu are the same. All these people have their totems from their mother's side. That is where I get my totem, from my mother. But the land, I get that from my father, where he comes from. I cannot get my mother's land. But my father's totem, I have nothing to do with that.

'The totem stories do not tell me how I got the land. That is up to my father. My father's land tells me where he got his totem from. I am all right in my father's totem. If my father was Eagle, I could not be Eagle. My mother's totem is Big Rock, so I follow Big Rock. I know my father's singing and how he got his land. I cannot sing my mother's songs but I sing my father's songs, but I still have my mother's totem.

'My mother's totem means that it helps me in my mother's place, where my uncle, her brother, is, and that is where I get my wife from. The totem is for kinship and marriage.'

Myths and sacred stories of Arnhem Land Aborigines tell of the exploits of the totem heroes. They are not just stories and songs. The Arnhemlanders have endless secular tales of the past. The myths are deeply religious, and recount the deeds of the dreamtime ancestors who give meaning to life. They provide the basis for the social organisation.

Myths and stories, rituals and ceremonies are inextricably bound together. The rituals re-enact the myths as they are sung to the accompaniment of the didjeridu and clap sticks. The performance of the rituals ensures the continuation of the eternal spirit of the totem, of that spirit within them, and the preservation of the whole world.

45

The most important rituals and ceremonies are those connected with initiation, when the novice is 'born again' into the clan, post-initiation rites dealing with creation and the continuing revelation of the law; fertility and increase ceremonies involving natural species, man and the seasons; and mortuary ceremonies. All are connected one way or another with the totems and the songs associated with them.

The *ubar* is one of the most important of the western Arnhem Land ceremonies. Lamilami said, 'One big ceremony was the ubar. That is the one that tells about creation. We see the Milky Way up on the sky and we say that the Milky Way up in the sky represents the ceremony ground of the ubar. There is the kangaroo dance, and the dances of the frill-neck lizard and the bandicoot, and how they came into being. The story is up there in the sky. It tells you. There is a lot of dancing with that ceremony and it takes about two or three weeks to finish.

'Both moieties, *dua* and *yiritja* join in a dance like that. This is a secret one, but not a separate dance for one particular moiety. They still dance the ubar now. The ubar was connected with creation. The ubar has all about marriage and children and things like that.'

Part of the myth in the ubar cycle tells of King Brown Snake, or in some places the male Rainbow Snake, who was betrothed to a girl. She refused to sleep with him because she had Water Snake as her lover. King Brown Snake was therefore very angry. He made a hollow log or ubar and left it on a track in the bush. He turned himself into a snake and hid inside the log. The girl and the mother saw the log when they were out hunting. Thinking that it might contain some small animal they put they hands inside and were bitten by King Brown Snake. They died and King Brown Snake went on to another place.

The ubar ceremony is associated with creation, fertility and increase. The hollow log is usually thought of as the uterus of the great Mother. The Gunwinjgu sometimes identify her with the female Rainbow Snake. Among the Maung, the inside of the ubar is the uterus of the Mother, and the ubar itself is the penis of the male Rainbow Snake.

The ubar ceremony takes several weeks to perform. The dancers are summoned from time to time by the booming of the log as it is struck. Rainbow Serpent plays an important part in the ritual, as he or she typifies the wet season rejuvenating and revitalising the earth. Wallaby dances signify and bring about the necessary increase in food and people.

Rainbow Snake is an important feature of Arnhem Land myth and ritual. In north-eastern Arnhem Land he is either male or female and is sometimes identified with Lightning Snake. Usually female Rainbow Snake brings the wet season, floods and rain. She has an aversion to blood, especially that of a menstruating woman or of childbirth. She is said to swallow pregnant women if they stand too close to billabongs or water holes. Myths speak of her coming over the sea from the north-west. She is often associated with a mythical figure Waragag, whose sacred place is Tor Rock.

The *maraiin* or sacred rituals of western Arnhem Land are also very important. They are connected with creation, instruction in the law, and increase. A wide variety of sacred objects such as the ubar, decorated poles, wooden objects and figures of birds, animals and fish, grass figures and painted stones are used. In north-eastern Arnhem Land sacred objects include *rannga* poles and posts, carved human figures and long didjeridus.

The story of Whale tells how the people of western Arnhem Land obtained maraiin objects. Whale moved throughout the country killing everyone who came in his way. As the survivors were about to kill him, he cried, 'I will show you the ceremonies before I die.' So he showed them the ceremonies and the sacred objects before he swam out to sea and died.

In north-eastern Arnhem Land the two great fertility mothers are the Djanggawul sisters, a *dua* singing. The cycle of myths associated with them tell how they and their brother came across the sea from the north-east. During their journey they stayed at Bralgu Island, now the traditional home for the spirit of the dead. They arrived in a bark canoe on the east coast of the mainland in the path of the rising sun. At Milingimbi they are called the 'daughters of the sun'. They embody the life-giving power of the sun and the increase which it brings.

The Djanggawul sisters brought with them a variety of sacred objects including the sacred mat, symbolising the female uterus. This mat also contained the sacred *rangga* emblems. They also had other sacred objects in their dilly bag.

The Djanggawul sisters were thought to be the creators of the Aborigines of north-eastern Arnhem Land. The Sisters brought them out of the sacred dilly bag. They also left a variety of animals and plants for the people. These are indicated by numerous sacred sites. The biggest *dua* rituals commemorate their activities.

Part of the Djanggawul cycle tells how men usurped the cere-monial power of the women. When the Sisters came to a certain place, they built a shelter in which they hung the sacred dilly bag containing the emblems. While they were away collecting mangrove shells their brother and some men whom the Sisters had created, stole the dilly bag and its objects. When the Sisters returned and saw what was done they began tracking the men. When they arrived at the place where the men were, they heard them singing the stolen songs. The men had also usurped the power inherent within the songs. The Sisters decided that as the men had stolen the sacred things they would now be responsible for the songs and ceremonies.

The Wawalag Sisters *yiritja* myth cycle and ceremonies of north-eastern Arnhem Land are usually associated with initiation and circumcision. The two Sisters and their children came into northern Arnhem Land from the Roper River area. After many adventures on the way, they came to a sacred water hole. Here the elder sister gave birth to a child during a storm. The afterbirth blood attracted the attention of the Python living in the hole, who swallowed the two sisters. Python did not swallow the children because they were *yiritja*.

The *kunapipi* ceremony is closely associated with the Wawalag mythology. The name *kunapipi* refers to the fertility Mother or to Rainbow Snake. The rituals are connected with increase and fertility and may last several months. The kunipipi has only recently been introduced into Arnhem Land from the south. Lamilami said that dancers from Bulman and Bamyili brought the ceremony into Arnhem Land when they came and initiated some of the old people. Since that time the kunapipi has become very popular. He added, 'The kunapipi has problems for Christian people. They can dance part of it but not all.'

The ceremony starts with the summons of the bullroarer representing the voice of Rock Python or Rainbow Snake. Initiates are 'swallowed' in the first part of the ceremony and then 'vomited up' to symbolise their entrance into the sacred life. Parts of some of the major ritual cycles including that of the Wawalag sisters are sung and danced by both men and women. An integral part of the ceremony is the mutual exchange of women. This symbolises goodwill and friendship between all. Many kunapipi songs and dances are highly erotic, portraying the power of sexual forces in nature and man.

The death of an Aboriginal person in Arnhem Land profoundly affects the whole community. Work immediately comes to a halt. Close relatives weep and wail for hours, gashing themselves with knives and axes until the blood flows. Others express their sorrow and sympathy by respecting the dead person.

Mortuary ceremonies following death, though differing from place to place, usually have certain common features. When a person dies his hut or house is roped off and a large flag flown. The use of flags appears to have come from north-eastern Arnhem Land, although the custom may have originated with the Macassans. The dead person's name must not be used. Close relatives observe strict food taboos.

In former days the corpse was often smeared with ochre or painted with totemic designs and placed on a platform or in a tree. Ritual cannibalism was sometimes practised, when a small portion of the person's flesh was eaten in order to get something of his spirit. Sometimes a kidney of a man was removed, stored in a small dilly bag and hung around the eldest son's neck. During fights he would bite the kidney fat to give him the needed strength of his ancestor.

After a time the bones were collected and placed in a bark container bearing totemic signs. Sometimes the bones were placed in caves. In other areas they were placed in logs which were buried vertically. In eastern Arnhem Land wooden grave posts were carved, probably a relic of Macassan days.

Nowadays the corpse is interred. Special close relatives prepare the body for burial and dig the grave. The service is usually taken by the resident chaplain or by a missionary. Customs are now changing significantly. Much more singing takes place while the body is being brought to the grave; the relatives now engage in more ceremonial at the time of committal; and the part played by the chaplain appears to be regarded in some places as being almost superfluous. There are noted exceptions to this trend.

Soon after a person dies the relatives hold an inquest regarding his death. Even though the deceased may have been very old and appeared to have died of natural causes, there is always the feeling that someone caused his death. Sorcery and rituals are performed to try to find out the person responsible. The culprit is usually someone of a clan with whom there has been a longstanding feud. Any necessary action is then taken.

The dead person's spirit is thought to hover in the proximity of the camp immediately after death. The spirit is unable to leave until it has been sung away to the land of the dead, which Christians conveniently term heaven. This singing usually involves recounting the deeds of the dead person and also those of the totem heroes to whom the dead man's spirit returns.

When the spirit of the dead person reaches the land of the dead it is there for ever. The ancestral spirits at the same time are invoked and brought back to the camp to break the taboos placed on the relatives. They are appeased when they see that the possessions and the dwelling of the deceased are actually or ritually burned, and the whole place cleansed with smoke. After this they return to their place. Further mortuary rituals are often held involving additional singing of the totems' exploits, so that they may see how the clan is progressing. Sometimes the hair of the dead person is cut off and placed in a sacred dilly bag.

Mortuary ceremonies are increasing in importance and length. More people are attending them. The ceremonies are also taking much longer and are becoming more complex. This is probably a reaction to the growing materialism being experienced through the inroads of Western materialism. Revival of traditional religion is a usual feature when cultures are under threat.

On one occasion I was warmly welcomed to attend a part of a mortuary ceremony, with the proviso, 'But do not bring your camera, Bapa'. We sat for the whole day on the sand while various parts of the ceremony were held. The main party were seated close together under a typical shelter of four posts and a thatched top. There were about forty men, naked to the waist, and wearing totem signs. The four didjeridus droned on while the white-haired song leader with his clap sticks sang for hours. I noticed that a number of the men under the shelter seemed to be a little uncomfortable seated on the sand. As I looked harder I noticed that at least twelve of the forty were sitting on tape recorders, which clicked on when the serious singing started! Their singing could be heard in the camp for days afterwards.

Aborigines of Arnhem Land universally believed in good and evil spirits. The bad spirits lived in deep caves in the escarpment, or among the rushes of the swamps, or in dark places of the forest. They caused people to become sick and die. They also lived in the 'dangerous' and secret places. Unauthorised entry or desecration meant punishment and death.

The good and friendly spirits were the Mimis. They are portrayed as stick men in rock and bark paintings. Lamilami said that 'Mimis usually live in the Gumadir River area. In the dry season they would live in my area, on the mainland south of Goulburn Island. Sometimes we would see them afar off just like smoke. The people would say, 'The Mimis are dancing. They have all come for a dance.' They have a song and a dance called the Mimi dance. They have a lot of stories and legends about Mimis that they tell to the young people. How they are and how they live. They are supposed to be very thin. They paint Mimis sometimes in caves and on bark huts, like Mimis going out hunting, or Mimis going out for wild honey, or Mimis going out gathering roots and berries. The Mimis do not go out on windy days. They stay in the caves. They are so thin that they might break!

'There were also other spirits,' Lamilami continued. 'Good spirits and bad spirits. Good spirits were friendly. Sometimes people might see something in the nights. They would be hunting and see some lights, something very strange. They would say, "That is the good spirit who has shown his light and told them that something will be happening."

'The good spirits bring good news. If someone was sick they might have a bush doctor. Sometimes he might be a bit of a cheat. He might not be a good doctor and these good spirits would tell these people or the tribe that that bush doctor is not very good. They would also tell good fortunes about the future and what would happen to them. They would sometimes show people the way if they got lost in the bush.

'Everything that the bad spirits do is bad. The first thing is to kill someone. Say if I am in the bush somewhere. I might see a strange light, then I would get frightened and think, "The bad spirits are coming". Sometimes I might figure out that I have seen something. It is the bad spirit. Then I would get sick thinking about what the bad spirits had done. And then I might die. That is what the bad spirits do.

'The people say that a bush doctor can send bad spirits to make certain people die. Or they might have good spirits and send them to kill the bad spirits. The bad spirits lived in certain places and the good spirits lived in other places. They would get a bush doctor to get some sort of a leaf that he would burn. He would throw it and drive away the bad spirits. He would rub his sweat on them and say that the spirits have gone. These days they give bush doctors money or material for doing this. In the olden days they would give them fishing nets or a dilly bag or an arm band.'

The power that sorcery still has over many Aboriginal people in Arnhem Land came home to me forcibly one day when I was visiting one community. News went round that a parcel had been left outside the hut of one family. All the community quickly gathered on the football field. Everyone went. After several hours of talking and staring at the parcel, several men were deputed to unwrap it. They did this with great care, using sticks instead of their fingers. Eventually they unwrapped the object. It was a carved piece of wood about six inches long. This caused great consternation among everyone. The atmosphere was electric.

No one knew who had brought the parcel. The purpose nevertheless was quite clear. Someone had died in another community and the parcel was sent to try and find out by sorcery who had been responsible for his death. If the guilty person had been present at our gathering, I am sure the emotional and psychological build-up was such that he would most certainly have confessed. As it was, no one did. So the parcel was tied up and everyone went quietly back home.

Aboriginal art and artefacts, magic and sorcery, were closely connected with myth and ritual. Bark and rock paintings portrayed the totemic heroes, and sometimes some of their exploits. Body painting was an integral part of the ritual and ceremony. Sacred objects were carefully carved or fashioned, painted and decorated. The art forms are unique and fascinating but, sad to say, are in danger of commercialisation and exploitation.

Arnhem Land Aborigines cut the bark for their paintings from tall stringybark trees. The wet season is usually the best time to cut the sheets, which often measure two metres by sixty centimetres. The bark is dried on a small fire, flattened out on the ground, and kept in place by wooden stretchers each end.

They use four basic colours: red, yellow, black and white. The red ochre, iron oxide or haematite, and the yellow ochre, limonite, come from rivers and watercourses. The white ochre is gypsum or pipeclay, and the black is either charcoal or manganese. Most Groote Eylandt paintings have a black base, as manganese is readily available there. Red and yellow ochres are difficult to obtain in some places, and is a profitable item of trade during large ceremony times. When a small group of Aborigines and I landed once on a very isolated part of the coastline, several elders showed me some very old bones, another group went looking for some sacred paintings, while several went off searching for red ochre. This last party came back with handfuls of the bright red stuff, to the loud acclaim of everyone present.

Aboriginal artists grind the various ochres into a fine powder. They mix each colour with water on a separate large stone, sometimes adding a fixative at this stage. The fixative is made from orchid juice, wax, honey or egg-yolk. They make brushes from twigs, strips of bark or hair and feathers.

They paint with very great skill, not wasting any time. Earlier paintings were often only those of totems or mythical stories. Many of these paintings have secret signs and symbols, which are known to only a handful of people. Only certain people should paint these sacred pictures. Secular paintings now cover a wide range of stories,

Reverend Lazarus Lamilami (*Photo Hamilton Aikin*)

Arnhem Land is a northern paradise. During the Wet countless streams tumble through narrow gorges such as this one in western Arnhem Land (*Photo N.T. News Service Ltd.*)

but are still executed in a traditional manner. Nowadays some Aborigines are experimenting with hardboard and European-style paint, which are more durable.

Large galleries of rock paintings occur throughout Arnhem Land and the offshore islands. Many of these paintings have deep religious significance and occur in very sacred places. Other paintings portray items of interest such as Macassan praus, European steamships, and a white person shooting with a rifle. Paintings of the Tasmanian tiger indicate that this animal once roamed Arnhem Land. Hand stencils of artists and their relatives are very common. Ground holes for ochre are often seen close to the galleries.

The earliest rock paintings cannot be dated with any certainty. More recent works often overlay older ones. No sure guide comes from the subject matter and the style. Radiocarbon dating is difficult. Some rock paintings are well preserved. I have seen those on Chasm Island described by Matthew Flinders in 1803, and they are still in very good condition. Others, such as those of the Macassan praus on south-eastern Groote, are weathering badly. Some in western Arnhem Land are being rubbed off by buffaloes. Experts suggest that the earliest paintings may be about 2000 years or even older.

Aborigines also paint their bodies for ceremonies. They sometimes just daub red and white ochre on their faces and bodies. At initiation they often paint elaborate representations on the bodies of the initiates. At other ceremonies they paint themselves with the design of the subject of the dance.

Speaking about painting, Lamilami said, 'When people dance, the markings they put on are for the song not the actual totem. If a *yiritja* does a bark painting he must put on a *yiritja* painting. If he is *dua* he must put on a *dua* painting. You know the clay they use. The yellow ochre is *yiritja* and the *dua* use the black charcoal stuff.'

Painting, singing and dancing, and the stories connected with them, are all essential features of Aboriginal culture. Nature, the land, animals and people were all part of the living world of these first Australians. Their rich traditions have existed with very little change for countless centuries. Now, suddenly, during the short time of three centuries these age-old traditions have come under terrible threat. They could cope with the seasonal visits of the Macassan traders. They have found it almost impossible to cope with the destructive forces of Western imperialism, technology and culture.

6
We liked the Macassans

'We liked the Macassans,' Djawa said to me one day. We were sitting down under a spreading tamarind tree on the beach at Milingimbi. 'We liked them because they gave us food and axes. Sometimes they gave us cloth. That is where they cooked their trepang,' he said, pointing with the long Macassan pipe which he invariably smokes. 'And this is where they anchored their praus, and pulled their canoes up the beach.' Djawa is one of the grand old Aboriginal men of the community, and is chairman of the Town Council.

Most Aborigines living on coastal Arnhem Land and Groote Eylandt say much the same thing. 'They were good people,' a group of four old Umbakumba men told me some years ago. I was sitting with them on a blanket on the hot sand under one of their corrugated-iron shelters. 'They gave us rice and axes and tobacco. Some of our relations went back to Macassar with them for one year or two years.'

Lamilami spoke the same way. 'The people used to say that the Macassans were good people. They were kind people and they made many friends with the Aborigines. I do not mean to say that they made friends because of the Aboriginal women. No. They made a friendship with Aboriginal people because of the work that they did. They worked together and became friends.'

These nostalgic memories of the 'good old days' beyond living memory overlook numerous instances of enmity and bitterness. At different times Macassans and Aborigines killed each other. The Macassans welcomed the protection of the British at Port Essington. Aboriginal women in most places were kept well out of sight. There were the bad times as well as the good. There were the disadvantages of this alien culture as well as the advantages. One thing is clear however. The seasonal Macassan visits were less traumatic for Aborigines than their permanent contact with white settlers.

The Macassans were Indonesians from the great trading centre of Macassar in southern Sulawesi. The Dutch had captured Macassar in 1669 and had established a centre of European colonialism and trade. Macassar was also an important trade link with the newly-founded Singapore. For centuries it was the outlet for the trepang trade with China.

Trepang is the Anglicised form of the Macassarese 'teripang', the name of a sea animal known popularly as the sea slug, the sea cucumber or *bêche-de-mer*. Trepang usually grow to about fifty centimetres long, although some measuring over one metre have been found. They vary in colour, and can be black, grey, brown, or white, or occasionally blue or red. They abound in the shallow waters of the northern and eastern coasts of Arnhem Land and the numerous off-shore islands. They are clearly visible at low tide, lying on the sea floor. Their skins are tough and leathery, and they exude water and slime when squeezed.

All the trepang caught by the Macassans in Australian waters went to China. The Chinese used the animals in soups, braised it with vegetables or fried it. They claim that when trepang is cooked properly, its jelly-like texture brings out the flavour of the other foods. Trepang were also reputed to have aphrodisiac qualities.

The Macassans called the great south land which they visited *Marege*, which may mean the area or the Aborigines themselves. They made their outward journey on the *bara* or north-west monsoon, which blows regularly from December to March. They fished for trepang during these summer months of the Wet, returning home on the dry south-east trades.

They made their outward journey in fleets of praus, passing round Timor and crossing the five hundred kilometres stretch of the Timor Sea in about four days. They carried out this feat of navigation without instruments of any kind. The praus were small boats of from ten to forty tonnes. They were made of wood with rattan or mat shelters on deck and normally carried two rectangular sails and a single mast. The most frequent landfall was Melville Island or the Coburg Peninsula.

The exact number of praus that came each year is hard to determine. Matthew Flinders and other maritime visitors to the coast give varying estimates. Dr Campbell Macknight, who has made an extensive study of the subject, estimates that there would have probably been from thirty to sixty praus on the Northern Territory coast in an average season during the first half of the nineteenth century. As the crews numbered about thirty, the number of Macassans annually visiting the Arnhem Land coast at this time would have exceeded 1000 and may have been in the vicinity of 2000. They would have greatly outnumbered the coastal Aboriginal people.

No one knows how long the Macassans had been coming to Australia. Earlier historians spoke of hundreds of years. Later estimates are more conservative and suggest that they probably started arriving in the latter part of the seventeenth century. That would mean that they were visiting Australia for a period of just over two hundred years.

The visits at the beginning were probably haphazard and un-co-ordinated. As the trepang supply became more assured, then the journeys became more organised. The visits ceased abruptly with the enforcement of the White Australia policy through the levy of an exorbitant tax.

Macassan praus carried considerable quantities of water in bamboo containers, rice, rice cakes, chickens, tobacco, spirits (mostly Dutch gin), tamarind fruit, iron cooking pots for curing the trepang, stoneware, earthenware bowls, ceramic plates, bowls and cups, bamboo rods for building curing sheds and rough shelters, assorted implements including knives, tomahawks and axes, cloth and dug-out canoes. Some had a small cannon mounted on the bow. Cooking facilities were limited to a large iron pan, placed on sand in the stern. The tamarind fruit was used to flavour rice and would have been a useful antiscorbutic. The spreading, shady, tamarind trees marking most Macassan sites on beaches on the Arnhem Land coast indicate the widespread use of this fruit.

Tamarind trees now flourish on the beaches of the Top End coasts. They sometimes confuse the Macassan site searchers, as their presence does not automatically mark a former Macassan camp. Many times I have sighted tamarind stands from the air or from a boat standing off-shore. A subsequent examination of the place often reveals no traces of Macassan occupation. On the other hand almost every Macassan site has tamarind trees.

The marking of a Macassan site by tamarinds came to me quite dramatically at one time on Groote Eylandt. The Umbakumba Aborigines assured me that there was a Macassan site on the northern side of the channel between Lake Angwurrgwurrigba and the sea. I found the place, but the whole lay-out was completely atypical. Casuarinas were growing instead of tamarinds. There were not nearby mangroves. The stone lines were not set out as usual. It just did not seem to be an old Macassan camp. The mystery was solved when an old European trepanger told me later that this place had been one of his trepang sites. He did not think the Macassans had worked there. My misunderstanding with the Aborigines about this being a Macassan site was probably due to a confusion in language, and the Aboriginal association of trepang with Macassans.

Macassans were regular visitors to the two early British settlements on the Coburg Peninsula. One major reason for the establishment of Fort Wellington in Raffles Bay between 1827 and 1829 and of Port Essington from 1839 to 1849 was to exploit the Macassan trade connections between Australia and the Netherlands East Indies. Sixty-four praus visited Raffles Bay in 1829: of the 1056 men who had left Macassar, thirty-seven had died on the voyage, three had been speared by Aborigines, and one had died at Raffles Bay.

The Macassans visited Port Essington annually and established good relations with the British there. One of them, Bapa Padu, who had been visiting the Arnhem Land coast for about thirty years, expressed great pleasure at finding the British there in 1839. He said that their presence would give the Macassans protection from the Aborigines, who, at this time, were very hostile.

The British in turn endeavoured to establish permanent trading relations with the Macassans. They were unsuccessful as the Dutch in Macassar discouraged them by heavily taxing any British goods which they brought back. The British also tried to persuade the Macassans to settle at Port Essington, offering them land at a low rental. The offer was not accepted.

From 1883 the South Australian Government forced the Macassans to pay for licences to fish for trepang, pearls, pearl and turtle shell, and levied a duty on all goods brought to barter with Aborigines or to pay for the services rendered. Alfred Searcy was the first sub-collector of customs. This colourful character was transferred from Port Adelaide to Darwin in 1882 for the purpose. Praus were intercepted as they passed through the Bowen Strait between Croker Island and the mainland. The Government continued to levy fees and dues until they finally, in 1906, prevented the Macassans from coming.

When the Macassans came they spread out in small groups all along the coast and into the Gulf of Carpentaria. They appear to have returned to the same places each season. Their camps were sheltered sand coves near good trepang grounds. Well-known trepang sites are at Port Essington, Port Bremer, Raffles Bay, Croker Island, Copeland Island, South Goulburn Island, Anuru Bay, Braithwaite Point, Entrance Island (Liverpool River), Milingimbi, Elcho Island, Arnhem Bay, Melville Bay, Port Bradshaw, Gray's Bay, Bickerton Island, Groote Eylandt and some islands in the Sir Edward Pellew Group.

Lamilami spoke about the Macassan site on Croker Island. 'It is just on the west side of the island. From the mission it is about eleven miles down to this place they call White Cliff. We call it Wanggirgurug. At that place we now see a couple of graves where the Macassans have died. They say one man was stung by a sea wasp or something and died. I don't know what happened to the other one. There are tamarind trees at the place. The remains of the stones where they cooked the trepang are buried now. When the tide comes in and washes the sand away you can see the stones. At low tide we pick up old broken pottery and things like that on the sand bank.'

Lamilami also spoke about the arrival of the Macassans. 'Whenever the bara started to blow from the west the people would be very happy because they knew that their friends are coming back and because before the Macassans went back they promised to bring something for them. They would bring back an axe which we call *lidburruk* and those big knives that we call *badi*. They were about two feet six inches long. They would bring back cloth or calico which we call *liba*. The people used these materials for putting round their bodies to cover themselves. They would bring back rice. As a present they might bring back a big bag which they would call *djungulu*. They would bring back mats which we would call *djabiri*. These mats were made in Macassar. They would teach Aboriginal people how to weave sails for dug-out or bark canoes. These sails were made from very fine reeds from the billabong or from pandanus.'

The Macassans appear to have set up their camps on the beaches in almost an identical manner at each place. They chose places where they were protected from the north-west monsoon but close to shallow waters where trepang could be easily collected. They camped near fresh water, and close to mangroves, whose bark was used for tanning and whose wood for fuel. They built stone fireplaces at right angles to the shore-line, starting about twenty metres from high water mark. Aboriginal families would camp nearby.

Groups of Macassans and Aborigines would establish subsidiary camping places on various beaches in the vicinity. At these places they would then collect, spear or drag-net trepang from dug-out canoes. When they had collected enough trepang at these places they would transport it to the main centre. Here it was processed.

The Macassans appear to have used several methods in curing the trepang. They employed Aborigines to help them in this work. Sometimes they would boil the animals, then gut and clean them. These were then buried in sand overnight. When dug up next morning the skins would come off, leaving the white flesh exposed. They would then be boiled again, dried and then smoked.

At other times the Macassans would bury the trepang in a large hole in the sand as soon as it was brought ashore. Hot water was poured over the hole. The next morning they would remove the trepang, skin it, squeeze out the innards and wash it. They then boiled, dried and sometimes smoked it.

In many cases it seems that the Macassans undertook a final curing of the trepang just before leaving for Macassar. They assembled at several vantage places, and pooled the trepang which had been collected during the previous few months. They boiled this up again in water mixed with mangrove bark which kept the trepang for its journey back to Macassar and then on to China.

The Macassan who had the overall responsibility of a number of praus was the *bunggawa*. He was assisted by a *rimba*, who, according to Lamilami, 'did all the sitting down and writing and things like that. He would do nothing but just write and talk with the people. He would write down how much trepang came in, how many people were employed to work, and things like that.'

Relations between the Macassans and Aborigines varied from time to time. The main causes of friction were the use and payment of Aboriginal women and the inadequacy of payment for work done. Sometimes killings took place, but again usually as the result of arguments or reprisals. Lamilami told how Aborigines massacred a number of Macassans at Brogden Point in reprisal for the killing of Aborigines on Entrance Island at the mouth of the Liverpool River. In spite of these incidents old Aboriginal men from every part of the Arnhem Land coast speak of the good old days when the Macassans came. Doubtless some of the unpleasant details have been forgotten. Obviously some of the benefits have been exaggerated. But they all say that their older relatives looked forward to the visits by the Macassans and to the items which they brought.

Some anthropologists exaggerate the extent of the sexual relations between Macassans and Aboriginal women. There is no doubt that liaisons took place. But statements given by the old men from different areas do not suggest that this was widespread. This claim is supported by the fact that there are not many part-Macassan part-Aborigines in Arnhem Land at the present time. This is all the more remarkable when it is remembered that the Macassans made annual visits for more than two hundred years.

'There were some relations between Macassans and Aboriginal women', Lamilami said. 'We have someone there on Croker Island. I think his father was a Macassan. He was accepted by our people as a full Aboriginal. It was very seldom that men would give their wives to the Macassans for tomahawks or for gin. But mainly the Macassans would make friends with the Aborigines because of good friendships, working with each other.'

Before the Macassans left for home on the south-east trades they gave gifts to the Aborigines in payment for the work which they had done. Lamilami said, 'They left a lot with the people: drinks, big bags of rice, cloth, calico and tomahawks. They would give them these things for the work they had done. That was their wages. One would get four big bags of rice, some material and some axes and knives and stacks of grog. Then another the same and another the same.'

The farewell parties on the beaches which the Macassans held just before they left for home appear to have been boisterous affairs. Accounts of drunken capers, fun and dancing come from all parts of the coast. Lamilami said, 'First of all they would get all the people together and have a sort of ceremony (celebration). There was drinking and fun, running after each other and knocking each other down on the beach and throwing them into the sea and all this. And then after the party they would go.'

A number of Aborigines went to Macassar with the returning trepangers. A few appear to have married and stayed there permanently. Most came back to Arnhem Land on the next monsoon. Occasionally they stayed at Macassar for two seasons.

Lamilami spoke about this. He said 'When the Macassans were ready to go away they would take some of our people with them. My father's brother was the eldest one. He went away with the Macassans during the east wind which we call *djimuru*, the dry season wind. On the next *bara* he didn't come back. Some of the others came back and told our people that my father's brother and some of the others stayed back at Macassar. Some stayed back because they wanted the Macassans to teach them how to build dug-out canoes. That's when my uncle stayed back. Then came the next wet season after that and he didn't return again, so they wondered what had happened to him. I think the third time some of the people went back to Macassar to see him. When they returned they said he was there and they said he got married or something like that, and he couldn't come back.

'Only a few Aborigines got married in Macassar. Many people went to Macassar and then returned back on the next monsoon. But few would stay here until the following December and then they would come back. There are now no people that I know of who are alive who went to Macassar and came back. The last one died in 1973 and another one I think a year before that.'

Macassan influence on the Aborigines of Arnhem Land was fairly considerable. The Macassans introduced the use of iron, so that iron spear heads and fish spear prongs supplanted wooden and stone ones. Steel axes and tomahawks were used instead of cumbersome stone implements. Macassans also taught Aborigines how to work systematically for wages. They introduced them to rice and rice bags, glazed and unglazed pottery, tobacco, pipes, alcohol, writing, paper and books, tamarind trees and their fruits. The Macassans brought the Aborigines the knowledge and use of the dug-out canoe and sails, enabling them to make longer and safer journeys by sea and along rivers.

A number of Macassarese words became part of the Aboriginal vocabularies in all coastal communities in Arnhem Land. One important word is *balanda* from the Macassan word for Hollander, or white man. This word is in constant use today in the Top End communities. Other words are *bara* — the north-west (monsoonal) wind; *badi* — a long knife; *biradja* — rice; *bunggawa* — the boss man; *djambagu* — tobacco; *djulu* — matches; *jara* — knife; *jura* — letter, paper, writing; *lantirrung* — light; *liba* — cloth; *lipalipa* — canoe; *nuna* — European woman; *jarrang* — horse; *rupia* — money.

Arnhem Land Aborigines often sing about the Macassans. They sing about how the Macassans came on the west wind. They have a number of stories about them and what they did. They also sing of the east wind taking the Macassans back to their land. These songs are not sacred, as nothing from Macassan religion has come into Aboriginal ceremonial or ritual.

Aborigines in Arnhem Land like to paint Macassan praus. Several years ago I asked one old man living at Umbakumba to paint a prau for me. After initial trouble in getting a suitable piece of bark, he set to work. In an incredibly short time he presented me with his bark painting. He had no external model, no picture and no other painting to refer to. The image was clear in his mind, the hull containing the dug-out canoes, the pointed prow, the raised poop and the characteristic rectangular sail. All these features had been imprinted on his memory even though he must have been only a boy when he saw a prau.

Aborigines have also painted Macassan praus on the rock walls and ceilings of caves. I have described the paintings in the Marrangala cave in the remote south-eastern peninsula of Groote Eylandt in my book *Totems and Tamarinds*. Another fine collection of prau paintings is found in the rocks between Cooper Creek and the coast in western Arnhem Land.

'We liked the Macassans,' said old Djawa. 'They brought us many things. They came here for many years, and you can see where they got their water at the Macassan well. That is the place where all the tamarind trees are.'

7
Balanda

'They (Aborigines) knew the white people of Victoria (Port Essington) and called them Balanda, which is nothing more than
"Hollanders", a name used by the Malays, from whom they received
it.' Thus wrote the intrepid Ludwig Leichhardt in his journal on
16 November 1845, as he journeyed from Moreton Bay to Port
Essington on the Coburg Peninsula. He had reached the South
Alligator River and had talked with the Aborigines there. From
time to time they had visited the white settlers at Victoria, and
had learned a little English.

Balanda is the word which the Aborigines of Arnhem Land
nowadays use when referring to Europeans or white people, in
English or in the vernacular to each other. Sometimes the word
has no racial overtones; frequently it is a term of disparagement.

Balanda ships heralded the coming of the white man to Arnhem
Land. The first visitors were from the Dutch East Indies. Then
came the maritime and overland explorers from colonies in the
south of the continent. They were followed by four unsuccessful
attempts to establish settlements in the North. The attempts failed
as Balanda were unable to adapt to life in these isolated tropical
outposts. But they were the forerunners of the permanent white
frontier which was to have traumatic results for the Aborigines of
Arnhem Land.

The first known Balanda to explore the tropical shores of the
northern coastline of Australia were the Hollanders or the Dutch.
The Portuguese may have preceded them, and the Chinese, Indians
and Arabs before them. If they did, they left no verifiable record.

The first known account of the sighting of 'Nova Hollandia'

as the Dutch called Australia, was made in March 1606 by Captain Willem Jansz in the yacht *Duyfken*. Jansz sailed for about 320 km down the western side of Cape York Peninsula, but was disappointed with both the land and its inhabitants.

The Dutch made further journeys of exploration to the 'great south land' during the seventeenth century in their search for gold and for spices, but the inhospitable shore and the hostile Aborigines deterred any attempt at settlement. Willem Joosten van Colster in the *Arnhem* sighted Cape Arnhem, and probably the Wessel Islands and the Arnhem Land coast from Cape Grey to Cape Arnhem in 1623 as he made his way back to Amboina. Abel Janszoon Tasman sailed round the Gulf of Carpentaria, and saw Groote Eylandt and much of the Arnhem Land coast. No written account of his journey is known, but one of his maps suggests that he surveyed the entire Arnhem Land coast. As a result of their explorations a number of places on the northern coastline have Dutch names, such as the Gulf of Carpentaria, Groote Eylandt, Cape Arnhem and Cape Van Diemen. These names appeared on Dutch maps, were used by subsequent maritime explorers, and have come down to us to the present day.

Negative Dutch opinion regarding the northern coast of 'Nova Hollandia' and its inhabitants found support in the observations of the Englishman, William Dampier, who spent about two months in the Melville Island area in 1688. He recorded that the 'Inhabitants of this country are the miserablest people in the world. The Hodmadods of Monomatapa, though a Nasty People, yet for wealth are Gentlemen to these; who have no House, and skin Garments, Sheep, Poultry and Fruits of the Earth, Ostrich Eggs, etc. as the Hodmadods have: And setting aside their Human Shape, they differ but little from Brutes. They are tall, straight-bodied, and thin, with small, long limbs. They have great Heads, round Foreheads and great Brows. Their Eye-lids are always half-closed to keep the Flies out of their Eyes . . .'

In 1756 Gozal in the *Rijder* and Asschens in the *Buis* explored the Gulf of Carpentaria and eastern Arnhem Land. On the western side of Cape York Peninsula, in the vicinity of present day Weipa they met a number of Aborigines. They said that they had 'two dogs, not unlike so-called Bengal jackals'. The explorers described their huts as 'primitive dwellings, merely consisting of sheltered places under the trees, partly covered in with bark.' They said that the 'natives mainly subsist on the roots of trees and wild fruits such as yams or tubers, together with small quantities of fish which they catch in their canoes . . .' Their overall report on the Gulf country and Arnhem Land was more favourable than that of their predecessors, but there was no suggestion of settlement on these uninviting shores.

The next Balanda to explore the northern coastline of Australia were the British. First was Captain Matthew Flinders, who constantly urged the use of the name 'Australia' for the whole continent instead of 'New South Wales' or 'New Holland'. His voyage took place from 22 July 1802 until 8 June 1803 in the *Investigator*, an old 334-ton sloop. During his meticulous survey of much of the Australian coastline, Flinders mapped the eastern and part of the northern coast of Arnhem Land. Flinders was not impressed by the flat, monotonous beaches and the absence of any high country in the interior. He also was unable to establish friendly relationships with the Arnhem Land Aborigines, even though he had on board a Port Jackson Aboriginal named Bungaree. This was largely due to the fleeting contacts which he made during the running coastal surveys in which he was engaged. He normally called the Aborigines 'Indians', but occasionally spoke of them as 'Australians', which was quite a novel term for those days.

Flinders' observations regarding the rock paintings on Chasm Island on the north Groote Eylandt coast are of interest. He recorded that 'these drawings represented porpoises, turtle, kanguroos, and a human hand; and Mr Westall, who went afterwards to see them, found the representation of a kanguroo, with a file of thirty-two persons following after it. The third person of the band was twice the height of the others, and held in his hand something resembling the *whaddie*, or wooden sword of the natives of Port Jackson; and was probably intended to represent a chief ...'

At Blue Mud Bay his party had an unfortunate clash with the 'Indians' despite Flinders' desire to be on friendly terms with them. In their second encounter one Aboriginal was killed, about which Flinders wrote, 'I was much concerned at what had happened, and greatly displeased with the master for having acted so contrary to my orders ...' He was surprised at the aggressive attitude shown by them here and stated, 'I can account for this unusual conduct only by supposing, that they might have had differences with, and entertained no respectful opinion of the Asiatic visitors, of whom we found so many traces, some almost in sight of this place.'

At Caledon Bay they met several Aborigines who did not show 'that timidity so usual with the Australians.' They were prone to stealing, and to teach them not to steal, he seized an Aboriginal youth of fourteen named Woga (surely an ancestor of the great old man Wongu or Wonggu of the area during this century). Woga was reluctantly released after several days for, as Flinders records, 'He was a sprightly lad whom our treatment would soon have reconciled, and in any future intercourse with his country men . . . he might have been of service.'

Flinders gave an interesting description of the Aborigines of Caledon Bay. He said they were similar to Aborigines he had observed elsewhere in 'Terra Australis' except that those here 'had lost the upper front tooth on the left side.' He could not describe the women as they had 'seen only one female and that at a distance'. He was astonished to find that they practised 'the Jewish and Mahometan rite of circumcision . . . but with what view it may be done, or whence the custom were received, it is not in my power to state'. He said that spears were the only weapons he saw, and that their obvious knowledge of firearms had come from the Asiatics, the Macassans.

Flinders was forced to abandon his detailed survey of the Arnhem Land coast at Arnhem Bay in March 1803 because of 'the rottenness of the ship, the state of my own health and that of the ship's company'. He then sailed round Australia, arriving back at Port Jackson in June 1803. He was disappointed not to have finished the survey, but had accomplished much. Some of his maps are still used.

Phillip Parker King was the second British naval officer to explore the northern coastline of Australia. He completed Flinders' unfinished task, and carried on the fine tradition of hydrography established by his illustrious predecessor. His careful exploration of the northern coast of Arnhem Land was of the greatest importance for the understanding of this distant shoreline.

King made four exploratory journeys between 1817 and 1822, three times circumnavigating the Australian continent. Three of these voyages were made in the *Mermaid*, a tiny vessel of only 83 tons, with a full complement of nineteen persons. The fourth was undertaken in a larger vessel, the 170-ton brig, *Bathurst*. His survey of the Arnhem Land coast took place during his first and second voyages.

From the outset, King's contacts with the Aborigines of Arnhem Land were marked by conflict. This appears to be the result of fear on his part and those of his ship, and stealing and provocation on the part of the Aborigines. Seldom during his voyages did he appear to take the time to try to befriend them. He always mistrusted them, though frequently for good reason. As with

Flinders, his continual movement from place to place did not allow extended contact.

The conflict started with King's first meeting with Arnhem Land Aborigines at Goulburn Island, the first place where he anchored on this part of the coast. His flags and tools used on shore were stolen, so a canoe was seized until the goods were returned. The Aborigines retaliated by swimming out to the *Mermaid* and stealing the whale boat. When King saw them the next morning he wrote, 'This afforded us a good opportunity of expressing our anger at their attempt to steal our boat and of shewing them that we were not Malays, that we fired a shot from a six-pounder carronade over their heads, the report of which for a moment scared them; but their alarm was only momentary, for they soon afterwards recovered from their fright and continued to watch us as before.' Later that morning three of the shore party were 'slightly wounded' by large stones which the Aborigines hurled down on them from the cliff tops. As a result King provided his crew with an armed guard when working on shore, and sailed from the island earlier than he had planned.

Several weeks later King and his party met 'three natives' when they landed on Croker Island. They quickly hid. King wrote, 'They were perhaps deterred from approaching us from our numbers, and from the muskets which each of us carried; for our experience of the disposition of the natives at Goulburn Island had taught us prudence, and no boat was, after that affair, permitted to leave the vessel without taking a musket for each man.'

On the other hand King got on well with the Macassans and shared with them their distrust of the Aborigines. He wrote, 'Upon mentioning the natives of the coast, and showing them the stone-headed spear that we had found, they evinced their dislike to them very plainly, — they called them "Maregas", Marega being, as we afterwards found, their appellation for this part of the coast.'

Although King was unable to make friendly contact with the Aborigines, his exploration of the north Arnhem Land coast was of great importance for the future history of the Top End. He carefully mapped the whole coastline, naming many of the islands, bays, promentories and rivers. He explored the Alligator Rivers, which were so named because of numerous crocodiles there. ('Alligator' was the popular name at that time for an Australian crocodile.) He greatly admired Port Essington, which he predicted would 'become a place of great trade, and of very considerable importance'. He explored the Liverpool River, which Cadell later urged should be the site of the capital of the Northern Territory.

Flinders and King were clearly unimpressed by what they saw. The seashore was inhospitable and uninviting. The hinterland was barren and infertile. The natives were acquisitive and aggressive. Yet despite their unfavourable reports, the Balanda decided to commence settlement there. They took forty-five years to succeed, and the first four attempts were failures.

The British Government decided to start a settlement in Northern Australia in response to challenge. King's report told of renewed Dutch interest and proposed exploration of the area. The French, too, were casting covetous eyes on this somewhat dubious area, following the explorations of Captain Nicholas Baudin in the north-west and Melville Island in 1800 and 1803. Baudin's maps marked 'Nova Hollandia' as 'Terra Napoleon'. The Colonial Office was under extra pressure from merchant interests to develop trading links with Singapore and with the Macassans. In the end they instructed the Admiralty to despatch a naval vessel to take formal possession of the north coast, and to establish settlements in the Apsley Strait area, between Melville and Bathurst Islands, and at Port Essington on the Coburg Peninsula. The command was given to Captain J. J. Gordon Bremer of H.M.S. *Tamar*.

Captain Bremer accompanied by two transports brought the founding party to Port Essington on 20 September 1824. He took formal possession of the country at Point Record, but could not find water. He sailed on to Apsley Strait, where he took possession of Bathurst and Melville Islands on 26 September 1824 and established the settlement at King's Cove, on Melville Island. The new site was called Fort Dundas in honour of Sir Philip Dundas 'the noble Lord at the head of the Admiralty'.

This lonely outpost of imperial Britain consisted of Captain Maurice Barlow of the Third Regiment of Foot ('The Buffs') as the commandant; one subaltern and twenty-three privates; Lieut. C.C. Williamson and twenty-five marines; one assistant surgeon; three commissariat clerks; three mechanics; and forty-four volunteer convicts.

When Bremer left on 13 November 1824, he considered that the settlement had been well established and could look forward to a bright future. A substantial fort, a pier, officers' quarters and huts for the soldiers and convicts had been built. He stated that the soil was good for vegetables and 'valuable trees' and that water was plentiful. He admitted that mosquitoes and flies were troublesome, and that there had been several unfortunate clashes with Aborigines. Bremer's optimism, unfortunately, did not take into account the dramatic climatic change of the Wet.

Top: Egrets in the swamplands, the main refuge for large numbers of birds. Bottom: The bird life of Arnhem Land is varied and magnificent. Here jabiru storks feed in harmony with white ibis

TOP RIGHT: Groote Eylandt women. These bark dresses were usually worn in the presence of strangers (*old photo*). TOP LEFT: Spearing fish from dugout canoe, Groote Eylandt, 1934. BOTTOM: Living on the beach at Groote Eylandt, 1924

He also underrated the tenacity and hostility of the Aborigines.

As the Wet came rolling in from the north-west, the settlers' enthusiasm quickly left them. The convicts, acting as beasts of burden, soon succumbed to the heat and humidity and the continual drenching from the incessant rain. Food and medicine became scarce. The white-ant riddled buildings disintegrated in the face of the driving rain. The gardens were destroyed and animals ran wild. Gloom and depression overcame commandant and convicts alike. Quarrels broke out. The terrible isolation became almost unbearable.

Because of the lack of horses and the chronic condition of the convicts, Captain Barlow obtained thirty water buffalo from Timor in the *Lady Nelson*. (In the following year this ship was captured by pirates near Baba Island and its crew murdered.) The buffalo that survived the trip back to Fort Dundas and others imported later became the originators of the vast herds that roam Arnhem Land today.

The privations and problems of the settlement were compounded by the aggression of the Tiwi, the Aborigines of Melville Island. Bremer and Barlow had been unsuccessful in their attempts to befriend them. As the months passed, axes, tools, a crosscut saw, a boat and a handcart were stolen. No one moved outside the fort unless under guard. The same conditions continued after the arrival of Major John Campbell in 1827 to relieve Captain Barlow of what he termed his three years' stint 'in hell'. Aboriginal attacks on the fort now took place almost daily.

The violent deaths by spearing of the surgeon, Dr John Gold, and the storekeeper, John Green, added terror to the lives of the dispirited garrison. The two men were speared in retaliation for the arrest of one of the leading Aborigines. Dr Gold's body had thirty-one spear wounds; Green's had seventeen, and his head had been smashed in.

Life by the seashore of delightful Melville Island now became intolerable. Campbell implored the Colonial Office to be relieved of his responsibility for this place on 'this vile island', or to abandon the settlement. He pointed out that the climate was impossible, sickness was rampant, the soil was bad, and the animals were dying. Only several trading vessels had visited the fort, and no Macassans had been seen. Above all the Aborigines were incorrigible and dangerous. Campbell could have complained also of the terrible isolation of this lonely place.

The Colonial Office eventually heeded Campbell's complaints and ordered the withdrawal of the garrison. As the forlorn band of pathetic Balanda sailed away on 31 March 1829, they established a pattern of failure for three future settlements in this far-off shore. They could not adapt themselves to the climatic extremes of the Wet and the Dry. They could not come to terms with the original inhabitants of the land.

The second northern settlement was commenced at Fort Wellington, on the Coburg Peninsula in 1827, but was abandoned two years later. The Colonial Office had commissioned Captain James Stirling of the H.M.S. *Success* to find a more suitable place than Fort Dundas. Considering Croker Island to be unsuitable, Stirling chose Raffles Bay, which had been named by Captain P.P. King in 1818 in honour of Sir Stamford Raffles, the founder of Singapore. The harbour was safe, the soil good, and water was plentiful. Stirling spent just over a month helping the commandant, Captain Henry Smyth, and the newcomers to settle in. Smyth had a detachment of soldiers, a party of marines, a surgeon, two women, five children and a few convicts.

Once again the prospects for the success of the new colony at first seemed to be reasonably high. A garden was started, the livestock flourished, and they had plenty of provisions. By October, however, even before the onset of the rains, the settlement was in dire straits. Almost fifty out of the total population of seventy-six were sick. The gardens had dried up, and the stock were faring poorly. The new settlement was beginning to succumb to the usual pattern of frustration and despair.

Relations with the Iwaidja, the local Aborigines, could not have been worse. Smyth was brutal, and believed that a dead 'black' was the answer to the troublesome 'black'. As the conflict worsened, he offered five pounds for every 'black' taken dead or alive. As a result a number of Aboriginal men, women and children were massacred.

Fortunately for all concerned, Smyth was invalided south, and his place was taken by Captain Collet Barker, who was an entirely different person. Barker arrived on 13 September 1828 with a fresh contingent of troops and convicts. He immediately put the tiny colony in order and established friendly relations with the Aborigines.

Large numbers of Macassans now began to frequent the area, as Raffles Bay was near some of their traditional trepanging grounds. The British welcomed the establishment of this large trepang camp close to the settlement. The Macassans, for their part, were pleased to be able to carry out their fishing and curing activities safe from Aboriginal attack and the threat of pirates.

Just when the settlement seemed to be finding its feet, the Colonial Office ordered the abandonment of both Fort Dundas and Fort Wellington. Fort Dundas had been a failure, Barker acknowledged, but Fort Wellington showed promise. He pointed out that the climate was healthy, that the Aborigines were now friendly, and that the Macassans and Chinese could be persuaded to settle there. Barker argued to no avail. The settlement had to go. And so on August 1829 the garrison sailed away from the sandy shores of this pleasant harbour in the Arafura Sea, and left the land once more to the Aborigines.

Ten years later the British Government made a third attempt to establish a garrison in tropical North Australia. The site chosen this time was Port Essington, so named by Captain King in honour of Vice-Admiral Sir William Essington. King had said that this port 'is equal to any harbour I have seen. From its proximity to the Moluccas and New Guinea, and its being in the direct line of communication between Port Jackson and India ... it must, at no distant period, become a place of great trade.'

Captain J.J. Gordon Bremer, who had rejected Port Essington fourteen years earlier, was commissioned to establish the new settlement. The Colonial Office once again had been persuaded of the need for this northern outpost to forestall any Dutch occupation of the area; that the place would be a strategic centre for establishing trading relations with the Macassans; and that it would be an important victualling centre for vessels trading between London, the Far East and Port Jackson. Captain Bremer was given three ships, the *Britomart*, the *Alligator*, and the *Orontes* to transport the royal marines, their families and their supplies to this new establishment. The commandant was Captain John McArthur. The new settlement was called Victoria, in honour of the young and well-loved Queen.

As in the case of the other two settlements, the early days of Victoria offered high hopes of success. Bremer spoke optimistically of a place where he said there would soon be '500 inhabitants, exclusive of the military authorities' and a municipal corporation capable of imposing taxation for local requirements.

Small numbers of Aborigines visited the new settlement soon after it was started. They gave no trouble, except in wanting any article which appealed to them. They went out exploring with the marines and lay down outside their tents at night. Some set up a camp on the shore nearby, and exchanged fish, crabs and oysters for Balanda food and clothing.

After a year the number of Aborigines camping near the tiny

settlement grew. They had with them their women and children. They frequently entertained the marines with their singing and dancing. By now they realised that pilfering would result in a whipping. At the same time they had come to trust the newcomers and became quite friendly with them.

In 1840 friction between Captain John McArthur and Captain W.W. Chambers, his second-in-command, flared up because of Chambers' severe punishment of Aborigines for petty offences. McArthur ordered Chambers to refrain from further flogging of Aborigines, and wrote to Governor Gipps in Sydney, seeking support for his authority at Victoria. The tension eased when Chambers left the garrison.

Good relations with the Aborigines were restored and Commandant McArthur showed great concern for their wellbeing. He tried to help them, and to 'improve' their way of life. He cared for them when they were sick, and at their request he arbitrated between them in their quarrels.

McArthur was also concerned for the spiritual welfare of the Aborigines. In 1846 Father Angelo Confalonieri and two other Roman Catholic missionaries undertook to help. Father Confalonieri's two companions were drowned when the *Heroine*, on which they were travelling, was wrecked in the Torres Strait. He was able to make his way with other survivors to Port Essington, where he took up his duties as 'Vicar General of Port Victoria'. He lived in a dwelling built for him at Black Rock Point, just south of Point Smith at the entrance of Port Essington. Here he was able to contact the local Aborigines more easily, and at the same time to live within reasonable proximity to the settlement.

During his first year Father Confalonieri was able to assist Captain McArthur and the surgeon to treat the Aborigines during a severe influenza epidemic. Many were dying and others were too weak to help themselves. They received reports that the epidemic was widespread along much of the northern coastal region of Arnhem Land. The help given by the Balanda at Victoria probably helped to prevent the extinction of the Aborigines of the Coburg Peninsula.

Mr Peter Spillett, the well-known Darwin historian, in his valuable book, *Forsaken Settlement* writes that Father Confalonieri 'continued to evangelise the Aborigines but without any degree of success. He endeavoured to attract as many children as possible of the Limbarkaregio tribe to remain in the area and teach them Christian prayers and observances. One of his greatest problems was the nomadic habits of the natives for they did not stay long enough to be taught ... He made an outstanding impression on all who met him by his facility to learn the Aboriginal language which in turn meant a better understanding of their mode of life. He was greatly liked by most of the Aborigines for the way in which he tried to reconcile tribal differences, his generosity in sharing his provisions and the way he adopted their nomadic way of life.'

The outstanding ministry of Father Confalonieri came to an end with his premature death on 9 June 1848. He was buried at Victoria at a service attended by the whole settlement, who had deeply respected and admired this earnest, zealous missionary. He had been a faithful priest working alone under very great difficulties. He did not witness any conversions, but had made those of the settlement know the importance of language and culture studies of the local Aborigines.

Just prior to his death an Aboriginal was killed by a member of the garrison. Sergeant William Masland had shot the Aboriginal, who was trying to escape from lawful custody. Captain McArthur was horrified by the killing, which was the first act of violence committed against the Aborigines at Victoria. Masland was later acquitted after his case had been heard by the Supreme Court in Sydney and referred to the Colonial Secretary. McArthur's deep distress and the seriousness with which the killing was viewed indicate the concern of the Commandant and Colonial Government regarding the treatment of Aborigines in Arnhem Land at that time. That such attitudes and acts were not emulated by white men in the later history of the North is a tragedy.

The killing of the Aboriginal had a further unfortunate sequel. The relatives of the killed man took vengence by killing Neinmal, a great favourite with the British settlers. Neinmal had stayed several years with the naturalist John MacGillivray, and had helped him with his collections. Neat and tidy in his habits, he was learning to read and write at Victoria before his untimely death cut short a promising life.

Several notable maritime explorers visited Port Essington. The first of these visitors was Captain J.S.C. Dumont d'Urville in the *Astrolabe* and the *Zelee*. Captain d'Urville had a poor opinion of the Aborigines of the Coburg. He commented that they were aware of some of 'the vices of civilization', one pronouncing the word '"brandy"', indicating with a sign that he wished to drink some'. He was impressed with what he saw of the new settlement, now six months old. He spoke of friction between Macassans and Aborigines camped there. He noted that the British were not at all worried about the Aborigines camped nearby, and had established friendly relations with them.

Another important maritime expedition to visit Port Essington was that being undertaken in the *Beagle*, first under the command of Captain J.C. Wickham, and then under Captain John Lort Stokes. The *Beagle* made four separate visits to Victoria between 1837 and 1843, during this last major sea exploration of Australia. The young naturalist Charles Darwin had been a member of the expedition but not during its visits to North Australia.

Stokes wrote enthusiastically of Port Essington when he first saw it in 1839. He said, 'The expanse of water presented to our view in standing up Port Essington quite delighted us. It is in truth a magnificent harbour, and well worthy of having on its shores the capital of Northern Australia, destined, doubtless, from its proximity to India, and our other fast increasing eastern possessions, to become not only a great commercial resort, but a valuable naval port in time of war.' He described the settlement in glowing terms, stating that 'the dwellings of the settlers had an air of neatness, pleasing to the eye'. He continued, 'Among the other buildings in progress was the church, which, planted as it was on the northern shores of the Australian continent, was expected to form a nucleus from which off-shoots might by degrees draw within its influence the islands in the Arafura Sea, and thus widely spread the pure blessings of Christianity.'

Stokes said that the 'natives were found by the settlers ... very friendly, and their assistance proved valuable': they did not use a boomerang but 'the throwing stick' or 'wamara'. He said that he only saw one musical instrument which he called an 'ebroo' which 'produces a kind of droning noise'. He continued, 'It is generally made use of at corroborees or dances, some of which express feats of hunting and war, while others are very indecent.'

On his final visit to Port Essington, Stokes wrote in his exalted style that 'we naturally experienced some regret on our departure, and were led to speculate, with interest, on its future destiny'. He considered that though the settlement was remote and solitary 'the experience of the past teaches us confidently to expect that wherever a knot of Englishmen locate themselves, there are deposited the germs of future greatness.' He claimed that it might not be a Gibraltar but 'its importance, as a commercial station, is incalculable' and that 'Victoria must one day ... be the centre of a vast system of commerce, the emporium, in fact, where will take place the exchange of the products of the Indian Archipelago for those of the vast plains of Australia'.

Despite Lort Stokes' expectations, Victoria, Port Essington, suffered the fate of the other two settlements. That it should have been abandoned was no fault of the ever-optimistic Captain McArthur, who had applied himself with singular devotion to the difficult task of its administration throughout the entire eleven years of its life. Like its predecessors, the colony had fallen victim to isolation, stagnation, and the inability to obtain a firm foothold in the soil. Produce was grown, but not in economic quantities. The proposed trade with the Macassans and their permanent settlement had not begun. Its role as a victualling port between eastern Australia and the Indies had not materialised. Cogent reasons for its continued support ceased, so Victoria was abandoned.

On 30 November 1849 the British deserted this beautiful but lonely spot on the Coburg Peninsula. Port Essington once more became silent, its silence broken only by the gentle lapping of the waves on the beach and the distant screech of the black cockatoo. The Balanda had gone and the Aborigines were once again left to themselves.

Victoria, Port Essington, had been the destination of the incredible overland journey of the inexperienced explorer, Ludwig Leichhardt. On 1 October 1844 Leichhardt with a party of nine had left Jimbour on the Darling Downs. After an astonishing feat of endurance, he and his party, now reduced by three, arrived at Victoria on the 17 December 1845. They had travelled more than 4800 kilometres over the Great Divide, across the harsh Gulf Country, and through forbidding Arnhem Land.

When they came to the East Alligator River, the Aborigines became their guides, so that they eventually reached Victoria, where they were given a very warm welcome. Leichhardt wrote, 'I was deeply affected by finding myself again in civilized society, and could scarcely speak, the words growing big with tears and emotion; and, even now, when considering with what small means the Almighty had enabled me to perform such a long journey, my heart thrills in grateful acknowledgement of His infinite kindness.'

Leichhardt's remarkable journey stirred the imagination of the colonists of the South, and his description of the pastoral potential of the Top End quickened their interest in the area. Further interest came through Surveyor A.C. Gregory's expedition from the Victoria River in Western Australia, across the Gulf Country, to Brisbane in 1855 and 1856.

Interest was further heightened four years later when the South

Australian Government offered £2000 to the first explorer to cross the continent from south to north. There were two contenders for the race and for the prize. The first was John McDouall Stuart; the second was Robert O'Hara Bourke assisted by his lieutenant, John William Wills. Stuart and his small party successfully made the journey after incredible hardship and two abortive attempts. He travelled north from Adelaide, eventually reaching Van Diemen Gulf on 24 July 1862. His route was later followed by the surveyors of the Overland Telegraph Line. The modern Stuart Highway from Alice Springs to Darwin follows his track. The modern motorist whizzing along the 1538 kilometres of tarmac at 120 km/h rarely gives a thought to the amazing exploit of this wiry little Scot, who blazed the trail for them.

Stuart did not win the race. He was beaten by Bourke and Wills, who had started from Melbourne with a vast cavalcade in August 1860. They perished on their return trip. The honour for the importance of achievements of the two contenders must rest with Stuart.

Stuart's journey and the report which he made led to the annexation of the Northern Territory by South Australia. Writing of the land between the Roper and the Arafura Sea, Stuart said, 'I believe this country to be well adapted for the settlement of a European population; the climate being in every respect suitable, and the surrounding country of excellent quality and great extent ... If this country is settled, it will be one of the finest colonies under the Crown, suitable for the growth of any and everything — what a splendid country for producing cotton.' Large-scale white settlement on pastoral properties in the North now became a distinct possibility. Balanda were starting to brace themselves for the coming confrontation with Aborigines over the sensitive issue of land.

But Stuart had fallen into the trap of so many visitors to the North! He had travelled in the cool conditions of the early months of the Dry. The country was at its best. The climate was magnificent. He did not experience the extremities of heat and barrenness of the later months of the Dry, and the tropical deluges of the Wet. Once again the white man misjudged the North.

The South Australian Government annexed the Northern Territory in July 1863. This vast area of over 134 million hectares, occupying more than one-sixth of the Australian continent, was ceded from the colony of New South Wales. South Australia acquired her northern territory because of the pastoral and supposed agricultural potential. By questionable means she wrested this doubtful prize from her rival contender, the Colony of Queensland. South Australia's small population was later to regret her precipitate and somewhat presumptuous action.

The site chosen for the temporary settlement was Escape Cliffs on Adam Bay at the mouth of the Adelaide River. Captain Wickham in the *Beagle* had discovered the bay and the river, naming the bay after Vice-Admiral Sir Charles Adam, and the river after the Queen Dowager. While on shore at Adam Bay, two of the *Beagle's* complement, Fitzmaurice and Keys, were surprised by a large number of Aborigines on the cliffs above who threatened to kill them. They escaped by amusing the Aborigines by dancing and shouting. As Stokes wrote, 'It was therefore, not a little surprising to behold this paroxism of rage evaporate before the happy presence of mind displayed by Mr Fitzmaurice, in immediately beginning to dance and shout, though in momentary expectation of being pierced by a dozen spears.' Because of this incident the area was called Escape Cliffs.

The choice of Adam Bay as the site of the new settlement was unfortunate, as was the appointment of B.T. Finnis as the government Resident. Finnis refused to consider any other site, was an unsatisfactory leader, and in 1866 was recalled. The exploration of the surrounding country to find a better place was unsuccessful. The attempt made during the Wet by the experienced McKinlay east of the Adelaide River was little short of a farce. Finnis' successor, Manton, was not much better. One thing, however, must be said for him. He saw the advantage of Port Darwin over Adam Bay as 'a site for a town and part of the first settlement'. On 11 January 1867 he transferred the settlement to Port Darwin. The fourth attempt to start a white colony in the North had been a failure.

The South Australian Government was still not convinced that Port Darwin was the right place for the northern capital. In 1866 they sent Francis Cadell to explore the northern coast of Arnhem Land. Cadell strongly favoured the Liverpool River as being the most suitable site, and spoke highly of the surrounding country. How different the future of the Arnhem Land Aborigines would have been had this site been chosen, situated as it is right in the central coastal area! There probably would have been no Arnhem Land Reserve, and possibly only a few Aborigines would have survived.

The South Australian Government continued undecided until insistent demands and legal action taken by holders of land orders in Adelaide and in England forced their hand. A site had to be chosen, the land properly surveyed, and lots allocated as quickly as possible. This time they chose the right man, Surveyor-General G.W. Goyder, who in turn chose the right place, Port Darwin. Goyder arrived there on the *Moonta* on 5 February 1869, and by August had surveyed not only four townships, but a further 660 000 acres. Goyder spoke highly of the country around Darwin, saying that it was 'a first-class country for large stock, such as horses and cattle ... parts of the table land is well suited for cultivation ... ' Future settlement was now assured. The Balanda had come to stay. From now onwards two entirely different cultures were to meet in head-on collision. One was almost to annihilate the other.

8
They must be protected

The impact of white settlement on Aboriginal culture in the Top End during the nineteenth century was devastating. Consequently protection and control became the twin philosophies underlying government Aboriginal policy during the first half of the twentieth century. The South Australian Act No 1024 of 1910 was 'to Make provision for the Better Protection and Control of the Aboriginal Inhabitants of the Northern Territory'. The Commonwealth Aboriginals Ordinance No 9 of 1918 was set up for 'the care and control of aboriginals and half-castes and the children of such people . . . the establishment of reserves, the licensing of aboriginal institutions and the removal of natives thereto, the regulation of employment and education'.

Before these laws there had been little protection and almost no control. Aborigines were a dying race. They were being shot and driven from their traditional lands, or they were killing themselves with white vices. The only means of saving them was to provide reserves and control their activities. The plea of the few who cared was, 'They must be protected'.

The situation in the nineteenth century was tragic. Wrongs existed on both sides. There is little doubt that had governments in the twentieth century not acted to protect, a greater number of Aborigines of the Territory would have continued to be massacred or would have 'just faded away'. This grim fact was brought into sharp focus by the indifference and inactivity of the South Australian Government during their forty-seven years' administration between 1863 and 1910. During those tough, rough years there had been virtually no protection, only gross injustice.

South Australian administration from 1869 until 1889 were boom years for this new white frontier of the North. The Overland Telegraph Line linking Adelaide with Darwin and the rest of the world was opened in 1872. Shortly afterwards the news of the discovery of gold at Pine Creek flashed over the telegraph, bringing hundreds of gold diggers to the Territory. Gold mining also brought the Chinese, who flocked in by their hundreds from elsewhere in Australia and overseas. (They later were to provide the backbone of the workforce.)

During the big pastoral boom between 1880 and 1882 much of the Northern Territory was leased for pastoral purposes. In 1881 the whole of Arnhem Land made up of more than 95 828 square kilometres was held under eleven leases. Bitter confrontation between the settler and the Aborigines of Arnhem Land had begun.

Two pastoral ventures in Arnhem Land during the next two decades highlighted the conflict. In the 1880s MacCartney started Florida station on the Goyder River. He built the homestead and cattle yards and established a large herd. But from the outset, he clashed constantly with the Aborigines and lost large numbers of cattle. The result was inevitable. He abandoned Florida in 1893 and turned his attention to Auvergne on the Victoria River. The Aborigines had won the first round.

The second venture was tragic and resulted in bloodshed. In 1903 the Eastern and African Cold Storage Company leased almost the whole of eastern Arnhem Land. Their lease occupied just under 50 000 square kilometres. The Company transferred about 5000 head of cattle from Elsey, Hodgson Downs and Wollogorang stations to the old Florida site and to places on Blue Mud Bay. This bold experiment, like so many others in the Top End, also failed. Stock spread out over such a vast area could not be herded. The grasses were unsuitable. Above all the local Aborigines were aggressive and acquired a great taste for beef. In 1908 the project folded up and the surviving cattle were taken to Hodgson Downs.

Once again the Aborigines won, but this time the price they paid was high. Relations between the Eastern and African Cold Storage Company and the Aborigines could not have been worse. From time to time the Company employed two gangs of up to fourteen Aborigines under a white or a half-caste to hunt out and shoot up the 'blacks' on sight. Many Aboriginal men, women and children were hunted like animals and shot. A number of the old men at Roper River have told me many stories of these shootings. Doubtless some accounts have become exaggerated over the years. But the fact remains that they happened. As a consequence many tribes in the Roper area are now almost extinct. The Roper River community has no major tribe or language. Creole, a form of pidgin English, is now the accepted means of communication.

Throughout the Territory, the nomadic Aborigines succumbed in one way or another to the inexorable advance of the white frontier. They retaliated where they could with spears, but these were no match for guns. They committed atrocities and killings of whites when they could. Whites reacted by shooting at sight, or by sending police punitive expeditions to massacre men, women and children, 'to teach the blacks a lesson'.

These were hard years for the white settler toiling in scorching heat or pouring rain to establish his holding. Conditions were harsh and life was lonely. They were also hard years for the blacks as they saw their land being taken from them. The very source of their life was threatened. There are two sides to the story. There were aggression, killing and treachery on both sides. Inevitably the superior arms, greater mobility and better resources of the white man prevailed. The lack of defined frontiers of the nomadic Aborigines was also a factor. The black man retreated, was killed, or came to terms with the invader, in what Professor Elkin has termed 'intelligent parasitism'.

There was no justice for the black man. Police, though called sub-protectors, were always on the side of the settlers. After all, the settlers were white men and 'civilised'. They provided welcome hospitality for the weary policeman riding for days in those lonely, inhospitable regions.

Most whites considered the 'blacks' to be sub-human and beyond reprieve. Their attitudes are typified by words of Alfred Giles of Springfield station at Katherine, which he wrote in 1887, 'Moral laws they have none, their festive dances and corroborees are of the most lewd and disgusting character, their songs, rites and ceremonies utterly revolting and fiendish ... the possibility of the existence of chastity among their women ... is ... preposterous ... White men are not infallible, and perhaps not infrequently fall victim to the blackfellow's cunning and his wife's allurements, but the mistake made by those who know no better is that the poor fellow who gets knocked on the head in the endeavour to protect his property is deserving of blame, because he abducted or seduced the lubra, and therefore they justify his killing him, whereas I have shown that in nine cases out of ten, the blackfellow sends, and insists — often against the woman's will — on her acting as his decoy.'

The first Government Resident in Palmerston (Darwin) to try to help the Aborigines was the Honorable J.A. Langdon Parsons. In 1885 he recommended that they should be protected by the creation of reserves, although he realised that they 'but imperfectly meet the case'. He said that large reserves ought to be proclaimed 'because the native life is essentially nomadic, and because the imperious demands of hunger take him where the waterlily roots, yams and game are to be found'. His plan to protect the disadvantaged Aborigines in this way fell on deaf ears in Adelaide. Nothing was done.

One gleam of hope, however, appeared in the darkening gloom surrounding the future of the lives of the Territory Aborigines. The Church commenced its ministry among them. Some doubt the effectiveness of Christian evangelisation of Aborigines; others hold that it morally is wrong. But whatever the views on missions may be, the work of the Church, with its roots throughout Australia and overseas, brought a new dimension of information and understanding for white Australians in the South and a more compassionate attitude towards the black Australians in the North.

Early Christian missions had their failures. The Jesuit mission, started at Rapid Creek in Darwin about 1883, closed after a few years. Similarly the second Jesuit mission, established at Port Keats near the Daly River in 1886, was abandoned about 1900. The Catholic Church was forced to turn its attention to the offshore islands as a base for its activities, starting at Bathurst Island in 1911. Aborigines here were not subjected to white 'civilising' pressures.

In 1908 the Anglican Church Missionary Society (CMS) started a mission on the Roper River, and the story of its ministry is told elsewhere in this book. The Government Resident of the day declared that the mission should have been commenced closer to Palmerston, where, he claimed, the need was the greatest. The CMS on the other hand emphasised that it wished to work among traditional Aborigines away from the demoralising influences of the towns.

The South Australian administration of the Territory was not a success. Its attitude and policy towards Aborigines in the Territory had been irresponsible. By the time that the Aborigines Act of 1910 was passed irreparable damage had been done. Too little was done too late to protect them. Within a year control of the Territory came under Commonwealth administration, to whom was transferred the complex and tragic plight of the Aborigines of the North.

On assuming power in 1911 the Commonwealth Government embarked on a vigorous policy of protection and control of Aborigines. The South Australian Aboriginals Act of 1910 had foreshadowed this move and reflected this policy. The Aboriginals Ordinance of 1911 amended the South Australian Act and was gazetted in January 1912.

This legislation provided for an Aboriginals Department under a Chief Protector and for the establishment of reserves and leases for missions. Provision was made for the rigid control of Aboriginal movement and employment, and rules were made for his welfare and protection. The definition of an Aboriginal included that of a half-caste, who was described as being the offspring of an Aboriginal mother and a non-Aboriginal father. The Chief Protector became the legal guardian of every Aboriginal and half-caste child up to the age of eighteen years. Special protection was to be afforded to half-caste children.

Dr H. Basedow, a medical scientist, was appointed Chief Protector of Aboriginals and given two Assistant Protectors. Basedow resigned after six weeks. In 1912 Professor W. Baldwin Spencer was appointed Chief Protector and Special Commissioner for one year. Mr W.G. Stretton later took his place. Attempts were made to establish schools for Aborigines at Pine Creek and Darwin; and small subsidies were given for the Anglican and Roman Catholic Missions at Roper and Daly Rivers.

Spencer's *Preliminary Report on the Aboriginals of the Northern Territory* underlined the need for their protection and control. He presented this report after nearly twelve months' careful investigation. Debunking the claim that Aborigines 'have no morality', he spoke of their moral code relating to marriage arrangements. He commented, 'It may also be said that generally speaking, the uncivilized native is honest, with probably not more exceptions than amongst whites.'

Spencer's attitude regarding Aboriginal intelligence and temperament reflects the outlook of his day. 'The Aboriginal is indeed a very curious mixture; mentally, about the level of a child who has little control over his feelings and is liable to give way to violent fits of temper, during which he may very likely act with great cruelty. He has no sense of responsibility and, except in rare cases, no initiative. His memory in many cases is wonderful so far as subjects are concerned that affect his life and mode of conduct. When once he has seen any place, or any particular object, he knows it for all time.'

Commenting on Aborigines living in townships, Baldwin Spencer said that they 'have long since become degenerate and have lost all their old customs and beliefs ... The supplying of aboriginals with opium and spirits and a wholesale prostitution of native women are common and constant practices among the great body of Asiatics and form the most serious evil that the Department has to contend within the settled and more especially the mining districts ...' He spoke of Aborigines living on large pastoral properties. 'Though comparatively few natives are employed on any station ... yet there is always a native camp in the vicinity of every station, where there is a smaller or larger group gathered together, attracted by the chance of securing food from the station.'

He spoke of the 'widespread habit of prostituting the lubras' and of 'the rapid degeneration of the native in contact with Chinese'. He deplored the absence of white women in the Territory, which was the main cause of the prostitution of Aboriginal women. He added, 'It is most important that all Protectors should be married men and emphatically no one except a married man should be a Superintendent of a reserve or native station or settlement.'

He spoke of the need for medical officers, for provision for treating contagious diseases, for the trial of Aborigines, for the establishment of 'an Aboriginal Reformatory' and for the proper treatment of half-castes.

Turning to future policy regarding Aboriginal affairs he recommended that the 'care of the aboriginals of the Northern Territory should be made a national responsibility'. Aborigines living in and around the two townships of Darwin and Pine Creek should be gathered 'together into a village or compound'. Here there should be a school, and a garden to employ people on a set wage, part of which would be banked. The inmates should be confined to this compound between sunset and sunrise. No 'native should be allowed to leave Darwin without the consent of the Superintendent or a Protector'.

Baldwin Spencer maintained that 'the real problem' was that of nomadic Aborigines 'who form almost the whole Aboriginal population of the Territory'. He said that 'there is no other practicable policy but that of the establishment of large reserves, if the aboriginals are to be preserved, and if any serious effort is to be made for their betterment'. The reserves must be large, contain abundant food supplies and be located where tribes 'are allied in their customs and are more or less friendly'. Each reserve should be under the control of a married Superintendent who would have overall control and responsibility. There should be schools for learning and 'moral training'. The primary object of the stations

Arnhemlander in dugout canoe. With the coming of the Macassans, the earlier flimsy, bark canoes were supplanted by these wooden dugouts (*old photo*)

Rock painting, Deaf Adder Gorge, western Arnhem Land. Many of these paintings have deep religious significance and occur in very sacred places

on the reserves 'must be to train the natives in industrial habits. Until such time as they acquire these habits there is no chance whatever of raising them from their present condition.'

The policy of protection by segregation on reserves comes out clearly towards the conclusion of his report where he stated, 'From the point of view of the Aboriginal Department, it is of primary importance that the reserves should be retained for the use of the natives, with the idea of isolating them and preventing them from coming into contact with other people'.

Any hopes of immediate implementation of Baldwin Spencer's Report were forgotten in the nation's preoccupation with the 1914-18 War. After the war in 1918 Aboriginals Ordinance was passed and subsequently amended in succeeding years. This legislation provided for the care and control of Aborigines and their protection in reserves on licensed institutions. Provision was made for Aborigines to be moved there, to control their business affairs, to regulate their employment and to provide moral protection for females and children.

Practice, however, did not match the policy and the provisions of the Ordinance. Frequent changes in government and personnel and the shortage of money hindered its application. Overseas countries began criticising the Australian Government for neglect or abuse of Aborigines. The high hopes of 1911 were not being realised.

Baldwin Spencer's recommendation for the formation of reserves for the protection of Aborigines were in line with earlier agitation for their formation. In 1910 the Association for the Advancement of Science expressed concern about the treatment of Aborigines in the Territory. The Association for the Protection of Native Races was formed in 1911 to bring pressure on the Commonwealth Government to legislate to prevent further deterioration of Aborigines in the newly acquired Northern Territory. In its first Annual Report in 1912 the Australian Native Races Protection Society stated that meetings had been held 'for the purpose of pressing upon the Federal Government the necessity for making adequate provision for the large population of Aborigines inhabiting the newly acquired Northern Territory'.

Church and mission bodies and their supporters also requested the creation of large reserves. The Anglican CMS started the Roper River Mission in 1908. The Methodist Overseas Missions (MOM) commenced work on Goulburn Island in 1916. CMS and MOM missionaries were on the spot; they knew the situation first hand. Although they were tiny outposts staffed by a few white people, the missions nevertheless were linked to southern supporters. The supporters in turn were able to engender wide public interest in Aborigines among influential groups throughout the community.

The MOM complemented its missionary activity with attempts at legislative reform. They were not very successful. When establishing the Goulburn Island Mission they asked the Commonwealth Government to declare that mission leases were reserves, in line with Baldwin Spencer's 1913 recommendations. Commenting on this intention a Government memorandum declared that such a move was about 'as reasonable as would be a suggestion to segregate wallabies!'

In July 1918, the Anglican Bishop of Carpentaria, the Right Reverend Henry Newton, recommended 'a bold and big policy' for the Arnhem Land area. The Northern Territory at the time was under his ecclesiastical jurisdiction. He wrote, 'I would suggest that the authorities be approached and asked to declare the whole of the North East of the Territory a Reserve for Aborigines ... I would suggest that the whole of that area be closed to white settlement for at least fifty years and that Missions be established to get in touch with and influence the people before the country is opened to settlement and then policy can be defined.'

In the 1920s a variety of churches and organisations continued their agitation for the formation of reserves. The Anglican CMS and ABM (Australian Board of Missions) constantly advocated this action through the United (later, the National) Missionary Council (NMC). The MOM continued to apply pressure through their own channels and through the NMC. The Australian Association for the Advancement of Science in 1926 requested that the Government should make Arnhem Land 'a permanent reservation for the use and benefit of Australian Aborigines'. The Association for the Protection of Native Races (APNR) whose members had church, scientific and humanitarian interests, demanded that 'adequate reserves should be set apart for the natives wherever they may be segregated, and enabled to live as far as desirable under their own native conditions ... ' The Anti-Slavery and Aborigines Protection Society of London, closely associated with the APNR, maintained a keen interest. In 1925 the Aborigines Protection League petitioned Parliament 'praying for the creation of a separate state in Northern Australia'.

Anthropologists were also among the agitators. Though not many in number they joined some of the organisations demanding reform. Others spoke out as individuals. W.L. Warner declared that missionaries should not be allowed into the Arnhem Land reserves when proclaimed 'for they were part of a civilisation that was poison to native people.' Dr F. D. Walker was appalled at the medical state of the Territory Aborigines and in 1928 urged the Minister of Home and Territories, to provide 'reserves for full-bloods.'

The first legislative move by the Commonwealth Government in response to this growing agitation came in 1927. The Minister for Home and Territories refused a royal commission or select committee of inquiry, but agreed to appoint Mr J. W. Bleakley, the Chief Protector of Aborigines in Queensland, to enquire. He began his work in 1928 and his report was made public in 1929.

Bleakley's review of the conditions of Aborigines living in towns and in the country revealed continued neglect and lack of protection. The new missions in Arnhem Land, except Roper River, came in for favourable comment. He said that 'these missions are all working on the right lines; the officers making themselves conversant with the native language and customs and endeavouring, without unduly pressing the white man's civilization upon them, to induce them, by the education of the young, to see the advantages of the settled and industrious life.'

Bleakley countered anthropologists' objections to mission activities and institutions. He said that the 'native, once having come in contact with the white man or alien and acquired a taste for his foods and luxuries, is not likely to longer remain a contented savage'. Missions ought to be encouraged and used. 'The cost of management is less, and the missions can obtain the type of worker who undertakes the work from missionary, and not mercenary, motives and is likely to have more sympathy with the people.' He also said that the Government was already overtaxed in the development of the country, and it would be better for the Administration if it could 'confine itself to the direction of the work required'.

Bleakley put forward a seven-point program for future administration. Government should establish 'a native state with self-government on the proposed reserves'; there should be 'complete segregation of all wandering natives' as 'the shielding of the race from the evils of contact with civilized races is urgently necessary'. Also needed were the 'establishment of cattle stations for Aboriginals', 'compulsory general education of Aboriginal children', 'education in citizenship', the 'formation of Aborigines Advisory Board' and 'the employment of a trained anthropologist for the scientific study of the race'.

The proposals which Bleakley made reflect the Queensland

Government's policy and thinking. The key words underlying his recommendations were segregation, protection, training and control. The formation of reserves was essential to his theory. Mission institutions on the reserves would be the handmaid for education and the processes of 'civilisation'.

Despite the report the Government was still hesitant. In April 1929, the new Minister for Home and Territories, Mr C. L. Abbott, called a conference to discuss Bleakley's recommendations. Various interested parties once again put their case and the conference unanimously agreed to request the Government to proclaim Arnhem Land a reserve. In June 1930 the Government finally agreed, and proclaimed the Arnhem Land Reserve in 1931.

The struggle for the reserve had been long and tiresome. Different groups had played a major role in forcing the Government to act. Other societies and individuals had helped. After twenty years' struggle the reserve was proclaimed 'for the use and benefit of the aboriginal inhabitants of Australia'. Since that time the Arnhem Land Reserve has enabled Aborigines to be protected and missions to engage in evangelisation and civilisation. The area and its people have also been a haven for continued research and scrutiny by anthropologists, sociologists and medical experts.

Although the battle to get the Arnhem Land Reserve was won, the condition of Aborigines there and elsewhere throughout the Territory still left much to be desired. Government policies of protection and control were not matched by corresponding action on the part of the administration and the population at large. There was a great gulf between policy and attitudes, between the legislative Act and human acts. White killings by blacks and massacres by whites or by police punitive expeditions still took place.

Public indignation was once again aroused by the Caledon Bay killings and the subsequent trials of the Aborigines concerned. The eventual release of the central character Tukiar, and his unexplained disappearance raised speculation suggesting police retaliation. The strange and tragic twists in the unfolding drama of the plight of this black man from a remote area of a distant reserve captured the imagination of the world. The injustice meted out to one Aboriginal man brought a greater measure of justice to many. Tukiar's story is told later.

The Tukiar incident raised questions regarding the condition of the Aborigines in the Arnhem Land Reserve. Methodist missionaries lodged strong protests over the Japanese pearlers' exploitation of Aboriginal women. All was not well. The reserve was not inviolable. Because of this, in 1935 the Commonwealth Government commissioned Donald Thomson of Melbourne University to investigate and report on the situation.

After seven months' stay with the Arnhem Land Aborigines, Dr Thomson reported that there was no shortage of food, but that the people were diminishing rapidly in number and were 'already on the road to extinction'. He recommended that 'native tribes ... be absolutely segregated, and it be the policy of the Government to preserve intact their social organization, their social and political institutions, and their culture in its entirety; that the native reserve, Arnhem Land, be created an inviolable reserve for the native inhabitants, and that steps be taken at once to establish and maintain the absolute integrity of this reserve; that steps be taken to remove the anomaly by which watering depots have been recently established on the native reserves for the convenience of pearling crews'; that 'the whole policy of administration of native justice be revised; that the change of policy of the Commonwealth Government be marked by the separate establishment of a separate Department of Native Affairs under a trained director.'

Although Dr Thomson strongly insisted on 'inviolable reserves' he indicated that these needed to remain only 'until and unless a sound working policy and one in the best interests of the Aboriginals is established, tested and proved by experience over a long period among the natives who are already detribalised'.

In this Interim General Report and in his 1935-36 Report, Dr Thomson claimed that the history of the continued contact of Aborigines with whites indicates that 'they have suffered everywhere, at first disorganization of their social order, degradation and ultimate decay'. He believed the efforts being made to teach nomadic Aborigines agriculture were 'quite incompatible with their native life and culture'. He was also highly critical of mission institutions and policies. These, he said, destroyed Aboriginal nomadic life-style. 'The collecting of natives not detribalised into compounds or institutions, should be prohibited,' he said. 'If it is desired to teach Christianity to these people, it should be insisted that the Christian teacher or missionary be prepared to visit the people in their own country, and not to gather them about a station or mission school.'

More enlightened protection instead of control begins to affect Government attitudes after the presentation of the Thomson Report. The 1937 Payne-Fletcher Report on the agricultural development of the Territory gives the Aboriginal population of the Territory at the time as 17 315. Of these 3449 were in employment,

1400 were dependants, 2560 were in institutions (including missions) and 9906 were 'bush blacks'. The report advocated protection from exploitation, the safeguard of health, and training and education for a full life in an endeavour to make Aborigines useful citizens and self-supporting. The Report also made further recommendations regarding judicial matters affecting Aborigines.

In 1939 the Government announced a 'new deal' for Aborigines. It was published as the McEwen Memorandum, named after Mr J. McEwen who had been appointed Minister for the Interior in 1937. In formulating this new policy McEwen had sought the advice of Professor A. P. Elkin, a leading exponent of Aboriginal advancement. He also had noted the opinion of Mr E.W.P. Chinnery, Director of District Services in New Guinea, that the Territory Aborigines were as capable of being 'civilized' as the New Guineans.

The Memorandum commenced a marked change in policy. The Government would move from preservation by protection to an endeavour to assimilate Aborigines to the conditions of Western civilisation. Reserves like that of Arnhem Land would now be viewed only as temporary places of preparation. At the same time it was realised that the processes of 'civilising' could not be thought of 'in terms of years, but of generations'. Under this new policy, missions were seen to be essential to the 'civilising' process. They should be subsidised if they agreed to implement Government policy. District Officers working among Aborigines would receive anthropological training at the University of Sydney. Facilities for medical treatment for those in remote areas would be improved. Training programs for young Aborigines would be started. The McEwen Memorandum advocated incipient assimilationism, which undoubtedly would have been apparent earlier had it not been for the disruption caused by the Second World War.

The Government initiated the new deal with the appointment of Chinnery as Commonwealth Government Adviser on Native Affairs, and first Director of Native Affairs in the Territory, in February 1939. His task would be the implementation of the new policies. This was made extremely difficult through the war years, especially between 1942 and 1945 when the Territory was under military control. Arnhem Land during these years was the frontier for Japanese attack from the North. The mission at Goulburn Island was machine-gunned, and that at Milingimbi was bombed. The RAAF took over most of the mission airfields. White and half-caste women and children were evacuated South. A number of Arnhemlanders served with the armed services in Arnhem Land

and elsewhere in the Top End. New horizons began opening up to them just at the time when Government endeavoured to implement the new deal for them.

In 1947 the Department of the Interior announced plans for a revised version of the 1939 McEwen Memorandum, which had not been implemented fully because of the war. This paved the way for the dramatic change in policy from protection and control to assimilation. A new day was dawning. The slogan 'They must be protected' was now superseded by 'They must become like us'.

9
They must become like us

The initiatives taken by the Department of the Interior in February 1947 were the first stages in implementing the McEwen ideal of assimilation. The policy was translated into practice by the Welfare Ordinance of 1953. The formulative stages of the new welfare era had begun. Aborigines were now to be given much more than protection. Their numbers were not declining but increasing. They must now be assimilated into the wider Australian society. They must be changed from being nomads into people living settled lives in communities. They must be taught health and hygiene and worthwhile trades and occupations, so that they might become 'indistinguishable from the other members of the Australian community'. They must become like us.

As missions were indispensable agents in implementing this new policy, Professor. A.P. Elkin of Sydney University invited missions to a one-day conference on 17 February 1947 to encourage them to adopt the new plan. Professor Elkin said that any mission in the North 'must have a positive economic and welfare policy. In addition to the spiritual, it should set out to teach the native to meet the new era of civilisation, which must, of necessity, make its impact on him in the future.'

Professor Elkin continued, 'The day of his nomadic existence is fast coming to an end. The Aborigines must be trained for new activities of life, which will include an economic development and a means of self-support in a new world which leaves no room for a simple food-gathering economy. Included in the training, there must come the reward or recompense with goods or money, so that they can keep themselves ... Nomadic Aborigines can be turned into gardeners, station hands, artisans, mechanics and the like ... This has to be done by the missions. Along that way lies their physical salvation ... The N.T. Administration does not want the Aborigines to be living the life of parasites. It needs their work, their help, their industry. Every mission should be a community based on activity, based on training the natives for industry, the doing of things of value to themselves and to Australia.'

Professor Elkin went on to outline Government's proposed program. Each mission should have its own store, to teach Aborigines the use of money; village life should be developed so that they might use simple furniture and cutlery; employment opportunities with reasonable wages must be offered; payment in money should be made for all that is done 'to enable them to learn the value of money'; missions should be more adequately staffed; and Aboriginal girls should be trained in the dispensary. Referring to education he said that that was 'a specialised job on its own. One of the aims is literacy in the native tongue and in English. Every missionary sent forth in future must learn the language of the people under his care ... '

Mr (later Sir) Paul Hasluck initiated parliamentary moves to implement the new policy. On 8 June 1950 he moved a resolution calling for co-operative action between the Commonwealth and State Governments for Aboriginal social advancement. He pointed out that two-thirds of the Aboriginal population were in contact with the white community. Therefore for 'either good or ill, the future of those Aborigines lies in close association with the white community.' He continued, 'Their future lies in association with us, and they must either associate with us on standards that will give them full opportunity to live worthily and happily or be reduced to the social state of pariahs and outcastes living without a firm place in the community. In other words, we either permit this social evil to continue or we remedy it.'

Hasluck became Minister for Territories in 1951. In September of that year he arranged for a conference on Aboriginal welfare to be held in Canberra, to try to effect closer Commonwealth-State co-operation in the advancement of native welfare. At this conference the policy of assimilation was outlined and its implications clarified.

In Parliament in October Hasluck reaffirmed that 'assimilation is the objective of native welfare measures. Assimilation means, in practical terms, that, in the course of time, it is expected that all persons of aboriginal blood or mixed blood in Australia will live like white Australians do ...' He said that segregation as an alternative was out of the question, because two-thirds of the Aborigines 'are either detribalised or well on the way to losing their tribal life'. Segregation, as a policy, he claimed, would be to build up an ever-increasing body of people who belong to a separate caste, 'a series of minority groups living in little bits of territory of their own'. On the other hand, in 'pursuit of a policy of assimilation, the settlement and the mission station can be used for the advancement of the native peoples and as a refuge for those of them who need protection during a transitional period.'

He concluded by saying that the major argument for a policy of assimilation was that it was 'a policy of opportunity. It gives to the Aboriginal and to the person of mixed blood a chance to shape his own life. If he succeeds, it places no limit on his success but opens the door fully. Segregation of any kind opens the door into a peculiar and separate world for coloured people only.'

Amending legislation to implement the new policy was introduced into the Northern Territory Legislative Council in January 1953. Half-castes were omitted from the definition of 'aboriginal', thus giving them full citizenship. At the same time if a half-caste requested care, or the Director considered that a half-caste needed care, the Director, with the Administrator's approval, could declare such a person to be an Aboriginal. The legislation stated that 'the time was not yet ripe for the full-blooded aborigine' to be exempted from the provisions of the Ordinance. The legislation therefore applied to all Aborigines, except those who gained exemption from its provisions. Few were granted this privilege during the twenty years of the 'welfare era'.

In the same month the Director introduced the Welfare Bill which omitted references specifically to Aborigines. The provisions of the ordinance applied to any State ward, Aboriginal or non-Aboriginal. Clause 14 of the Bill stated that the Administrator could declare a person to be a ward if that person by reason of his manner of living, inability to manage his own affairs, standard of social habit and behaviour, or personal associations was in need of special care and assistance. It was clear that almost all full-blood Aborigines in the reserves and on cattle stations would become wards.

The duties of the Director of Welfare under the Bill, amongst other things was 'to promote their social, economic and political advancement for the purpose of assisting them and their descendants to take their place as members of the community of the Commonwealth.' He was to provide for their educational, vocational, medical and monetary needs. He was to 'supervise and regulate the use and management of institutions' other than those of the Government, and also the reserves. Restrictions on alcohol were covered by the Licensing Ordinance.

The Welfare Bill, especially Clause 14, came under strong criticism in the Legislative Council. The acting Crown Law Officer condemned it as offending 'against the principles of basic justice'. The Deputy Director of Health said that it was 'one of the worst pieces of legislation' he knew, 'harsher and more oppressive than the legislation in any other part of Australia'. The Director of Works said that it transgressed 'the principles of British Justice'. Yet when debate on the Bill resumed in June 1953, there was little opposition and amendment, and the Bill was accepted. Further complementary legislation in the form of the Wards' Employment Ordinance was passed in September 1953.

The underlying policy of the new ordinance gained wide acceptance throughout the Territory. The 1949-1953 Report for the Northern Territory stated that 'Aboriginal policy is fundamentally conditioned by the fact that only about 800 natives live a fully tribalized life. Where the native tribal structure and way of life have not yet collapsed they are in a process of disintegration; a process that is inevitable. The policy of the Government is to so direct and encourage the re-establishment of the aborigines that they will eventually be assimilated as an integral part of the Australian community ...' The new ordinance was 'considered to represent the most important single step yet taken in the approach to the Aboriginal problem. This abandons the "protective" approach represented by the Aboriginals Ordinance and represents the positive "welfare" policy ... This legislation assumes that aborigines as well as white Australians in the Territory have full citizenship as a right and that this right is to be withheld only in cases where an individual is in need of special care and assistance.'

Although the framers of the new legislation claimed that the ordinance was non-racial, in actual fact almost all wards were Aborigines. Conversely almost all full-blood Aborigines were wards. In this sense the legislation was an hypocritical attempt to avoid the accusation of racial discrimination.

Although the Legislative Assembly passed the Welfare Ordinance in June 1953, its provisions were not implemented until May 1957. During these four years Aboriginal affairs continued to be administered under the provisions of the Aboriginal Ordinance. In October 1954, Mr H. C. Giese was appointed as Director of Welfare, but did not assume statutory duties until May 1957. Mr Giese continued as Director until the formation of the Department of Aboriginal Affairs under the new Labor Government in 1973.

The official policy of assimilation sought to change Aboriginal traditional ways of life to those of civilised white Australians. The 1957-58 Welfare Report stated that the aim of the Commonwealth Government with respect to Aborigines in the Northern Territory 'is to promote and direct social change amongst them in such a way that, whilst retaining connections with and pride in their Aboriginal ancestry, they will become indistinguishable from other members of the Australian community in manner of life, standards of living, occupations, and participation in community affairs. It is important for this process of assimilation that Australians should be ready and willing to accept aborigines in the wider community as fellow-citizens in all respects; it is equally important that aborigines should be encouraged to detach themselves from their present position of group separateness and solidarity and become merged as individuals in the general community.'

These views were repeatedly expressed during the next twenty years. The Native Welfare Conference held in Canberra in January 1966 stated that the aims of the assimilation policy were that 'all aborigines and part-aborigines will attain the same manner of living as other Australians and live as members of a single Australian community enjoying the same rights and privileges, accepting the same responsibilities, observing the same customs and influenced by the same beliefs, hopes and loyalties as other Australians.'

The Welfare Department outlined this same position to its staff in a *Handbook of Instructions for the Guidance of Settlement Superintendents and Staff under their Control*. This document said that the only future for Aborigines 'is to merge into and be received as full members of the European community'. This judgment was not based on race but on social standards. Aborigines must change by discarding their previous standards of conduct and social conventions and move into accepted patterns of the wider Australian community. They will change only if they have the right motives and these will be accomplished through incentives of work and food. Little change can be expected from older Aborigines 'apart from the acquisition of improved hygiene practices and some better work habits and skills'. Emphasis therefore should be on children and youth. They must be educated. At the same time they should not be separated from the adults, as 'family life is strong in these people'.

In its Annual Report for 1969-70, the Welfare Branch reviewed its wide-ranging activities in Aboriginal social welfare. These were 'child and family welfare, youth activities, the promotion of cultural, sporting and recreational activities, Aboriginal welfare, education and vocational training, the alleviation of distress, and the provision of assistance and advisory services to community bodies in the establishment and operation of community welfare services'.

Missions in Arnhem Land and elsewhere throughout the Territory were seen to be indispensable agents for the Government's assimilation policies. At a conference of Government and mission officials held in Darwin in 1953, Hasluck had said, 'The policy of the Government is to co-operate with the Christian missions and to give government support for the work of the Christian missions. We adopt that policy because we place high value on Christian teaching and the spiritual counsel and moral guidance of the Church in the uplifting of humanity, and because we recognise that the missions can also make a major contribution to those measures in health, education and training for citizenship, which open a path for the native people towards full racial acceptance in our community. Over the past seventy years in the Northern Territory, the missionaries have cared for natives at times when many others were neglecting them. They have shown compassion when others were indifferent, and they have held a faith when others said there was no hope. I wish to assure those present that I know and honour the record of missions.'

Church missions and government settlements had to settle nomadic Aborigines in communities in order that the assimilation process might begin. The Welfare Branch Annual Report of 1961-62 categorically stated that 'it is Government policy to establish settlements — operated by the Government or by Christian missions — to serve as training centres in social change for Aboriginals'.

The *Handbook of Instructions* indicated that such settlements would teach Aborigines 'the habits and skills of living in a permanent community'. They would provide welfare 'fitted both to their needs and to their stage of social development'. Education 'would give at least some basic skills in that vocation'. The settlement would 'introduce to all members of the group the general concept of work as a worthwhile aim in life', and 'prepare the younger age groups for a wider life outside the settlement and tribal community'. The settlements therefore were to be training centres where work and living habits and attitudes would be developed, skills taught, and education and health services provided.

The Department of Territories, in an article called 'The Tools of Assimilation' written in January 1962, said that the assimilation policy would have three stages. The first phase was the congregating of Aborigines into missions and settlements so that they 'will become familiar with their use and function in the larger pattern of society'. The second stage was training 'within a somewhat restricted non-aboriginal community. The extent to which these persons will proceed further into the wider community will be determined largely by individual self-confidence. At this point, the aboriginal is still in need of guidance; at the same time he will be moving away from the special dependence typical of persons still in the first phase.' In the third phase the Aboriginal will be employed; 'side by side with other Australian workmates to whom he is now a true competitor for all benefits offered within the wider society, he will come to experience the full impact of competitive society.'

The Welfare Branch which was established under the Welfare Ordinance became a monolithic structure. Its main function was the welfare of wards, almost all of whom were Aborigines and half-castes. Its administration included the management of settlements, Aboriginal education, settlement nursing, hygiene services, and feeding schemes, Aboriginal vocational training and employment, mission administration, legal counsel for Aborigines and construction work on settlements.

The activities of this gigantic structure frequently came under criticism from legislative and administrative bodies. Unsuccessful attempts were frequently made to transfer the general non-Aboriginal welfare to another authority. The Director steadfastly opposed these moves on the ground that the separation of welfare for Aborigines and non-Aborigines would amount to racial discrimination.

The large amount of money allocated to the Welfare Branch also brought strong reaction from the Legislative Council and from Territorians at large. For example in the 1961-62 financial years £1 011 984 was spent for the welfare of wards (almost all Aborigines) out of a total of £4 640 048 for the whole of the Department of the Northern Territory. Other general welfare services under the control of the Welfare Branch used only £52 326.

Resentment against the high proportion of money spent by the Welfare Branch led the elected members of the Legislative Council to prepare a 'Remonstrance' for presentation to Federal Parliament. An original clause in the Remonstrance read, 'Of all the moneys expended in the Northern Territory by the Commonwealth Government, a large proportion is wasted in a futile, albeit altruistic attempt to advance the aborigines of the Territory.' This clause was deleted, but the Remonstrance had little effect in changing official attitudes.

Dr Colin Tatz, in his doctoral thesis dated 31 March 1964 and entitled 'Aboriginal Administration of the Northern Territory', examined after ten years the evidence for the actual gap between the assimilation policy and its administration. He concluded that during the first ten years of the administering of the Welfare Ordinance on missions and settlements, wages had not increased; employment was still 'of the general labouring type'; Aborigines were still unskilled and unqualified despite training programs. He indicated that unemployment and sickness benefits and tuberculosis allowances in practice were not being given to Aborigines; that there was still 'considerable disease among Aborigines; humpies still predominated'; and that the educational program had 'done little to lift the literacy and educational standards of all Aborigines, including the pupils'.

Continuing his scathing indictment of the failure of the assimilation policy in practice, Dr Tatz stated that even though Aborigines now had the right to vote they were still 'ruled' from above. He said that they 'still do not participate in "municipal-type" management of their own affairs wherever they live. The village councils in which a few participate are without power, advisory, and largely ignored when their suggestions run counter to what the local superintendent deems "law". Even autonomy in tribal matters is diluted when church or personal values are "infringed".'

Tatz claimed that legally 'an Aborigine is still a controlled person. In the Aboriginals' Ordinance he was controlled as a minor because he was an Aborigine; in the present era he is a controlled minor because he is in need of care and assistance. His status may be said to have improved in one sense: intermarriage is possible without official permission and a ward cannot be removed or detained without a court's direction. But these changes are of no great moment in relation to the things he still cannot do: drink, enter into sexual relations of his own choice, and sell his labour and skill to his best advantage.'

Tatz concluded his detailed criticism of the outworking of assimilation policies by the Welfare Department by asking, 'What has the programme achieved? It has in a number of ways deprived Aborigines of incentives, incentives to maintain independence, to obtain food, to work for money to obtain food, to remain responsible for his family. In these senses the Aborigine has been pauperised. His residence on a settlement or mission, as an inmate of an institution, where he often gets something for nothing, where ration handouts save the need to forage or to work, where his family is catered for, where decisions on many matters are made for him by officials in his best interests, is in fact pauperisation . . .'

The reasons for the gap between policy and administration, Tatz claimed, lay in the 'failure to see the policy-administration continuum'; in domination of the Welfare Branch by uninformed officials in Canberra; in the view that the 'assimilation policy is something that belongs exclusively to the Welfare Branch and does not "apply" to anybody else'; and in 'the administration of general, non-Aboriginal welfare by the Welfare Branch'. He maintained that missions had accepted the assimilation policy and had accepted subsidies to do so but had implemented 'their own version of what is "right" for Aborigines and they [had] not always conform[ed] to official aims in the subsidised fields of activity.' He indicated that the care of Aborigines on pastoral properties has not been in proportion to their numbers, and that the tension between the Welfare Branch and the Northern Territory Council for Aboriginal Rights was unwarranted.

The final reason for failure was the all-important factor that 'Aborigines, the subject matter of administration, have yet to be viewed as part of the organisation.' He quoted Hasluck's advice to administrators in 1952 that to an increasing extent 'the ideas which the aboriginal himself has about his own future will be a factor in shaping that future.'

It is easy for an academic without some years of experience of the difficulties of the situation to criticise. Some of Tatz's observations were seen out of perspective. Some of the things which he attacked were improved during the next decade. For example, vocational training and allowances were introduced. A long-term program for better housing was started. Town Councils had more Aboriginal representation. Industrial and agricultural projects were commenced. At the same time his observations indicate basic inadequacies in policy and practice.

On the other hand an indication of the far-reaching activities and influence of the Northern Territory Welfare Division after almost twenty years' operation can be gauged from its Annual Report for the year ending 30 June 1972. By then Northern Territory Ordinances administered either wholly or in part by the Welfare Division were: The Social Welfare Ordinance, 1964-1967; the Child Welfare Ordinance, 1958-1971; The Adoption of Children Ordinance, 1964-1969; The Intestate Aboriginals (Distribution of Estates) Ordinance, 1961-1967; The Native and Historical Objects

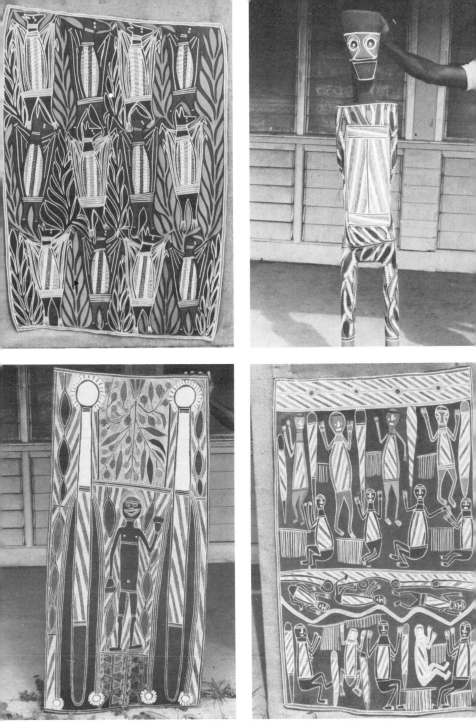

Bark paintings and carved figure at Milingimbi. These art forms, which are closely
connected with myth and ritual, are unique and fascinating

Early British settlement at Victoria, Port Essington, 1839–49 (*Photo from the copy in the Mitchell Library, Sydney*)

and Areas Preservation Ordinance, 1955-1960; and The Criminal Law (Conditional Release of Offenders) Ordinance, 1971, with the Parole of Prisoners Ordinance, 1971.

By 1972 various branches of the Division were responsible for different aspects of the work. Of these the Projects and Services Branch was concerned with welfare-type programs generally and for special advancement and vocational training programs for Aborigines; the Education Branch was responsible for the education of the majority of Aboriginal school children in the Territory; the Executive Services Branch was responsible for providing support services for the Division including works programming and funds; the Research Branch was responsible for a program of basic and applied research in respect of all the activities of the Division.

On 30 June 1972 the total staff establishment of the Division was 1123 made up of 862 permanents and 261 temporaries. Of the permanent staff, 117 were in head office; 30 in regional offices; 3 in district offices; 166 in training (teachers, patrol officers, social workers); 489 (plus 115 temporary) at settlements, schools, Kormilda College, Dhupuma College and Batchelor Vocational Training Centre; twenty-nine in other institutions and ninety-six temporarily in the mobile works force. The phenomenal extent of staff growth is evident when it is realised that ten years previously the staffing establishment stood at 412, of whom 253 were permanent and 159 temporary.

Financial expenditure on Aboriginal welfare by the Welfare Division for the year ending 30 June 1972 amounted to $8 017 234. This amount did not include staff salaries, office accommodation and expenses, or the costs of stationery and telephones at head office. These were paid by the Department of the Northern Territory. Assistance provided through missions amounted to $3 267 703, and through pastoralists to $228 546. Operation of care and training amounted to $2 959 677, education accounted for $502 678, and self-help, housing and building works cost $655 339.

Great advances in the material well-being of Aborigines had taken place during the two decades of the welfare era. Staff subsidies for missions and settlements in Arnhem Land and elsewhere throughout the Territory had increased dramatically. Educational facilities now included pre-school and post-primary grade and the transitional forms at Kormilda and Dhupuma Colleges. Extensive feeding programs for children and old people were implemented (though they were later abandoned) with child endowment and old-age pension moneys. Health services involved in- and out-patient care, Aboriginal nursing-aide training and leprosy rehabilitation. A large number of houses were built though in many cases they were for the burgeoning non-Aboriginal mission, government, educational and medical staff. Large stores and supermarkets were established and prospered. Vocational training and industrial and marine enterprises were initiated with varying success. Attempts were made to involve more Aborigines on Councils, in semi-skilled positions, as works supervisors and in general employment situations.

Despite these undoubted benefits, the policy of assimilation and its administration through the Welfare Ordinance suffered several fundamental defects. The change in emphasis from protection to welfare had been a great advance in policy, but it was by no means the final answer. Extensive welfare did not and could not meet basic 'soul needs' of Arnhem Land Aborigines and others in the Territory. Aborigines were still Government wards, not people in their own right. They were institutionalised and managed for their welfare, instead of being free people determining what they themselves wanted. They were educated and given vocational training in artificial communities and under paternalistic control. They were second-rate workers, given a training allowance because they had not yet achieved sufficient status to equal even the uneducated labourer outside the reserves.

In the later years of the welfare era, Aborigines were given more say in the handling of their own affairs at different levels. But the final say still rested with the non-Aboriginal Superintendent, the Director of Welfare, and his numerous agents. Prohibitions, controls, rules and regulations were made *for* Aborigines but not *by* them. They lived in artificial communities made up of many different clans and tribes. These were communities run by non-Aborigines, not by the people as in a free society where the majority made its choice. Missions became little theocratic states. Government settlements were worse, employing excessive numbers of non-Aborigines.

Assimilation policies of the welfare era had been a step forward from earlier protectionism. But they had bogged down. Aborigines were just not being assimilated, despite the devoted services of large numbers of welfare and mission personnel and the expenditure of enormous sums of money. In 1972 almost all Aborigines were still wards and looked like remaining so. Something dramatic had to be done. The change was started when Labor swept into power in December 1972.

The policy of assimilation assumed that all Aborigines had

to be assimilated into white society. Their outlook, their way of life, and their customs had to be changed. They had no choice. They had to be cared for until they could care for themselves. Differences of culture would then largely disappear. Perhaps the whole Aboriginal race would disappear in what could be called 'beneficent genocide'. Racial tension would cease because there would be one race. Even if this final stage was not accomplished for generations, one thing was necessary. They must become like us.

10
We still want
the missionaries

The Anglican Church Missionary Society (CMS) and the Methodist Overseas Missions (MOM) have been the only two Christian missions to work among the Aborigines of Arnhem Land. The CMS started at Roper River in 1908 and the MOM at Goulburn Island in 1916. Even before the missions started, white frontier settlement had already devastated Aboriginal culture in some areas. The missions did not destroy the culture that remained, as some often allege. Rather, they saved many of the Aboriginal tribes from disintegration and extinction, allowing them to revive and maintain much of their cultural past.

When the Aborigines did not die, the missions did everything in their power to have them protected and segregated into reserves. They institutionalised them on their mission stations for evangelisation and civilisation. During the 1950s and 1960s the societies became instruments of the Government's policy of assimilation. During the 1970s they co-operated with Government in their newer policies of self-determination and self-management, adopting a servant role under the direction of the Aboriginal Councils.

The missionaries were the first to care for the desperate plight of the downtrodden Aborigines. They tried to save the souls of the first Australians, soiled with their own sins and those of the white invaders. They sought to heal their bodies, scarred with the diseases of the Asiatics. These men and women of God taught them to become literate so that they could read the Bible. They also wanted them to have the simple skills in the three Rs so that they would start being able to cope with the white man's ways. They also taught these nomads of the northlands agriculture, industry and hygiene so that they could settle down and live like 'civilised people'.

The policies of the missionaries have been censured and their methods criticised. They nevertheless were men and women of compassion. Many worked for years in searing heat under the most appalling conditions. They were few in number and were usually isolated for months on end. They had few comforts and slender resources. But they were motivated with the highest ideals, and had it not been for their labours, there would have been few Aborigines at all left in Arnhem Land.

The CMS started working in Arnhem Land at Roper River in 1908 as the result of an impassioned plea for Aborigines made by Bishop Frodsham of North Queensland at the Australian Church Congress in 1906. The Bishop said, 'We have an airy way of speaking about Australia being a white man's country. But Australia first of all was a black man's country, and I have never heard that a black man invited us to take his property from him ... We have developed the country, and we have civilised it, but we have certainly done very little to preach the Gospel to the people we have dispossessed. The blacks have been shot and poisoned while they were wild and dangerous. They are now left to kill themselves with white vices where they have been "tamed" ... but very few have received at our hands, either justice or consideration.'

Bishop Frodsham continued, 'The Aborigines are disappearing. In the course of a generation or two, at the most, the last Australian blackfellow will have turned his face to warm mother earth, and given back his soul to God Who gave it. Missionary work then may be only smoothing the pillow of a dying race, but I think if the Lord Jesus came to Australia he would be moved with great compassion for these poor outcastes living by the wayside, robbed of their land, wounded by the lust and passion of a stronger race, and dying — yes, dying, like rotten sheep — with no man to care for their bodies and souls.'

The CMS took up the challenge to care for the neglected Aborigines. In 1908 they started a mission on the northern banks of the Roper River about 110 kilometres from the estuary. This was to be the first of a series of missions which they hoped to establish on the east Arnhem Land coast and on Groote Eylandt. Lack of staff and finance and appalling conditions prevented the planned expansion for a number of years. In 1921 the first Groote Eylandt Mission was founded at Emerald River following journeys of exploration by the Rev. H.E. Warren from 1916-21. The Emerald River Mission was transferred to Angurugu in 1943 because of the close proximity of RAAF personnel stationed at the mission airfield. The Society did not start work at Numbulwar on the Rose River until 1952.

CMS made their policy clear when they started the Roper River Mission. In the 'Instructions' they gave to the pioneer missionary group they said, 'In going to the Roper River of the Northern Territory, you, my brethren, are entering upon a service of distinctly national character. One of the most sacred obligations resting upon the people of this Commonwealth is to give to the original possessors of this Continent — the Aborigines — the benefits of our Christianity and civilization ... You are going to a service of great urgency. The Aboriginals need to be properly protected, properly taught various industries, and adequately cared for. Above everything else they require the uplifting influence of the Gospel of our Lord and Saviour Jesus Christ; and your supreme work is to present that to them.'

The CMS from the outset stipulated that the Mission should be industrial and agricultural, as well as educational, medical and spiritual. The Instructions given to two missionaries in 1913 stated that 'You are to give yourselves, at the outset at any rate, to this branch [agriculture] of the Mission, which, we repeat must be specially developed ... And we wish most earnestly to warn you against the fatal mistake of doing the work yourselves instead of training the Aborigines to do it. The Committee ... is convinced of the absolute necessity of encouraging industrial work amongst members of child races such as the Aborigines of Australia ... so that men and women connected with the Mission may soon be placed in their own homes and upon their own plots of ground, and be so taught that they shall eventually be able to live independently of material help from the Association.'

Mission policy at that time, and for many years later, was institutionalism for civilisation. The Mission considered that the only way in which nomadic, isolated bands of 'uncivilised natives' could be civilised would be to gather them together into institutions, to build houses for them, teach them trades, look after them physically and spiritually, and in this way, raise their general living standards. The Bishop of Carpentaria reiterated this view in 1939, saying, 'Whilst our work among these people is primarily evangelistic ... we have also to try to lead them away from their nomadic, food hunting stage of culture when they can live happily in family communities and produce their own food supply ... This training takes infinite patience, for it is no use trying to advance too quickly by using implements that in his

106

generation the Aboriginal will never be able to purchase for himself.'

This early pattern of institutionalism for civilisation was an incipient form of assimilationism, which became mission and government policy in the 1950s and 1960s. It should be realised, nevertheless, that the CMS missions were staffed only by a few missionaries, assisted in some cases by half-castes whom they had trained. The numbers of Aborigines involved was not great and fluctuated considerably. The Groote Eylandt Mission was devoted solely to the care of half-castes from 1924 until the early 1930s. Aborigines were still very nomadic until the 1950s, and in many cases well into the 1960s. The institutionalisation process was slow, and the settled communities did not clearly emerge until after World War II and the large injection of finance during the welfare era.

The CMS took over the responsibility of Oenpelli in 1925 at the request of the Commonwealth Government. This Mission is almost on the western boarder of Arnhem Land. Oenpelli previously had been the home of Paddy Cahill, a famous Northern Territory bushman, who had started shooting buffaloes in the region in the 1880s. Cahill established a dairy herd there in 1906. The Commonwealth Government, at the instigation of the Administrator, Dr Gilruth, purchased Cahill's farm in 1916, and moderately successful attempts were made to produce butter. The wharfies declared this butter 'black' when taken to Darwin, as Aborigines had been involved in its manufacture. The whole project collapsed with the Darwin general strike in 1919 and the removal of Dr Gilruth.

The history of Oenpelli has been one of hard work by a small group of dedicated men and women. Aboriginal and mission Aborigines have engaged in stockwork there over the years. The transport of stores was a perennial problem until recent years, as the area becomes one vast inland quagmire during the Wet. When communications began to improve, Western cultural forces made serious inroads into this adjacent Aboriginal mission. Many Oenpelli Aborigines have dissipated themselves with the vices of Darwin. The high consumption of alcohol from the neighbouring Border Store on the western bank of the East Alligator River at one stage almost resulted in the complete disintegration of the Oenpelli people. In recent years timber milling at Murganella, prospecting, and the proposed mining at Nabarlek not far away have brought fear and frustration to them. They also live close to the uranium province with the possibility of a large mining town being built nearby.

During the 1930s the CMS had missions at Roper River, Emerald

River on Groote Eylandt and at Oenpelli. They cared for the half-castes whom they segregated from 'uncivilised blacks and pestilent whites' on Groote Eylandt. Mission policy and activity was rigorously administered from the South. During this decade, a CMS missionary, Mr K. Langford-Smith, for the first time used an aeroplane to bridge the long distances over rugged terrain and virgin bush. This venture did not last long, but later became the vision of another CMS missionary, Mr Alf Wilson. The years 1933 and 1934 witnessed the noted 'Peace Expedition' of two CMS missionaries, the Revs. H.E. Warren and A.J. Dyer, assisted by Mr Donald Fowler. The peace party met the Caledon Bay Aboriginal killers and persuaded them to go to Darwin to prevent a police punitive raid in which the whole tribe would have been annihilated. The story of the Caledon Bay killings is told in chapter 17.

The year 1931 saw the culmination of the efforts of the CMS, in conjunction with the Methodist Overseas Missions and interested people in the South, for the proclamation of the vast Arnhem Land Reserve of almost one hundred thousand square kilometres. The Aborigines would now be protected and able to start in isolation on the long task of being trained. They would start trying to bridge the culture-gap of twenty thousand years.

The Aborigines in Arnhem Land did not and could not live in complete isolation. First of all they had missionaries living among them. Most of these were white Australians. The MOM also had Fijians, Baduans and Tongans. Japanese pearlers, white and Malay trepangers, and white beachcombers sailed along the coasts and established their camps at vantage points. Buffalo hunters roamed the bush in the west, and pastoralists in the South often made inroads into the supposed 'inviolate' reserve. The Aborigines themselves often moved out of the Reserve, spending time in towns like Darwin, Pine Creek and Katherine, or working on cattle stations. Complete segregation was not possible.

The establishment of the Qantas flying boat base at Port Langdon on the north-eastern coast of Groote Eylandt in 1938 brought Aborigines into further contact with non-mission white people. Soon afterwards Fred Gray set up his settlement at Umbakumba on the opposite side of the bay. The Aborigines who settled there supplied labour, fish and vegetables to the Europeans at the base. The CMS took over Umbakumba in 1958 and managed the place until 1966. After that time it became a Government settlement. The Anglicans maintained a presence there by providing a chaplain and, for a number of years, several nursing sisters.

The CMS Roper River Mission was completely swept away by a

disastrous flood in 1940. The Mission had frequently not had a very happy history since its commencement in 1908. Living conditions had been bad, the fragmented tribes were often difficult to handle, and sometimes the staff were unsuitable or incompatible. The overall situation improved with the rebuilding of the Mission about eight kilometres upstream. The buildings were more adequate, and the CMS made a determined effort to improve the staffing situation, resulting in better morale among the staff and Aborigines.

World War II greatly disrupted CMS missionary work in Arnhem Land. All white and half-caste women and children were evacuated South. The three tiny missions had to carry on with a skeleton staff of one or two white missionaries. The RAAF took over strategic airfields. Many Aborigines went walkabout, especially as food and medicines became scarce. A number of Aborigines and their families went to Darwin to work with the Army. Others remained at the Mission carrying out basic duties, and tracking Allied or enemy airmen who had been shot down.

In 1950 the controversial 'tobacco question' strained relationships between CMS and the Government, and brought division among the missionaries themselves. In December the Government ordered the missions to issue tobacco to the Aborigines under their care, as part of their rations. When the missionaries on the three CMS stations refused on the grounds that Aborigines were becoming addicted to tobacco and using endowment and other moneys to buy it, the Administrator of the Territory threatened to withdraw CMS licences to work in the Reserve. A compromise solution was adopted whereby it was agreed that missions should make tobacco available for sale in mission stores. It was also agreed that tobacco would not be made available to children, and that parents could not use endowment moneys for its purchase. Some of the CMS missionaries resigned because of the controversy.

The CMS started the Numbulwar Mission at the mouth of the Rose River in 1952 at the request of the local people. A number of Nunggubuyu people resident at Roper River had asked if they could be repatriated to their own country and so the move was made. After a few years, buildings were constructed from locally milled cypress pine, an airstrip was completed and a garden planted.

The five CMS missions of Roper River, Angurugu and Um-bakumba on Groote Eylandt, Numbulwar and Oenpelli developed dramatically during the welfare era. The Government injected large sums of money for capital works, staff subsidies, educational and health programs. Former forlorn-looking missions now expanded rapidly and took on a brighter appearance. Schools, hospitals, stores and additional housing for missionaries and educational workers sprang up. Housing for Aborigines lagged behind, and it was not until the 1960s that determined efforts were made to build Aboriginal houses. The greatly needed linguistic work was started through Government subsidies.

In 1966 the CMS handed over the administration of Umbakumba to the Welfare Branch and in 1968 handed over Roper River. This meant that they had the overall responsibility for only three missions: Oenpelli, Angurugu, and Numbulwar.

Like other missions the CMS considered that the administrative changes introduced with the new policy of self-determination in 1973 came too quickly. The features of this policy are discussed in chapter 12. The Society maintained that it had been practising a kind of self-determination through village and community councils for a number of years in the past. They also claimed that until the communities were incorporated and the Town Councils legalised, then they would have the ultimate responsibility in administration, not the new Aboriginal Councils. This gave the unfortunate impression that the CMS was still wanting to maintain its former paternalistic role and to deny Aborigines their full rights of self-determination.

The administration of the CMS has been dominated from the South until recent times. In 1937 an Aborigines Committee was formed to administer the Society's work in the North. In 1962 the CMS adopted a policy of decentralisation with the appointment of a Field Superintendent and a Field Council. The Aborigines Committee in the South still maintained an important function. A further change came in 1977 with the replacement of the Field Council by a CMS Advisory Committee dealing solely with missionies, and a CMS Consultative Council concerned with the service of the Society to Aboriginal communities.

A further feature of CMS Arnhem Land missions has been the relationship between the missionaries and the bishop of the diocese in which they have been serving. The whole of the Territory was part of the Diocese of Carpentaria until 1968, when the Diocese of the Northern Territory was formed and the Right Reverend K. B. Mason was consecrated as bishop. Cordial relations have existed between the CMS, its missionaries, and the diocese. Moves are currently being started which could result in all 'mission' workers being members of a diocesan home mission organisation.

Each of the five Anglican communities has its own church. The Diocese of the Northern Territory is obtaining church lands leases for these churches and the adjacent vicarages, as town plans are being drawn up for the communities. Each centre for many years has had its own chaplain, an Anglican priest, supported by the CMS. A major move in indigenisation took place when the Bishop made the Reverend Michael Gumbuli deacon on 3 November 1973 and priest the following day at Roper River. He is the first, and at the time of writing, the only Anglican Aboriginal priest in Arnhem Land.

During the past seventy years a large number of CMS missionaries have served the Aborigines of Arnhem Land with distinction. Some have worked for long periods of time. The contribution of others has been of much shorter duration. They have worked under difficult and frustrating circumstances. They have made mistakes, and the CMS has made errors of judgment and policy. They were all children of their age just as we are children of ours. Yet with the assistance of half-castes and of the Aborigines themselves, they have prevented the annihilation of the Aborigines in the area. They have cared when others did not care. They healed and educated, taught skills and assisted in general welfare when little else was being done. They laid foundations which how enable Aborigines to take full responsibility for themselves and to manage their own affairs.

The Methodist Overseas Missions (MOM) commenced missionary work in Arnhem Land in 1916, when the Reverend James Watson founded the Goulburn Island Mission. Under an agreement of missionary societies known as 'comity of missions', the MOM was allocated the northern Arnhem Land coast for its work, the Anglican CMS was given the southern and eastern areas, and the Roman Catholic missions accepted the area to the west outside the Arnhem Land Reserve, including Bathurst and Melville Islands, Daly River and Port Keats. Thus Christian Aborigines of Arnhem Land are not Anglican or Methodist by choice, but by geographic chance.

Watson chose Goulburn Island for the first MOM mission after surveying western Arnhem Land for four months. He was able to start the work because of a generous donation from Mr R.J.M. McBride. This was the first of several large gifts which McBride made to MOM work in the North.

The modern belief that missions destroyed Aboriginal culture is incorrect. Aboriginal culture was under threat long before the missionaries arrived. Watson wrote in 1915, 'In Australia there are said to be from 40 000 to 80 000 aboriginals, the remnants of the original possessors and inhabitants of this continent. Opium, grog and vices have been doing their deadly work of decimation, and to us as a Methodist Church has been allotted some 16 000 to 20 000 of these people. We ought to have been amongst them fifty years ago! No, men and women of Methodism, "We are nowhere near the end of the war". It is the time for girding on the armour, not laying it aside.' Watson's calculation of 16 000 to 20 000 was far from accurate if he meant that this was the number of Aborigines then living in Arnhem Land. At the time there were probably about 15 000 Aborigines in the Territory of whom only about 3000 to 4000 were in Arnhem Land.

Watson was greatly assisted in his founding work by Messrs A.E. Lawrence and Mosesi Mansio. Both were laymen, one being a white Australian and the other a Fijian. Their appointment symbolised the invaluable contribution which lay missionaries and Pacific Islanders have made in the MOM missions in Arnhem Land.

Lay people have been indispensable. Mission work in Arnhem Land is very different from that in almost any other part of the world. In North Australia there has been a continuing need to provide all the physical supports for the communities living at the missions and the towns which evolved out of them. Missionaries, with Aboriginal helpers, had to fell timber and mill it, and build houses, schools, dispensaries, hospitals, workshops, stores and churches. They had to bring in all kinds of supplies by sea. Lay people also included nursing sisters, school teachers, linguists and social workers. Even now, when a number of the jobs previously undertaken by missionaries are being done by Aborigines, each of the communities, which number between five and eight hundred, needs outside supporting lay staff of between twenty to fifty non-Aborigines, and in some places more are needed. Expatriate lay people have always played an important role in the Arnhem Land missions.

The presence of Mosesi Mansio, a Fijian, marked the start of the MOM policy of involving Pacific Islanders in mission work. This policy was not employed by the CMS. Pacific Islanders were all missionaries from their own areas. They worked on mission boats, as gardeners, as builders, and in some cases as community advisers and ordained ministers. In 1977 the Minister at Croker Island was a Fijian, and those at Maningrida and Yirrkala were Tongan. With their traditional background they appear to relate more readily to Aborigines and their cultural situation than do most white people.

In the year that Watson, Lawrence and Mansio started the Goulburn Island Mission, Miss Amy Corfield arrived. She was the first of a long line of mission teachers, whose contribution was an integral part of the mission's work. For the first ten years the MOM used the dormitory system in educating the children. In the first half of the 1920s, every child coming to Goulburn Island had to enter one of the dormitories. In this way they were segregated from the undesirable aspects of tribal life. The Reverend T.T. Webb abolished the dormitory system soon after his arrival in 1926. He insisted that missionaries should make a study of the Aboriginal way of life, understand the people and respect their culture. He said that they should convince rather than coerce, and not adopt any policy which separated children from their families.

James Watson worked at Goulburn Island for three years before leaving for South. (He later returned to the North for several years to relieve a staff shortage.) Before leaving in 1919 he had chosen Milingimbi in the Crocodile Islands as the site of the second MOM Mission. Jennison, the missionary appointed to start the new mission, however, chose Elcho Island instead, starting work there in 1921. Shortly afterwards the new mission suffered a setback. The Elcho Island Naptha Petroleum Co. Ltd commenced drilling for oil almost in the centre of the proposed settlement. As a result the second mission was transferred under Watson's direction to Milingimbi in 1923.

In 1924 the MOM undertook responsibility for mission work in Darwin. Darwin had always been the main supply centre for the Arnhem Land communities, and increasingly it became the headquarters of the District.

During his period of service in the North Watson advocated the establishment of a third mission at Melville Island. This island was later called Bremer Island, and lies just north of present day Yirrkala. The MOM did not agree with Watson's recommendation and it was ten years before Yirrkala commenced.

In 1927 Harold Shepherdson ('Sheppy') and his wife began their fifty years' outstanding service to the Aborigines of Arnhem Land. Sheppy was a quiet person who went about his work as an engineer calmly and quietly. In 1936 he bought a plane in Adelaide with his own money and flew it to Darwin. This plane later crashed on Groote Eylandt, and Sheppy had to wait eleven years before he could get another. He then started flying regularly to outstations south of Elcho Island. Sheppy had a vision of Aborigines living in their own country away from the large mission settlements. He could be called 'the prophet of the homeland movement', a title also applicable to Alf Wilson of the CMS.

In 1935 the Reverend Wilbur Chaseling started the Yirrkala Mission to care for the Caledon Bay Aborigines and others in the area. The establishment of this Mission was the MOM's response to the Government's proposed punitive measures following the Caledon Bay killings. Warren of the CMS, who had led the successful 'peace expedition' in 1933-34, had built the small St David's Church at Caledon Bay. The CMS planned to start a mission there, but the MOM claimed that the area was within its jurisdiction under mission comity. As a result the MOM started Yirrkala.

The MOM also built Croker Island as a half-caste mission. The children were cared for first at Pine Creek and then at Goulburn Island, while the buildings were being constructed. They started living there in 1941, but shortly afterwards were evacuated South because of the threat of Japanese invasion.

In 1942 the MOM started Elcho Island as an outpost of Milingimbi. The Milingimbi airstrip had been taken over by the RAAF and the mission authorities realised that the mission was now a likely target for Japanese attacks. As a result they took the sawmill and other valuable equipment to Elcho as a safety measure. After the war the MOM approved the development of Elcho Island into a full mission station. Elcho Island (Galiwinku) has now the largest Aboriginal community in Arnhem Land, numbering almost one thousand inhabitants, excluding the large non-Aboriginal staff.

The five Methodist missions strung out along the length of the north Arnhem Land coast became Australia's front-line during World War II. All white and half-caste women and children were evacuated South. Mrs Shepherdson refused to leave and was cared for in a hideout in the hills about twenty miles south of Milingimbi. She later stayed in Darwin.

As was the case with the CMS missions during the war, a handful of missionaries continued to care for the MOM centres. These were greatly depleted in numbers. Many Aborigines went to Darwin and joined the armed services. Others tracked down grounded Japanese or Allied airmen. As Milingimbi was an important Spitfire base, the Japanese strafed and bombed it several times.

The Reverend Len Kentish was executed by the Japanese in May 1943 while a prisoner of war. He had been visiting the Arnhem Land coast communities when the naval vessel in which he was travelling was sunk by a Japanese amphibian aircraft near the Wessel Islands. After machine-gunning the survivors, the plane landed on the water and the pilot took Kentish prisoner.

114

He was flown to the Aru Islands where he was beheaded. Part of the tragedy of the whole affair was the fact that Kentish was a non-combatant. He had taken a liking to the Japanese, and had taught them English when he was in Darwin. His work and witness unto death is commemorated on Goulburn Island by the Kentish Memorial Grove, which is dedicated 'to one of Christ's finest missionaries who lost his life so tragically'.

The Fijian missionaries gave outstanding service during the war years. Foremost among them was Kolinio, who was ordained minister at Croker Island in 1945. In 1948 he returned to Fiji, having served the MOM missions faithfully for fifteen years.

The war years left an indelible mark on the Aborigines of Arnhem Land. They were now a changed people. They had witnessed the threat of the non-white Japanese to the whites of their country. Many had been to Darwin, and had received more money than they had ever had before. They tasted the white men's food and their liquor. They had worked under them in various jobs and they had shared a small part of their wealth. They had become conscious of the use of money and knew what it could buy. They could never be the same again.

The missionaries returned in greater numbers after the war, and the half-castes returned to Croker. Conferences aimed at improving Aboriginal welfare were held down South between the Government and the missions, Professor Elkin playing a leading part. The new policy of assimilation was now to be implemented. The MOM, like the CMS, was being called on to be an important agency whereby Aborigines might be brought to the same level of 'civilisation' as white Australians.

Arnhem Land now became a haven for anthropologists, photographers, film producers, geologists and authors. Aborigines were no longer despised Stone Age savages. Instead they became the objects of the minutest scrutiny by knowledge-thirsty, inquistive, white people. A new and more subtle form of exploitation was beginning.

The five Methodist missions developed rapidly with the implementation of the assimilation policies and the injection of large sums of money. Non-Aboriginal staff increased dramatically, larger schools and hospitals were built, and more houses were provided. Communal feeding was introduced to improve Aboriginal health. Mission stores were started, trading in a wide variety of goods, and tea, flour and sugar became standard items in Aboriginal diet. Money also became available for linguists who started to reduce Aboriginal languages to writing. They were able to pave the way for the bilingual education programs of the 1970s.

A greater proportion of Aboriginal children now went to school. Some furthered their studies for several years at Kormilda and Dhupuma Colleges. The function of these Colleges is discussed in Chapter 15. Many adults worked on training allowances at the mission. Increasingly they received money, moved around freely, and made frequent trips to visit relatives and to get drunk. They had more freedom and more money but greater responsibilities when self-determination became the accepted Government policy from 1973.

For the fifty years ending in the late 1960s, the mission boats were indispensable in carrying mission stores to and from Darwin and between the missions themselves. The sea journeys were tedious, often very rough, and sometimes dangerous. Missionaries and their families, usually unaccustomed to travelling at sea in small craft, suffered the tortures of seasickness. Several of the mission boats were wrecked. The main vessels used were the *J.M.McBride*, the *Larrpan I* and *Larrpan II*, the *Aroetta* and the *Warrawi*. Nowadays supplies come by barge from Darwin and Brisbane, and personnel arrive by air. Gone are the fearful days of the long and hazardous sea voyages.

Changes in mission and church administration have taken place over the years. In 1955 the Congregational, Methodist and Presbyterian churches agreed to work together in the Territory as the United Church in North Australia (UCNA). The amalgamation was by mutual consent and was not binding legally. The activities of UCNA at that time did not include the mission work of the MOM in Arnhem Land, which was not incorporated into UCNA until 1969. In June 1977 the Australia-wide Uniting Church in Australia embracing most of the congregations of the Congregational, Methodist and Presbyterian Churches, came into being. The activities of the United Church in North Australia are now directed through the Northern Synod of the Uniting Church.

Following the Government's promulgation of its policy of self-determination in 1973, the Aboriginal Advisory and Developmental Services (AADS) of the United Church conducted a commission of enquiry to reassess its role in Aboriginal communities in Arnhem Land. The report of the commission was entitled *Free to Decide* and has been the blue-print for UCNA's policies and activities in Arnhem Land since that time.

Free to Decide tries to respond to the new self-awareness of Aborigines as a result of the policies of self-determination and self-management. The report examines fundamental issues in Aboriginal communities, such as traditional and other power

116

TOP: The grand old man Wonggu and some of his twenty-two wives, Caledon Bay,
1934. BOTTOM: Tukiar, the central character of the Caledon Bay killings, and his wives.
At the time of the Peace Expedition 1933–34

Merara, one of the three Aborigines found guilty of killing the Japanese at
Caledon Bay

groups, the dependent economies of small and isolated communities, educational and vocational development, land rights, and Aboriginal custom and law. The report also outlines new UCNA perspectives in the light of changing circumstances.

The Uniting Church now does its work in Aboriginal communities through the active Christian congregations by the provision of community services and by the 'presence of community development staff who are free to live and work with Aboriginal people in their communities in ways which bring new awareness of both problems and possibilities, which offer new freedom in shaping life in their own style, pace and direction, to those who are blinded and enslaved by dependence'. Aboriginal Councils are encouraged to take full responsibility for all civil matters in the communities. Senior 'mission' staff now adopt the role of community advisers.

UCA defines a community adviser as 'a person primarily working with groups such as councils and associations which are not traditional parts of Aboriginal social structure. He is working with Aboriginal communities to enable them to function as intergrated working groups, facilitating inter-clan communication and corporate action so the groups can come to terms with the expectations of external agencies on the one hand and other groups within the community on the other.'

UCA has actively supported Aboriginal initiatives to return to their homelands. This had been the dream of Harold Shepherdson. Since the early 1970s there has been a dramatic increase in the number of tribal groups from UCA areas returning permanently or temporarily to their own country. The movement is particularly marked in eastern Arnhem Land, where large numbers of Aborigines have formed communities inland and down the east Arnhem Land coast.

The Uniting church has also been responsible for the spiritual care and oversight of the Government settlement of Maningrida at the mouth of the Liverpool River. The Government established Maningrida in 1957 initially as a ration centre, and as a place from which Aborigines could move to Darwin in the assimilation process. The depot quickly became a settlement, and had the strengths and weaknesses of the mission settlements elsewhere. Different tribes living nearby and on missions began camping at Maningrida, and communal facilities had to be quickly provided for them. During the 1960s a large number of non-Aboriginal staff employed by Welfare, Forestry and other Government departments worked there. In the 1970s the numbers became so great that they posed a grave threat to Aboriginal self-determination. On different

117

occasions the Aborigines expressed deep disquiet and dissatisfaction at the numbers and attitudes of many of the Balanda staff.

In 1973 the Anglicans and the United Church jointly formed the Combined Church Training and Research Centre Incorporated in Darwin, called Nungalinya College. The College seeks to respond to the needs of the two churches, especially in connection with training programs for the Aborigines of Arnhem Land and elsewhere throughout North Australia. The College has two main areas of concern. The first is community development. Facilitating courses for community workers, Aboriginal supervisors, and new and experienced staff are provided. The courses provide opportunities for discussion and exchange of ideas so that Aborigines and non-Aborigines may together assist forward policies of self-determination and self-management in the communities.

At Nungalinya College programs of theological education are undertaken by means of lessons recorded on cassette tapes. After preliminary orientation studies at the College in Darwin, students continue their studies with the cassettes in their own communities. They are helped in this work by local ministers or staff, who are approved tutors of the College. In some cases tutors and students work together in the vernacular. In any case every endeavour is made to make the theology relevant to the circumstances in which the Aborigines find themselves.

The Reverend Lazarus Lamilami, M.B.E., was one of the outstanding Aboriginal Christian leaders of Arnhem Land. He visited the Liverpool River as a missionary before Maningrida was started. On 5 November 1966 he was ordained at Goulburn Island, after assisting the missionaries over a number of years as a carpenter and lay reader. From that time until his death in Darwin in September 1977 he was a loved and revered pastor to Aborigines and non-Aborigines alike. He was at home in European and Aboriginal culture, and was able to build bridges of understanding between the two races. He would often say, 'Let us walk together, hand in hand'.

Most Aborigines of Arnhem Land say that they still want missionaries to work with them in their communities. They say that the missionaries' role is now different. They emphasise the point that missionaries 'are not the bosses now', although often in practice the missionary superintendent still has prestige and authority.

An Aboriginal recently said, 'It is our land and we have to say what we think ... we want the missionaries. We will organise things, organise the work, and all this, but we want the missionaries.' At the same time Aborigines have not been slow to realise their rightful authority. One said, 'At this stage we are free to employ the people we want and to fire them if we don't want them'.

Arnhem Land Aborigines still want to have people they know and can trust working alongside them. As one Aboriginal said to the 1974 AADS commission of enquiry, 'Are we going to live ourselves or is the mission going to be here with us? If we push you, the missionaries, away, the other Balanda will come and you know better than I do. We ourselves are just frightened of the other Balanda. I still myself know we want the missionaries to stay with us.' Another said 'We are pretty sure we still need someone to work with us, to teach us and train us for many things we do not know. We want this until we are ready to take over and have a company run just by Aboriginal people.'

The work of the expatriate now is advisory and that of the servant. Another Aboriginal said, 'To work with Aboriginals in the store we need an advisor to be there, not a manager, just one alongside before the eyes of the Aboriginal people so that the Aboriginal people can take over.'

The Anglican CMS and the MOM, later the United Church and then the AADS of the Uniting Church, have played a significant part in the protection and preservation of the Aborigines living in Arnhem Land. Their original role was directive. Their task today is different. If they are to stay, they stay by permission of the Aboriginal communities. If they are to continue to function they must do so in the role of the servant rather than the manager.

11
They took us
from our mothers

'They took us from our (Aboriginal) mothers and put us in a mission', a part-Aboriginal said to me one day. 'I don't think that they should have separated us from our mothers. The missionaries were good and did what they could, but we had no family. We often talked about this when we were growing up. We were given food and clothes and we had to work hard. We learned to read and write. But what is the use of all that if we do not know who our parents are? Some of us knew who our parents were. Some of us did not and that was very bad. They should have left us alone with our mothers. Our parents are more important than our food.

'My boy now says to me, "Eh, Dad!", and he knows who I am. I don't know who my father was. I tried to find out, but no one would tell me. I tried at that place where you know about births and deaths, but he would not tell me. I had a big row with them, but they still wouldn't tell me about my parents. I can't say, "Eh, Dad!" because there is no one. I don't know where I came from and who my parents were. I don't know what tribe I belong to. This worries me very much. They should not have taken us from our mothers.'

This cry of anguish is heard from many part-Aboriginal people. Some know who both their parents were. Some know only who their mothers were. Some just do not know who their mothers and fathers were at all. Many of the half-castes from Arnhem Land have worked hard and done very well for themselves. They have good jobs in the Top End or down South. Some of the men have become drifters and drunkards, and have not done well at all.

120

But they all have this in common. Their identity and the knowledge of their antecedents is of supreme importance for them.

In more recent times some part-Aboriginal children have been adopted at birth by sympathetic, well-screened, white parents. In many of these cases neither the part-Aboriginal children nor the adopting parents know the actual parents or mother. Such children have grown up in an atmosphere of love and affection. Yet they still experience periods of feeling rejection and frustration. They tell of bullying and abuse at school and of discrimination in the community. Often they rebel against their home and their environment. 'We want to go and find who our mothers are,' they sob. The best child-care cannot compensate for the emotional stability of blood relationships.

The treatment of half-castes for many years was shocking. Successive Governments of the Territory were guilty of inhumanity and indifference. During its forty years' administration in the nineteenth century the South Australian Government did nothing for them. Large numbers of whites and Chinese flocked into the North to develop pastoral leases or to try their luck mining. The only women available were Aborigines who were traded to the newcomers for flour, opium and grog.

During the first decade of the twentieth century the South Australian Government tried to improve the appalling conditions of Aborigines and half-castes. They were prompted by the Government Resident, C. J. Dashwood, who, in 1908, drafted legislation for their protection. In that year the Chief Protector stated that there were ninety-nine known half-castes in the Territory — forty-eight males and fifty-one females. He estimated that there were probably many more not known.

In 1910 the South Australian Government belatedly passed the Northern Territory Aboriginals Act 'to make provision for the better protection and control of the aboriginal inhabitants of the Northern Territory, and for other purposes'. By this Act a half-caste was defined as 'any person who is the offspring of an aboriginal mother and other than an aboriginal father'. The notion of a white woman marrying or having a *de facto* relationship with a non-white was at that time apparently unthinkable! The new Act set up a Northern Territory Aboriginals Department for the welfare of Aborigines and half-castes, and the Chief Protector became their legal guardian. Intermarriage between Aboriginal women and non-Aborigines could take place only with his permission.

The Commonwealth Government took over the administration

121

of the Territory in 1911 and amended the South Australian Aboriginals Act. In 1913 Professor W. Baldwin Spencer presented his *Preliminary Report on the Aboriginals of the Northern Territory* after twelve months' investigation. In his report he stated that 'the half-castes are in a most unfortunate position. There may possibly be 100-150 of them in the northern and approximately the same number in the southern part, where also there are quadroons who may be regarded as belonging to the white population.'

Professor Baldwin Spencer emphasised their plight. 'I think it may be said that though the half-castes belong neither to the aboriginal nor to the whites, yet on the whole they have more leaning towards the former. Certainly this is the case in regard to the females. One thing is certain and that is that the white population as a whole will never mix with half-castes.'

Spencer pointed out that they were a very mixed group. The mother was normally a full-blooded Aboriginal; the father could be a white man, a Chinese, a Japanese, a Malay or a Filippino. With the typically superior attitude of the time he continued, 'The mother is of very low intellectual grade, while the father often belongs to the coarser and more unrefined members of higher races. The consequences of this is that children of such parents are not likely to be, in most cases, of much greater intellectual calibre than the more intelligent natives, though there are exceptions to this.'

There have indeed been exceptions to this, more exceptions than would have been anticipated. The myth of the inferiority of Aboriginal intelligence has been exploded. Many part-Aborigines born about this time or soon afterwards have made good. They have won through in the face of prejudice and discrimination. Despite the obvious handicap of emotional disturbance and upset in their formative years, they have established themselves within a society which until recently was critical and racist.

White attitudes and the policy of the time regarding the care of part-Aborigines is reflected in Baldwin Spencer's recommendation. 'No half-caste children should be allowed to remain in any native camp, but they should all be withdrawn and placed on stations. So far as practicable, this plan is now being adopted. In some cases, when the child is very young, it must of necessity be accompanied by its mother, but in other cases, even though it may seem cruel to separate the mother and the child, it is better to do so, when the mother is living, as is usually the case, in a native camp.'

'The best and kindest thing,' concluded Baldwin Spencer, 'is to place them on reserves along with the natives, train them in the same schools and encourage them to marry amongst themselves. Any special cases in which a half-caste — a boy especially — shows any marked ability can be easily provided for and he can pass on from a native to an ordinary school or to some other institution. On the reserves the services of the more intelligent half-castes may be utilized in supervising the work of the aboriginals.' This view formed the basis of Government and mission policy for half-castes in Arnhem Land for the next forty years.

The continued plight of Aborigines and half-castes in the Territory led the Commonwealth Government in 1928 to commission Mr J. W. Bleakley, Chief Protector of Aborigines in Queensland, to conduct a comprehensive investigation into all aspects of the mixed and full-blood communities in the Northern Territory. His report was presented to Parliament the following year.

Bleakley wrote, 'Perhaps the most difficult problem of all to deal with is that of the half-castes — how to check the breeding of them and how best to deal with those now with us.' In order to 'check as far as possible the breeding of half-castes', he recommended that there be a 'strict inforcement of laws for protection and control of female aboriginals'. He said that white women should be encouraged 'to brave the hardships of the outback' and live in the Territory, and that the Government should make sure 'Protectors stationed in the bush are married men and have their wives living with them'.

Bleakley next turned his attention to the half-castes of the Territory, then numbering about 800, 'those now with us'. Of these, 306 were in Central Australia, 206 were in institutions, and a few were employed in the towns. About 400 were employed on cattle stations. The remainder, of whom probably a half were children, were in camps attached to the stations or in the bush. He was most anxious that 'the children should be rescued as early as possible'. All illegitimate half-castes, male and female, not otherwise being satisfactorily educated should be collected and placed in Aboriginal Industrial Mission Homes for education and vocational training. Their education was 'to aim at making them intelligent and able to protect themselves in business dealing', and the vocational training was to 'fit them to fill a useful place in the labour for the development of the Territories'.

Bleakley said that there were two current attitudes regarding the future of half-castes. The first was the 'complete separation of the half-caste from the aboriginals, with a view to their absorption by the white race'; the second was 'complete segregation from both black and whites in colonies of their own and to marry among themselves'. He obviously was in favour of neither. He said that past experience had 'shown that the half-caste with few exceptions, does not want to be separated from the blacks, in fact is happier amongst his mother's people. He is not wanted by the whites, nor does he want to be pushed into a society where he is always an outcast. He should certainly be rescued from the degradation of the camps and given the benefit of education and training, but will be happier if raised to this civilization in company with the young aboriginals of his own generation.' He favoured the marriage of half-castes with full-bloods 'provided the latter have been lifted to an equally civilized plane'. He observed that most marriages between the 'superior' half-caste or quadroons 'did not seem to be very happy ones. The best type of white man is not anxious to outcast himself in this way, preferring, if he must, to satisfy his lust with casual lubras until able to return to white society.'

Bleakley strongly favoured the continuation of mission institutions to care for half-castes as well as for full bloods. His reasons are given elsewhere.

The Government of the day accepted Bleakey's recommendations. They collected half-castes and sent them to the missions or to the half-caste compounds in Darwin and Alice Springs.

The record of the missions in caring for half-castes is far happier than that of Government institutions in Alice Springs and Darwin. The Anglican Church Missionary Society (CMS) and the Methodist Overseas Missions (MOM) were the two missionary agencies to engage in this work in Arnhem Land. The policies of both were much the same. The half-castes were to be isolated and given practical training so that they might eventually lead a useful life in white society.

The CMS started the Roper River Mission in 1908. This Mission became a centre for the nurture and training of half-castes from the first decade of its life. This was due in no small measure to the proximity of the Mission to the nearby pastoral properties. Darwin was too far away to send half-castes, and in any case, living conditions for them there were terrible. In 1917 the Superintendent, the Reverend H.E. Warren, said that the numbers of half-castes being brought in by the police and by him as Protector of Aborigines was increasing. Something would have to be done to remove them from the blandishments of unprincipled white men from over the river, and to stop them from running away.

Anglican mission and church leaders tried to solve the problem by establishing a half-caste mission on isolated Groote Eylandt in the Gulf of Carpentaria. Here half-castes would be segregated from undesirable elements in the Aboriginal camp near the mission, and be removed from the attentions of poor whites. They would have the opportunity of being trained in isolation to take their place in Western society.

The Bishop of Carpentaria supported this policy. On 12 August 1918, he wrote to the Victorian CMS saying, 'It is important that the half-caste children be treated and dealt with separately and distinct from Aborigines. There must be a separate establishment for half-caste children, and the teaching and training, next, of course, to religion. The tendency of the half-caste is to sink to the level of Aborigines. I would suggest that as soon as possible an establishment be formed at Groote Eylandt for the half-caste children, and that it be quite distinct from any work among Aborigines on the island . . .'

During the next eight years the CMS missionaries at Roper explored and prepared the Groote Eylandt Mission for the half-castes or 'Euralians' as they were being called. In 1922 the Bishop of Carpentaria reiterated the Church's isolationist policy for them. In a letter to Warren he said, 'The government has brought you many of these children, and now you must look upon their care as a separate work. They are half-Western, some more. For this reason I do not think it is right to allow them to associate with and learn the habits and customs of the Aborigines. They should be learning Western ways of life . . .'

The marriage of Timothy Hampton to Sarah Johnson in January 1924 indicates the good influence which the Mission had on the lives of the half-castes. Both Timothy and Sarah had spent most of their childhood at Roper. Both had been taught there and had been confirmed. They had greatly assisted the missionaries in the school and dormitories and subsequently became full staff members.

In September 1924 Warren took thirty-five half-castes from Roper to the Emerald River Mission on Groote Eylandt. The transfer meant that some of the half-castes were separated from their Aboriginal mothers, who had settled at Roper and married there. One such woman later told me, 'When we left the Roper River Mission in September 1924, to go to Groote Eylandt, I cried and cried because I was being separated from my mother. As the *Holly* was leaving the jetty, everyone was singing "God be with you till we meet again", but I just cried for my mother. She was the only person I really knew in the world.'

Segregated life for the half-castes on isolated Groote Eylandt had the advantages of nurture and teaching away from 'unprincipled whites'. But it was a lonely life for the half-castes. As they grew older the future seemed all the more uncertain. They were not allowed to marry full-bloods. A few married white men. Others married among themselves, an immediate solution with an indefinite and sometimes fragile future.

Captain (later Sir) Hubert Wilkins, the noted Australian Arctic and Antarctic explorer, quickly became aware of this during his stay at the Mission from January until April 1925. He wrote, 'Taken at an early stage, as they had been, from the sordid surroundings of "bush" life, these half-castes soon acquire a taste for modest culture, and, schooled by high and noble-minded people, they have acquired a gentle and respectful manner which compares more than favourably with that of children of the same age in more civilised localities ... The problem of their future life is difficult to solve. They are prohibited from marrying full-blood natives and would, indeed, be unfit for the life to which that might lead. Whether they will be content to live a community life and marry among themselves remains to be seen ... The future problem of these chocolate coloured people is one that leaves us sadly floundering for a satisfactory solution.'

The wholesome environment of the Groote Eylandt half-caste mission was so much better than the terrible condition of the half-castes in Darwin. The Methodist Church here viewed 'with sorrow and indignation' the shocking plight of the Darwin half-castes. In 1926 the MOM sent three children South to a home in New South Wales in order to save them from what they termed 'a vicious environment'. Later that year the Chief Protector of Aborigines in the Territory asked the Methodist Church to take over the care of the half-caste children in the Darwin compound. The Department of Home and Territories also promised to send all other half-castes in the northern half of the Territory to Groote Eylandt. Before these moves could be made Dr Cecil Cook became Chief Protector. His policies were different from those of his predecessors and included Government control of half-castes.

Meanwhile, Bishop Davies, who had succeeded Bishop Newton as the third Bishop of Carpentaria, maintained the Church's stance on the segregation of the half-castes and on their training on Groote Eylandt. The report of an address which he gave the Victorian CMS on 15 October 1926 says, 'The Bishop began by referring to the grave problem of the half-castes, particularly at Darwin and the locality. The whites in this part of the Territory altogether depended on the half-caste portion of the population to meet domestic needs. The most important side of the question was that relating to the children. The Bishop unhesitatingly stated that in his opinion the only solution to the difficulty lay in the complete segregation of the children. Groote Eylandt possessed great advantages for the segregation of these children, and he was of the opinion that every effort should be made to obtain them.'

Bleakley, also, in his 1929 report highly commended the work which the CMS missionaries were doing. He said that there were thirty-four half-castes on Groote Eylandt, fifteen males and nineteen females. 'The discipline seems excellent and the control firm, but just and paternal ... The staff of this institution appears to be admirably suited for the work.'

Bleakley nevertheless questioned the half-caste policy of the CMS. He wrote, 'The aim of the mission is to give these half-castes vocational training, encourage them to marry among themselves, and then, if they wish, go to employment on stations as married couples or remain on the reserves and maintain themselves by farming small plots ... The mission's present policy, of segregating the half-castes from both white and black and confining them to marriage amongst themselves, is not regarded as a correct one, nor likely to be successful, for reasons already outlined in the general report.'

Towards the end of the 1920s, the CMS changed its policy on its half-caste work on Groote Eylandt. Southern leaders became impatient at the lack of work among full-blood Aborigines on the island. Early in 1929 they adopted a new policy which stated that 'while the primary object of the Mission has been to bring the blessings of the Gospel on the Aboriginal people ... there has arisen the necessity to care also for a small proportion of people of mixed bloods called Euralians ... Much of the work, therefore in North Australia has been expended in connection with this section of the work, which is quite subsidiary to the real and original efforts of the Society.' This change in outlook corresponded with Dr Cook's views.

The CMS finally adopted its new policies in 1932, and the half-caste mission on Groote virtually ceased. Fourteen half-caste children of school age were transferred to Roper River so that they could be sent on to Darwin and Alice Springs. They were accompanied by several half-caste teaching assistants. Some of the older half-castes over school age were kept on Groote to help in the work at the Mission and on the *Holly*. As it transpired, Dr Cook would not allow the fourteen half-caste children to be sent on to the half-caste homes in Darwin and Alice Springs because of suspected leprosy. They therefore stayed on at Roper River together with the half-caste assistants, who gave excellent service in the school and dispensary.

Meanwhile the treatment of half-castes in Darwin was an utter disgrace. Church authorities continued to make representations to the Government regarding their disgusting conditions, but to little avail. Xavier Herbert in *Capricornia* graphically portrayed the tragedy of their lives.

The deplorable circumstances of the Kahlin half-caste compound in Darwin was discussed in Parliament in Canberra in 1939. Mr McEwen, the Minister for the Interior, said that about fifty half-caste girls, ranging from children three or four years old to young women, were 'accommodated in a small weatherboard cottage of not more than five or six rooms, the kind that normally would be regarded as suitable, perhaps, for a minor official, his wife and two children ...'

He continued, 'Not only were these fifty girls living in this place, but the building also served them for a school. The dividing walls had been torn out, and stretchers were packed over the whole floor as closely as they could be put. For their schooling the girls huddled on a narrow strip of verandah which was not accommodating beds, and there they were taught. I have since been informed that even the buildings had been taken over by the administration or the defence authorities, I do not know which, and the girls are being accommodated — under what conditions I do not know — in the compound for aborigines. That is the very opposite of what has been agreed upon as the proper care of half-caste people, the idea being to raise their status by keeping them away from the aborigines. I could not, without being unparliamentary, express the shame I feel that no money has been provided in the Estimates this year to correct that state of affairs.'

Some members of Parliament of the time expressed concern that the new compound for half-castes and full-bloods was to be located at Bagot. One such member said, 'It is too near the aerodrome, where 300 to 400 of our young men are to be trained for the Air Force. It is a disgrace to the Government that the compound should be located so close to the aerodrome. It is well known that many of the half-castes and aborigines in the compound suffer from venereal disease. Some of them are in a bad state. It is a disgrace ... seeing that we are sending our boys there for the Air Force training.' In the continuing debate, he reiterated '... we should not be sending our boys into a training camp so close to the filthy compound in which these natives and half-castes are living ... We should not set such a temptation in the way of our young men ... The natives and half-castes should be accommodated many miles away from Darwin and not close to the centre of the town ...'

The appalling conditions for half-castes in Darwin, the obvious success of the Groote Eylandt experiment and growing interest by the Methodist Church in a possible venture on Croker Island led the Anglicans to reconsider their policy. After extensive investigation and negotiation with the Department of the Interior, the CMS planned a new settlement for half-castes, again on Groote Eylandt, but this time at Angurugu. There would be a 'modern mission' where the half-caste boys would be taught 'cattle work, gardening, cotton-growing and marine pursuits' while the girls would learn domestic science and cooking.

Staffing difficulties, the destruction of Roper River by a disastrous flood in 1940, and World War II put a stop to these plans. The Government evacuated all white and half-caste women and children residing in war zones in the Northern Territory. Three hundred half-caste women and children were brought South, of whom between fifty and sixty came from Groote Eylandt, Roper River and Alice Springs. Most of these were housed at Mulgoa in New South Wales until the end of 1948.

After the war the Government reversed its approval for CMS to open a half-caste settlement on Groote Eylandt. Instead they offered a site on Coburg Peninsula for the work, claiming that it would 'be closer to the half-caste work of the Roman Catholics on Melville Island and the Methodists on Croker'. This was unacceptable to the CMS, so the Society abandoned its plans for a half-caste settlement and closed the Mulgoa half-caste home at the end of 1948.

Before the Mulgoa home closed, Mr Moy, the Director of Native Affairs, interviewed each half-caste adult and child. He asked them to tell him what they wanted to do. Some of the boys accepted his offer to go to a hostel in Adelaide. One lad, who had just gained his Leaving Certificate, was allowed to continue to stay on in Sydney in order to attend the Sydney Teachers' College. He allowed four of the girls who were already in suitable employment to remain. Two others wanting to do nursing training under CMS auspices also stayed in Sydney. He offered the remaining girls places in the Hostel at Alice Springs run by the (Anglican) Australian Board of Missions. Married couples who had come to Sydney and were not living at Mulgoa were allowed to do what they wished.

Meanwhile the Methodist Church continued its care for the half-

129

castes in Darwin. They appointed a Fijian minister to look after them and for other non-whites in the town. This minister commented, 'I have worked among my own people, the Rotumans, among Fijians, Australian half-castes and Aborigines, but in my opinion the most neglected people are the Australian half-castes.'

The Methodist Church also continued to negotiate with the Government for the establishment of a home for the Darwin half-castes. Government was now sympathetic. The situation was critical and something had to be done. But the Methodist Church could not agree where the home should be situated. Supporters in Alice Springs did not want the half-castes who were being cared for there, sent North. The Methodist Inland Mission suggested that a large lease in Central Australia should be taken out for the purpose of training half-castes in pastoral work. The Methodist Overseas Missions on the other hand wanted to rescue the Darwin half-castes and have them settled on Croker Island off the Coburg Peninsula. The final arbiter in the dispute was Professor Elkin, who opted for an island settlement. The MOM proposals won the day and they set about establishing a 'colony for half-castes' on delightful Croker Island.

While the site on Croker was being prepared during 1940, forty half-caste children were taken from Darwin and temporarily housed at Pine Creek. They stayed there in rough conditions until July 1941 when they were joined by twenty-eight half-castes from Alice Springs. The whole group was then transferred to temporary quarters on Goulburn Island. An additional twenty or so were kept in Darwin for medical treatment and joined the group later. Finally the group was transferred by the mission launch, the *Larrpan*, to Croker in November 1941, in time to settle in before the Wet. Even then only four cottages had been erected and these were not complete. But ninety-six children up to the age of eighteen were now on the threshold of a new life, segregated from white man's vices and black man's degradation.

Because of the worsening war situation the children did not stay long on Croker Island. The military authorities ordered them out along with white women and children lest they fall into the hands of the invading Japanese. Many of the aeroplanes which systematically bombed Darwin from February 1942 flew directly over Croker from Japanese bases in New Guinea.

The evacuation of the ninety-six half-caste children of Croker Island and accompanying staff under Margaret Somerville was a terrible ordeal for everyone. The whole journey took six weeks and two days. They set out on Easter Monday 1942. They were taken by the *Larrpan* to the mainland, then transported by several broken-down mission vehicles along bush tracks to Oenpelli. After resting there for about a month they were transported in rattling Government vehicles over rugged mountain ranges to Pine Creek. From there they went by rail in cattle trucks to Larrimah and by military trucks to Alice Springs. From here they went by rail to Adelaide, Melbourne, and finally to Otford, not far from Sydney. This was to be their home for the next four years.

Like their Anglican counterparts at Mulgoa, the half-castes at Otford fitted in well in their new home. They were readily accepted at the local schools and church. They made their mark under the ever-watchful and loving eye of Miss Somerville.

The decision to re-establish the half-caste children on Croker after the war did not pass without challenge. The founder of the Methodist Mission at Yirrkala, Wilbur Chaseling, considered that controlled contact with whites in the South, such as they were experiencing at Otford, would be far better than the isolation of the North. He was concerned that they would have nowhere to go when they had to leave the Mission at eighteen years of age. They could perhaps work on at Croker, marry and live there. If they went on to Darwin what would be their future? The Methodist Inland Mission also was critical of the half-castes' returning to the isolation of Croker for much the same reasons.

The MOM Board was adamant that they should return to Croker Island. The Government supported this view. There was also the fact that Croker had been maintained and developed by the devoted efforts of two missionaries in preparation for the half-castes return.

So return to Croker most of them did. Some of the older ones were now independent and stayed South permanently. An advance party of eight of the adolescent half-castes returned in July 1944. The remaining sixty-nine children returned in April 1946. They were welcomed by Rupert Kentish, who had now provided eight cottages and had cultivated a farm. Margaret Somerville was the only one of the original staff to return.

For the next twenty-one years Croker continued as a half-caste settlement. During almost the whole of this time Miss Somerville mothered this family with great devotion. There were on average between fifty and sixty children. The mission was run on a cottage home system with about ten children to each cottage. In this way children lived much the same lives as children do in a normal family. Domestic science and home duties were part of the training for the senior girls.

Government and mission philosophy underlying half-caste

child-care in this way was that of isolation and segregation. Away from the harmful whites and troublesome blacks, the children would grow up to live wholesome, disciplined lives. Many did so. Others did not. The two great problems were marriage and employment when the children grew older. Some of the Croker girls became pregnant through illicit sexual affairs. The resident staff encouraged marriage, but the Southern Board was not sympathetic. Some of the young men sought work in Darwin but often succumbed to the seductions of town life.

At the end of 1967 the half-caste mission of Croker was closed and the children brought to Darwin. They are now cared for in six Somerville Cottage Homes which are at Nightcliff, Stuart Park and Rapid Creek. All the children now are not necessarily half-castes, but are those handed over for care by the courts. In the first year thirty-five children were cared for in these six homes as family groups supervised by cottage parents. The present superintendent encourages children to find out who their parents are, and to build bridges of understanding and identity. This is a far cry from the policies initiated thirty years earlier.

Changes in community attitudes to part-Aborigines has been a feature of the past seventy years. In the early days men and women of compassion cared and acted while the white community despised and governments remained indifferent. Human bodies as well as human souls mattered to them. These people of compassion did what they thought was right. They took them away from meddling whites and unwholesome blacks, and taught them the 'better' way of the white man. This would enable them to grow up in isolation, intermarry among themselves and become people of the 'in between'.

For some of the half-castes this was the best way. 'Groote Eylandt is the only home I have ever really known,' said a respected part-Aboriginal woman. 'I loved my time there very much. Not that everything was easy. We were very isolated and life was hard in those days. The discipline was strict and some of the punishments were a bit harsh. All the same the happiest years of my life were spent on Groote Eylandt.

'We were brought to the Roper River Mission because it was part of the job of the police at that time to round up the half-castes and see that they were looked after properly. We were not wanted by our mothers' people and were ignored by the whites.

'The Mission was built on a small clearing ... We were not allowed to go outside the fence by ourselves, or to talk with anyone except the missionaries. We were not allowed to have anything to do

Sunday morning on South Goulburn Island Mission, early 1930s

Top: Mrs G. R. Harris and the senior girls, Angurugu Mission, 1948. Bottom: Medical care at Maningrida settlement. Initially established as a ration centre in 1957, it quickly became a settlement

with the natives who were camped at the edge of the Mission. We did not know how isolated we were until we had afterwards left there.

'We all loved Mr Warren. He was very strict but he was very kind to us all. He was the only father I had never had. We all called him "Daddy". When he would come back from his trips on the *Holly* he would always bring us something . . .

'The memories of my years with the Mission are not all good ones, and some things might have been better. But I can truly say that I was very happy there and was given a home when no-one wanted me.'

That the half-castes should have been isolated from arrogant selfish whites is understandable. Their separation from the 'degradation of the black man's camp' is open to question. Standards of health, morals and education were quite different. Yet there would have been the security of belonging to a group, and knowing they belonged. Mr Jim Lester, a highly respected part-Aboriginal from Central Australia said, 'I'm an Aboriginal man myself. I was brought up in the camp by my mother and step-father. I speak five Aboriginal dialects and a little bit of English. I'd like to tell you what I can remember about the 1930s. I suppose it was a Government law that made policemen come from Oodnadatta to look for part-Aboriginal kids to take them away . . . A lot of mothers were upset by the taking away of their part-Aboriginal children. They used to cry in the camp and everybody was very upset. They would talk about it and say, "I suppose my boy or girl is calling white people aunties and uncles now". When they used to think like that and talk about it, they got very sad. I remember this because I used to run away myself to the hills with my mother and the policemen never caught up with me.'

'They took us from our mothers' was not an infrequent cry. It had been universal. One man told me that when a round-up of half-castes was about to take place 'my mother quickly ground up some charcoal and painted me with it so that I could not be identified. I was not to be taken on that trip. I went on the next. My mother had forgotten to paint me!'

Did white men of a former generation take half-castes from their mothers because they really wanted to help them? Men of compassion certainly did. Perhaps others advocated segregation in order to pander to their pride and to salve their troubled consciences. It is even possible that they could not tolerate the thought of a girl with even a small percentage of white blood submitting to the embraces of a full-blooded black.

12
We are the bosses now

The Labor Government introduced sweeping changes in Aboriginal policy and administration when it gained power in December 1972. The changes were dramatic and revolutionary, and have far-reaching consequences for the foreseeable future. Aborigines are now given the right of self-determination. They are given the opportunity of determining their own future instead of being processed into the life-styles of the majority of Australian society. They are now able to choose the nature of the society which they wish to create. They seem certain to want to choose an alternative way of life, which, in turn, will have to be integrated into the wider Australian pattern. The policy of assimilation has now been abandoned; integration is the basis of the new deal. As a number of Arnhem Land Aborigines are saying quietly, but with understanding, 'We are the bosses now'.

During the latter part of the 1960s many people were becoming dissatisfied with the underlying philosophy of the policy of assimilation and its outworking in the Northern Territory. They questioned the morality of assimilating a minority group with its distinctive culture into a larger and more powerful majority. They maintained that this would inevitably mean the loss of identity and ultimately the destruction of a culture and of a race.

Two further factors led the Government to revise its thinking in its search for an Aboriginal policy for the seventies. The first was the 1967 referendum, in which the Australian people overwhelmingly recognised Aborigines as members of Australian society with full voting rights. The second was the judgment of the Supreme Court of the Northern Territory on 27 April 1971 that Australian law did not recognise Aboriginal title to traditional land. Greater efforts had to

134

be made to give Aborigines a greater sense of identity and to remedy this gross defect in Australian law.

New moves were outlined by the Prime Minister, Mr William McMahon, on 26 January 1972. He said that the Government had decided to make certain changes in the emphasis of its policies and to introduce new measures affecting land holdings on Aboriginal Reserves and elsewhere within its jurisdiction. A five-point 'Statement of Objectives' had been adopted and this would be 'a general directive to those responsible for the formulation and administration of Commonwealth policies affecting Aboriginal Australians'. The five objectives were: '(1) . . . they (Aborigines) should be assisted as individuals and if they wish as groups, at the local community level, to hold effective and respected places within one Australian society with equal access to the rights and opportunities it provides and acceptance of responsibilities towards it. At the same time they should be encouraged and assisted to preserve and develop their own culture, languages, traditions and arts so that these can become living elements in the diverse culture of Australian society.' (2) The Government 'recognises the rights of individual Aborigines to effective choice about the degree to which, and the pace at which, they come to identify themselves with that society . . . The concept of separate development as a long-term aim is utterly alien to these objectives.' (3) 'We also believe that programmes to give effect to such a policy must evolve in accordance with the effects of action so far taken and the needs of the times. They must take into account the expressed wishes of Aboriginal Australians themselves . . .' (4) The Government 'considers that a balanced strategy . . . requires a programme of action . . . which would (a) encourage and strengthen their capacity increasingly to manage their own affairs . . . (b) increase their economic independence; (c) reduce existing social and other handicaps facing them in health, housing, education and vocational training; and (d) promote their enjoyment of normal civil liberties and eliminate remaining provisions in law which discriminate against them.' (5) The Government also 'considers special measures will be necessary to overcome the disabilities now being experienced by many persons of Aboriginal descent.'

After reviewing the Government's policy and its achievements in the post-war years, Mr McMahon stated that his Government would create a new form of lease for land on Aboriginal Reserves, which would be called a general purposes lease. The Government would also provide additional finance for Aboriginal enterprises, and investigate 'ways of providing a simple, flexible form of incorporation for Aboriginal communities'. He said that the Government would also consult with Aboriginal communities affected by mining, 'so that their welfare can be taken into account when applications for exploration and development rights are being considered'.

Mr McMahon's new deal for Aborigines contained elements of self-determination, although assimilation still remained the basic policy. Aborigines were to have an 'effective choice about the degree to which, and the pace at which, they came to identify themselves' with the wider Australian society. They would be allowed increasingly to manage their own affairs, have incorporated communities, and have some say in mining on their land. At the same time the new policy was to be administered through the existing Welfare Branch. The 'concept of separate development as a long term aim' was 'utterly alien to these objectives'. Modified assimilation was still the ultimate goal.

The new proposals did not go far enough and came too late. Before they could be put into operation, the Liberal-Country Party coalition was roundly defeated in December 1972, and Labor swept into power. The new Government was able at last to put into practice their pent-up policies, and the ideals which had been frustrated during more than two decades in Opposition.

The Labor Party outlined its policy on Aboriginal affairs for the seventies at the Party's twenty-ninth Conference in June 1971. The Conference stated that the Office of Aboriginal Affairs would be upgraded to Ministerial level; that Aborigines would have equal rights and opportunities with all other Australians; that they would receive the standard rate of wages; that they would have adequate educational, housing, health and social services; and that all Aboriginal lands would be vested in a public trust.

Mr Whitlam changed Labor's Aboriginal land policy after meeting with Aboriginal demonstrators at the 'Aboriginal Embassy' on 9 February 1972. He now said that a Labor Government would 'establish community ownership of land in the Northern Territory by identifiable communities or tribes by way of freehold title'; would protect Aborigines against any discriminatory legislation passed by a 'fully elected legislative assembly'; and would make provision for Aboriginal legal aid. The part-Aborigines of the South thus played an important part in the granting of full land rights for traditional Aborigines in remote areas in the North.

Labor continued to promise enlightened legislation for Aborigines if it assumed power. In his election speech at the Blacktown Civic Centre on 13 November 1972, Mr Whitlam said, 'There is one great group of Australians who have been denied their basic rights to the pursuit of happiness, to liberty and indeed to life itself for 180 years

— since the very time when Europeans in the New World first proclaimed those rights as inalienable for all mankind'. These were, of course, the Aborigines. He castigated the McMahon Government for not acting since the 1967 referendum. He went on to say that there would be a separate Ministry for Aboriginal Affairs, that Labor would, among other things, 'legislate to establish land in Commonwealth territories which is reserved for Aboriginal use and benefit as system of Aboriginal tenure .. and vest such land in aboriginal communities'; 'establish an Aboriginal Land Fund to purchase or to acquire land for significant aboriginal communities and to appropriate $5 million per year to this fund for the next ten years'; 'legislate to prohibit discrimination on grounds of race'; and 'legislate to enable Aboriginal communities to be incorporated for their own social and economic purposes'.

When Labor won the 1972 elections, the new Government immediately began implementing its new policies for Aboriginal advancement. They certainly acted quickly. Many would claim that they tried to do too much, too hastily. But they set in motion a new concept for Aboriginal development which has not been superseded since, even by a change of Government. They established a new way forward for Aboriginal identity and land ownership, which will be the pattern of Government policy for many years to come.

The basic Labor philosophy is that of 'self-determination'. An understanding of this policy and its implications for those of us concerned with the Aborigines of Arnhem Land were discussed at three seminars held at Batchelor between March and August 1973. We came up with the definition that 'self-determination means that Aboriginal communities decide the pace and nature of their future development within the legal, social and economic constraints of Australian society'. The seminars hotly debated the latter part of the definition, regarding restraints. Each seminar reached the same conclusion. Aborigines must themselves determine what they wanted to do, but such decisions must be within the legal and economic parameters of Australian society.

'Self-determination' was clarified also by the Prime Minister, Mr Whitlam, in an address to the Ministerial Aboriginal Affairs Council in Adelaide on 6 April 1973, when he said, 'The basic object of my Government's policy is to restore to the Aboriginal people of Australia their lost power of self-determination in economic, social and political affairs. The Minister for Aboriginal Affairs, Mr Bryant, will be introducing into Parliament, I hope during the next budget session, legislation to enable Aboriginal members, determining their own decision-making processes, choosing their own leaders and executives in ways they will themselves decide as the primary instruments of Aboriginal authority at the local and community level.'

Further understanding of self-determination came from Mr B. G. Dexter, Secretary of the Department of Aboriginal Affairs, in an address entitled, 'The Commonwealth Department of Aboriginal Affairs — its functions and underlying principles', given at Monash University on 9 May 1973. Mr Dexter said, 'The underlying principles of the new Labor Government's approach to Aboriginal affairs are somewhat similar to those of the McMahon Government. The main principle is one of self-determination. The emphasis is on participation by Aboriginals in the making of policies and in decisions about their future and the programs that affect them ... Policies and programs must now be designed to enable Aboriginals to decide their own goals and to achieve them. Ideally, policies and programs should be open-ended, concerned with methods rather than with ultimate aims.'

The concept of self-determination rejects 'assimilation', which is based on the idea of the superiority of the dominant culture. It envisages instead some form of integration which has been defined as 'a process by which diverse elements are combined into a unity while retaining their basic identity. There is no insistence upon uniformity or elimination of all differences, other than those differences of each component which would disturb or inhibit the total unity. Integration, as differentiated from assimilation, is a two-way process which does not entail the disappearance of indigenous institutions and traditions. It implies consciously refraining pressure upon indigenous groups to abandon their culture ...'

The Labor Government emphasised four main spheres of activity in implementing its policy of self-determination. The first was the recognition of land rights. The Government set in motion the Woodward Land Rights Commission, foreshadowing subsequent legislation whereby the ownership of land in the Aboriginal Reserves of the Northern Territory and unalienated Crown land with traditional ownership would be vested in Aboriginal communities. The second sphere was that of consultation, and accordingly the National Aboriginal Consultative Committee (NACC) was convened to advise the Minister for Aboriginal Affairs. The third emphasis was bilingual education, which would provide primary education for Aboriginal children in their own languages as well as English. The fourth was the incorporation of communities, so that Aborigines through their own Town Councils might achieve their own goals.

In clarifying the policy of self-determination, the Department of

138

Aboriginal Affairs in a submission to the Senate Standing Committee on the Social Environment entitled 'Policies and Programs in Aboriginal Affairs' analysed some of the implications of the shift in policy in comparison with the past. The Department pointed out that one of the basic reasons for failure in welfare programs overseas 'was that they were designed by administrators and social scientists and that the client communities of the poor were not actively involved in developing the plans and carrying out the programs. It is difficult to think of any programs in Aboriginal affairs which have not been similarly designed and executed by white administrators and based on their judgments of the needs of the situation. Aboriginals have as a rule been involved only as more or less passive clients or recipients sometimes invited to endorse or comment on programs already approved.'

The submission stated that programs 'designed to develop and strengthen the capacity of Aboriginal people to manage their own affairs' were of central and crucial importance. The submission severely criticised Government and mission settlements. Such communities, the submission claimed, 'invite attention as the focal points of the failure of existing programs to develop Aboriginal independence. These "institutional communities" are relics of earlier phases when it seemed convenient to segregate Aboriginals in order to control and protect them or, more recently, when it was hoped to educate and train Aboriginals for "assimilation". As institutions designed to "process" Aboriginals into hard-working and well-behaved citizens of industrial society they have failed. Ever-increasing sums of money have been spent on their maintenance and development and their staffs have been steadily increasing, but there seems no evidence that more staff and more money are making them more effective. Far from sending out acculturated citizens ready and willing to seek a job and a house in the "wider Australian community", these communities have generally grown rapidly and have produced a generation of people who know no other life than the almost totally dependent existence of settlement-dwellers. Within them have emerged additional problems including delinquent youth, illegitimacy, drunkenness and petrol-sniffing, high rates of infant ill-health and adult under-employment . . .'

As a remedy to these tragic circumstances, the submission stated that thought 'is currently being given to ways in which these centres may be transformed into properly functioning, independent communities. These communities must lose their institutional character, and, as they cease to be managed by a staff in the manner of institutions, there should be an immediate shift of some responsibility to the communities themselves and a progressive increase in that shift. In this process white staff should become helpers and sources of advice rather than managers and supervisors ... The development of local responsibility can proceed by allowing Aboriginal residents decision-making power in matters about which they themselves are concerned, rather than by imposing a western-style local government system or by merely employing Aboriginals in the settlement staff structure. This can best be done by incorporating Aboriginal communities with powers to act in a wide range of issues of community concern, so that they may adapt their customary law and traditions to the needs of their present situation ...'

The submission also advocated the encouragement of the return of Aborigines to their homeland centres. 'They are establishing or seeking to establish small communities where traditional hunting and gathering can be combined with production of goods for sale to provide some cash income ... The establishment of such small outpost communities provides an immediate opportunity for Aboriginal groups to manage their own affairs ...'

Other matters covered by the submission included the need for the preservation of sacred sites, adequate land rights, assistance in coping with life in towns, provision for the economic independence of Aborigines, employment, Aboriginal enterprises, and reducing handicaps in health, housing and education.

The Labor Government accepted the recommendations made in the submission, which was a practical application of its policy of self-determination. Labor also set in motion during its three years in Government the enabling legislation and the administrative framework to effect these new measures.

Subsequent chapters deal specifically with the main issues, such as land rights, bilingual education, health and general welfare issues.

The first major administrative change came with the reorganisation of the Department of Aboriginal Affairs. Prior to this time the direct responsibility for Aboriginal matters in the Northern Territory had been held by the Welfare Division of the Northern Territory Administration, the Northern Territory Administration as a whole being responsible to the Comonwealth Department of the Interior. On 19 December 1972 the Department of the Interior ceased to exist and the Departments of the Northern Territory and Aboriginal Affairs were created. Under this arrangement the Welfare Division of the Northern Territory Administration was transferred in its entirety to the new Department of Aboriginal Affairs (DAA), and became its Northern Territory Division. The transfer included the Aboriginal Education Branch, and also the Community Welfare Section.

Further administrative changes followed soon afterwards. On 1 January 1973 the Department of Health assumed sole responsibility for the provision and control of nursing services to Aboriginal communities. Prior to this time the Welfare Division had been responsible for health services at Aboriginal communities and for the administration of the subsidised nursing sister scheme for pastoral property communities.

On 2 January 1973 responsibility for the employment of Aborigines was transferred to the Department of Labor. Prior to this time the Welfare Division had been responsible for the employment placement of Aborigines on the missions, settlements and on pastoral properties.

On 13 February 1973 the Department of Education took over the responsibility for Aboriginal education from the Department of Aboriginal Affairs. Aboriginal education now became part of the newly established Northern Territory Division of the Department of Education. Prior to this time the Education Department of South Australia had provided teachers for Aboriginal schools under the Welfare Division.

Research work previously undertaken by the Welfare Division now became the responsibility of the Australian Institute of Aboriginal Studies. The Institute was given the responsibility for recording and evaluating all sites of significance for Aborigines throughout Australia. As from February 1973 all research in this and other areas previously undertaken by the Welfare Division was phased out, and its Research Branch ceased to function.

These dramatic administrative changes greatly affected staffing and funding arrangements. Mr Ray McHenry became the Acting Director of the Northern Territory Division of the Department of Aboriginal Affairs, replacing Mr H. C. Giese who had been the first Director and then Assistant Administrator (Welfare). Over 570 positions were transferred from the Northern Territory Division of the Department of Aboriginal Affairs to other Australian Government Departments. Staffing establishment changes between 1 July 1972 (first stated figures) and 30 June 1973 (second stated figures) were: Head Office, Darwin, 117 to 97; Regional and district offices, 78 to 57; in training, 116 to 33; reserve communities, schools, colleges, vocation training centres, 604 to 239; other institutions, 62 to 119; mobile works force, 96 to 79. Thus the overall establishment for the new Northern Territory Division was reduced from 1123 to 624.

Administrative changes automatically meant new financial arrangements. Some of the appropriations such as Aboriginal Health and Education in the former Welfare Division were transferred to other government departments. Additional funds were made available from the Aboriginal Advancement Trust Account. The Department of the Northern Territory now allocated funds for DAA items of expenditure which had not previously been included in the operational votes of the Welfare Division.

The outworking of the policy of self-determination in the Arnhem Land Communities was traumatic. There were in 1973 the three government settlements, Maningrida, Umbakumba and Ngukurr; the five United (now Uniting) Church communities, Croker Island, Goulburn Island, Milingimbi, Elcho Island and Yirrkala; and the three Anglican missions at Oenpelli, Angurugu and Numbulwar.

Those who felt the changes most keenly were obviously the non-Aboriginal staff. Almost overnight they were being asked to change from directive to advisory roles. The whole philosophy of authority, work patterns, and administrative structures of the past would have to be re-arranged.

For many months Aboriginal and non-Aboriginal staff were confused. Some considered that the changes had come too quickly and that Aborigines had neither the capacity nor the training to cope with executive authority. Others said that self-determination was a political 'gimmick' which would soon pass when there was a change of Government. Some saw the new system as a threat to their careers or to their personal power and reacted accordingly. Others saw that here was a grand opportunity for Aboriginal control and the growth of Aboriginal responsibility, despite the swiftness of the events, and tried to make the system work.

The employers of staff also had to think through the implications of the new policy. The Department of Aboriginal Affairs, Church authorities, and mission boards had now to give way to decisions made by Aboriginal Town Councils. DAA and the United Church welcomed the moves and immediately appointed community advisers instead of superintendents. The Anglican CMS was more cautious, and maintained that superintendents should continue while the mission was still legally responsible and until Town Councils became incorporated.

Aborigines in Arnhem Land are unanimous in their approval of the policy of 'self-determination' and of the control of their communities. Most have said that they thought that the changes had come too quickly, and that too much was expected of them too soon. Several years had to pass until they realised fully what was involved, and where ultimate power lay. The non-Aboriginal concept of elected councils, and the way in which they made their decisions also had to be thought out and talked through. Various Aboriginal power groups vied with each other for control. The older men were not often fluent in English and did not understand committee-type debate. Many of the younger, more educated men did. Tension between the older and the younger often emerged. Yet despite all this, Aborigines know that they have the ultimate say, and the assumption of greater responsibilities has added to their sense of purpose. They say, 'We are now the bosses in our own country'.

That the system in its early stages should be abused was inevitable. Town Councils were sometimes manipulated by Aboriginal power groups or by white advisers. Community advisers varied in their understanding of 'advising', interpretations ranged from directing to passive inactivity and incompetence. Some accountants and business consultants took great financial advantage of the situation. Architects and building consultants sometimes received extremely high fees for services rendered to Housing Associations who built only a few houses. Some non-Aboriginal staff handed their responsibilities over to Aborigines without giving the necessary patient undergirding advice and encouragement. Representatives of some Government departments other than the Deparment of Aboriginal Affairs seemed to be unaware of the policy of self-determination and its implications, and continued to direct and to demand. There was misunderstanding and mismanagement, just as there were mistakes and misdemeanours. But these were all part of the growing experience for Aborigines and non-Aboriginal advisers and helpers until they were able to come to grips with the new situations and organise themselves to meet the different demands.

In March 1975 Senator J.L. Cavanagh, the Minister for Aboriginal Affairs, clarified the Government's policy regarding the role of churches and missions working in Aboriginal Communities. In an opening statement at the National Missions Conference held in Adelaide, he reviewed the important contribution of 'civilising and Christianising' which missions had made in the past. He pointed out that by 1972 Australian Government assistance to missions in the Northern Territory was running at $3.5 million each year and covered such matters as the cost of capital development, buildings, water and electricity supplies, roads and communications. He stated that; 'Assistance was, of course, limited to the secular activities of the missions in work of direct benefit to Aboriginal communities'.

Senator Cavanagh made quite clear the position of missions working in Aboriginal communities. He said, 'In the early days of the Labor Government it perhaps seemed to many missionaries that their days in the field were numbered and it would not be long before the Aboriginal communities, at the instigation of the Government, would politely or otherwise ask them to leave ... I sympathise with missions who consider they still have a secular role to perform in Aboriginal communities and I think it would be most unfortunate if they felt compelled or pressured into precipitated action ... Having said this I must make it clear that the Government can only support mission-conducted programs which coincide with its views as to the future of the Aboriginal communities. It has often been said that the Government's policy in relation to Aboriginal affairs is one of "self-determination" ... The Government accepts the views that programs and policies in Aboriginal affairs will be less effective if they are not supported by the Aboriginal people ...'

Senator Cavanagh continued, 'What we are aiming for, therefore, is a situation in which Aboriginals are free to determine their own future as part of the total Australian community and are not bound by the pre-conceptions of the past which assumed that any cultural adjustments would occur in one direction only and that Aboriginals would adjust to the dominant culture ... The Government looks to missions as a continuing source of assistance so long as those communities want them to remain. I suggest that communities will wish this only as long as the missions show themselves willing to recognise the developing aspirations of the communities and accept those aspirations for what they are ... We will retain the responsibility and the right, however, to consult with and advise Aboriginal communities in their relations with non-Aboriginals including missions, and I trust their relations with missions will continue to develop into a firm working partnership for the maximum advantage of the Aboriginal people.'

The activities of the Labor Government came to an end when the Governor-General, Sir John Kerr, dissolved Parliament on 11 November 1975. The Liberal National Country Party was subsequently elected and took office on 13 December. Labor was once again out, but its policies on Aboriginal advancement were continued by-and-large by the new Government. Self-management now became the key idea instead of self-determination.

The Department of Aboriginal Affairs continues to implement Government policies aimed at the advancement of Aboriginal people. Self-management, land rights and self-sufficiency are the three main emphases.

The provision of finance for community development programs is one of the main functions of the Department. The main sources of funding are the Grants-in-Aid Scheme (formerly the Aboriginal Advancement Trust Account), the Land Fund, and the Loans and Enterprises Funds. Separate provision also exists for assisting missions and funding Civil Works programs. During 1976/77 the allocation of funds under the Grants-in-Aid Scheme alone was $18.3 million.

The provision of expertise to other Government departments engaged in Aboriginal community development is another important function of DAA. This was necessary after health, education, social welfare and vocational training were transferred from the Welfare Division to the different departments. Liaison is established through interdepartmental committees, whose members keep each other informed concerning the policy and practice being adopted by each.

The Department of Aboriginal Affairs supports the homeland or outstation movement. The return by Aborigines to their land is an expression by them of their wish to retain their traditional life-style, and their response to social and cultural problems facing them in their relationships with European Australian society. Even if the movement is only a passing phase, it nevertheless enables them to work out future goals, provided they are left free to make their own decisions. DAA normally provides decentralising groups with a grant of up to $10 000 to provide initial water supply, shelter, communications and a store.

Decentralisation and the movement of Aborigines between their traditional land and the missions and settlements has been going on for a number of years in Arnhem Land. Both Harold Shepherdson of Elcho Island and Alf Wilson bought and flew their own aircraft as a means of contact and communication with small groups of people camped in different areas. In the late 1960s people began to move out from Maningrida. By 1977 the trickle had become a flood, so that in north-eastern Arnhem Land alone there were more than three dozen such decentralised communities.

In its 1975 *Report on Arnhem Land* the Council for Aboriginal Affairs, Dr H.C. Coombs, Professor W.E.H. Stanner and Mr B.G. Dexter, after visiting the area, said, 'There are in these movements both a challenge to and an opportunity for an imaginative development of policy and administration. The general situation seems clear. The movements, whether diffuse or definite and organized, are voluntary. They are taking place under traditional leadership. The tasks and burdens involved in the decisions to move are, though onerous, being assumed cheerfully and are regarded as rational and attainable. The controlling aim seems to be to re-establish an authentic Aboriginal society which will assimilate chosen European elements but will not necessitate a continuous white presence or the maintenance of a "worker-boss" relationship between black and white. It seems certain that to some degree being "in one's own country" is a material and psychological pre-requistie of independence and distinctively Aboriginal life style.'

These then are some of the reasons for the homeland movement: The move back to a traditional way of life, but with added and controlled European factors; the socio-religious affiliation with the land of the ancestors; the ferment caused by land rights agitation and the knowledge that Aborigines now have their own land and want to enter once more into their inheritance; the disenchantment of life in government settlements, missions and other white-controlled centres and the opportunity for self-development; the moral and practical support which the Government is giving to achieve these stated goals.

Gätjil Djerwurkburk, whose homeland centre is at Dhalinbuy (Cato River) said, 'We prefer to use "homelands" rather than "outstations" because more than anything the people have said that they are going home. When people first went to Yirrkala it was only their temporary home. They did not feel at home there. There were fightings between the clans.

'People went back to their homelands not just because of land rights. It was the people's move. It was not a holiday centre but a permanent place. They show this in their willingness in trying to improve the place. Their social life is completely different. What they act and do here at Yirrkala they never do when they go back to their homeland. They respect their elders. They know where they belong and feel part of that country.

'Education in the homelands is not confined to one program. It is a process. As it progresses that is the way it will develop. They learn basic literacy and numbers and English. There is storytelling about the area. The children are taught how to survive in the bush. There is a general learning about the environment. There is also adult education for old people.

'The economics of the homeland centres are from social services, craft and part of the proceeds of Aboriginal Business Enterprises. The main source of income is craft.

'People have their ceremonies and they are happy. They often express with tears, "I am at home in my country at last. I have neglected this my country". It is a bit like the story of the prodigal son. They have gone back home.'

Through moral and financial assistance to the homeland movement, and by implementing its policies in a wide number of areas, the Department of Aboriginal Affairs is firm in its determination to forward the policy of self-management. Finance enabling Aborigines to achieve this basic goal is fundamental. In July 1977 Mr D.O. Hay, the Secretary of the Department, said that priority 'should be given to projects which promote self-management. This goal incorporates three basic elements: independence/self reliance, responsibility, and the acquisition of managerial skills; all of which are readily applicable to any individual, family or local community group situation . . .

'Self-management could be enhanced if finance was directed to programs which (i) support the provision of services and facilities by Aboriginal organisations; (ii) encourage the development of specialist Aboriginal organisations to work with functional authorities in such fields as health, housing and education; (iii) support the review and evaluation of programs by Aboriginals and encourage their responsibility for success or failure of programs; and (iv) seek to develop Aboriginal management skills whilst operating.

'Aboriginality includes the recognition that Aboriginals have the right to retain, modify or develop their languages, culture, customs, traditions and lifestyle in their own way. It can be expected that Aboriginal people will be concerned to promote, manage and develop special interests arising out of their Aboriginality. Finance should be allocated as a priority to maximise options available to Aboriginals in such areas of interest to them as the management of their lands and property, the preservation of sacred sites, the expansion of bilingual and bicultural education and the operation of Aboriginal enterprise.

'In the development of a freely chosen lifestyle it is sometimes difficult for communities to survive in some locations because essential services are difficult to obtain. Before self-sufficiency measures can be considered, finance is required and may be provided for food, clothing, shelter, communications and health services, such as pure water and waste disposal.'

In 1977 the Government policy of self-management was quite specific. The main thrust of the Department of Aboriginal Affairs and mission and Church communities in Arnhem Land is the implementation of this policy in all aspects of Aboriginal life. Large numbers of Balanda still pose a great problem, as continued unrest at Maningrida shows. Small groups of non-Aborigines in key executive positions often unwittingly pose a threat to the idea. The expectation by most white people of assimilation of Aborigines into

Western life-styles in universal. The granting of land rights and the resurgence of Aboriginal culture in themselves posit a pluralistic society divided on racial lines. Yet despite all this one thing remains clear. Aborigines now have their own land. They now control their own towns. They decide who may or may not enter their country. They say, with pride and dignity, 'We are the bosses now'.

TOP LEFT: Reverend Harold Shepherdson ('Sheppy') (*Photo Australian News and Information Bureau*). TOP RIGHT: James Galarrawuy Yunupingu, Chairman of the Northern Land Council, 1978. BOTTOM: George Winunguj playing a didjeridu with the Adelaide Wind Quintet

James Galarrawuy Yunupingu shows the Yirrkala 'bark petition' to Messrs J. Long, Silas Roberts and R. I. Viner (Federal Minister for Aboriginal Affairs)

13
Without land
I am nothing

James Galarrawuy Yunupingu, an Arnhem Land Aboriginal from Yirrkala, in a recent open letter headed 'From Black to White' wrote, 'The land is my back-bone. I can only stand straight, happy, proud and not ashamed about my colour because I still have land. The land is the art. I can paint, dance, create and sing as my ancestors did before me. My people recorded these things about our land this way, so that I and all others like me may do the same.

'I think of land as the history of my nation. It tells us how we came into being and what system we must live. My great ancestor who lived in the times of history planned everything that we practise now. The law of history says that we must not take land, fight over land, steal land, give land and so on. My land is mine only because I came in spirit from that land, and so did my ancestors of the same land. We may have come in dreams to the living member of the family, to notify them that the spirit has come from that part of our land and that he will be conceiving in this particular mother.

'My land is my foundation. I stand, live and perform as long as I have something firm and hard to stand on. If there is a flood on my land I will have to swim and all Gumatj clan will have to swim, but not for long, we will surely perish, then we will be just like thousands of other people whose lands have been stolen away from them. We will be the lowest people in the world, because you have broken down my back-bone, taken away my arts, history and the foundation. You have left me with nothing.

'Without my land I am nothing. Only a black feller who doesn't care about anything in the world. My people don't want to be like you.'

149

Galarrawuy's passionate plea for his land is but one of a multitude of Aboriginal voices which are being heard today throughout Arnhem Land and other parts of the Northern Territory. They all say much the same thing. Their land is their life and the very 'backbone' of their existence. It is 'the history of their nation', and their sure 'foundation'. Without their land they feel that they are nothing.

The Aborigines of Arnhem Land have been living on their land for at least 20 000 years. This is where they hunted and gathered their food. This is where they lived and loved and died. This is their country.

They have a profound religious affinity with their land. They believe that their ancestors, the great totem heroes of the dreamtime gave them this land. They sing the songs of these heroes, and perform ceremonies associated with them.

Each clan or tribe has its own country. This was defined in the totem songs and dances. Where the great hero went, he made different physical features, such as rocks, pools, and trees. He gave them their country. Their ceremonies are the religious rites, the title deeds to the territory, which the totem made.

The land links Aborigines with nature and with eternity. Formerly they believed that they were conceived by the spirit of their ancestors, who entered their mothers. They were born into the heritage of their clan and its country. They were part of timeless nature and of the universe. Death was the return of the spirit to the ancestors.

This is why land is so important for Aborigines. The land has not just been their means of livelihood or the place where they have lived. It has been the centre of their religion and the voice of their soul. This is why their demand for land rights has not been just a political or moral issue. They have had to have the land to maintain their identity, and to retain their spiritual life.

Bunuk of Goulburn Island said, 'Land means something to my people. More than land, it means the past, present and the future. This is how I see it. Not only me but my people. This is how we see it, past, present and future. When we talk about the past, the stories, the legends mean something to us and when we talk about the present we talk about young people who go to school. They will have nothing to claim as their own, and this leads to when we talk about the future ... the stories, trees, sacred sites, stones and the old people. The old people still look forward to see that their land will be given back to us. We want to claim this country and own it as it has been in the past.'

A number of individuals, churches and organisations had been clamouring for Aboriginal land rights in the Northern Territory for a number of years. It was the Aborigines, themselves, who precipitated the matter. In August 1966 the Gurinji stockmen and their families walked off Wave Hill Station and set up their camp at Dagaragu, or Wattie Creek. In the following year they petitioned the Governor-General, Lord Casey, to assist them to gain tenure of their tribal lands from which they had been dispossessed. Nine long years were to pass before the lease for the Gurinji tribal land was handed to Mr Vincent Lingiari by Mr Gough Whitlam, the Prime Minister, on 16 August 1975.

Meanwhile on 28 August 1963, Aboriginal elders from Yirrkala had petitioned the House of Representatives. Their formal request was written in the Gumatj language on bark, the traditional material for paintings and communication. They asked Parliament to appoint a Committee 'accompanied by competent interpreters, to hear the views of the Yirrkala people' before permitting the excision of their land for bauxite mining by Nabalco. They stated that the procedures for the excision of their land and the fate of the people on it 'were never explained to them beforehand'; that decisions were taken 'without them and against them'; that 'the land in question has been hunting and food gathering land for the Yirrkala tribes from time immemorial; we were all born here'; that 'places sacred to the Yirrkala people as well as vital to their livelihood, are in the excised land, especially at Melville Bay'. They concluded their now-famous bark petition by stating that 'the people of this area fear that their needs and interests will be completely ignored as they have been ignored in the past, and they fear that the fate which has overtaken the Larrakeah tribe will overtake them'.

As a result of the petition the House of Representatives set up a Select Committee to examine their grievances. This Committee presented its report on 29 October 1963. The report contained legal agrument regarding Aborigines' right to title to the land. The Crown counsel also stated, 'When Australia was settled Aborigines of Australia were considered at that time not to have title to their land. The whole of our system of land tenure is built on that assumption, so there is no difference, so far as that is concerned, between eastern Australia and the Northern Territory. In point of fact, of course, this part of the country was part of New South Wales.' The conclusion was clear. Aborigines had no legal title to their land.

The Select Committee nevertheless recommended that the hunting rights of Aborigines over the mining area should be preserved, and that nobody else should be allowed to take any of the foods and materials which the people needed. They also recommended that sacred sites should be preserved, and that Aborigines should have some say in the relationships between themselves and the people of the proposed town of Nhulunbuy.

The Aborigines of Yirrkala continued the fight for their land. On 13 December 1968 three of their leaders, Milirrpum, Munggurrawuy and Daymbalipu, on behalf of the Yirrkala clans, issued a writ in the Supreme Court of the Northern Territory against Nabalco Pty Ltd. The action contested the right of the Crown to negotiate with Nabalco for the purpose of mining bauxite without the traditional owners' consent, and without compensation to them for the use of their land. The case was heard before Mr Justice Blackburn. Mr Justice Woodward, at the time Queen's Counsel, was one of three barristers representing the Aboriginal plaintiffs.

Mr Justice Blackburn gave his decision on 27 April 1971 in Alice Springs, after hearings in May and June 1970 in Darwin, and September, October, November 1970 in Canberra. In giving his judgment, Mr Justice Blackburn said that the evidence showed that the Aborigines belong to the land but the land did not belong to the Aborigines. He said that the doctrine of communal native title did not form, and never had formed, any part of the law in Australia.

He said, 'There are great and difficult moral issues involved in the colonisation by a more advanced people of a country inhabited by a less advanced people. These issues though they were rightly dealt with as relevant to the matters before me, were not treated as the foundation of the plaintiff's case.'

He then went on to say that the foundation of the argument was that political sovereignty over and title to the land became vested in the Crown by reason of Governor Phillip's actions in Sydney in 1788. From that time onwards the common law applied to all subjects of the Crown, including Aborigines.

'The claim is that the plaintiff clans, and no others, have in their several ways occupied the subject land from time immemorial as of right, that the rights of the plaintiff clans are proprietory rights, and that these rights are still in existence and that Nabalco's activities are unlawful in that they are an invasion of such proprietary rights.' Mr Justice Blackburn said that there was no place in his opinion for communal native title in the law as it stood, and that the Aborigines had obtained no grant from the Crown. A major element in their case had been that the Minerals (Acquisition) Ordinance 1953 of the Northern Territory was invalid; but the evidence showed that nothing had invalidated the ordinance.

No appeal was made to the High Court, but the judgment did not go unchallenged. Articles were written in legal journals, magazines and newspapers disputing the decision. The New Zealand decision by the Privy Council regarding Maori land rights was cited. A number of legal writers claimed that communal 'native title' did give a proprietary interest in land.

But all was to no avail. The Aborigines at Yirrkala lost their case, and their right to title to their land. To them it was a bitter blow. This is reflected in a petition which they made to the Prime Minister in May 1971, which read, 'The people of Yirrkala have asked us to speak to you on their behalf. They are deeply shocked at the result of the recent Court case. We cannot be satisfied with anything less than ownership of the land. The land and law, sacred places, songs, dances and language were given to our ancestors by spirits Djangkawu and Barama. We are worried that without the land future generations could not maintain our culture. We have the right to say to anybody not to come to our country. We gave permission for one mining company but we did not give away the land. The Australian Law has said that the land is not ours. This is not so. It might be right legally but morally it is wrong. The law must be changed. The place does not belong to white man. They only want it for the money they can make. They will destroy plants, animal life and the culture of the people.

'The people of Yirrkala want: (1) Title to our land; (2) A direct share of all royalties paid by Nabalco; (3) Royalties from all other businesses on the Aboriginal Reserves; (4) No other industries to be started without consent of the Yirrkala Council; (5) Land to be included in our title after mining is finished.'

The three signatories to the petition were R. Marika, Daymbalipu Mununggurr, W. Wunungmurra.

The view of the Yirrkala elders that Mr Justice Blackburn's decision 'might be right legally but morally be wrong' was shared by a large number of people throughout Australia. The validity of the judgment in law was no longer the issue. What was needed clearly and without delay, was some means whereby Aborigines might have title to the land which had been theirs for thousands of years.

The first attempt at reform was made by Mr W. McMahon, the Prime Minister. His policy statement dated 26 January 1972, started with the words, 'When the Supreme Court of the Northern Territory decided on 27 April last year [1971] that Australian law did not recognise Aboriginal title to land in Australia the Government decided to review its policies relating to the Aboriginal people and their aspirations'. He then outlined a five-point 'Statement of Objectives' and new procedures which should be adopted.

Concerning the land use by Territory Aborigines he said, 'We are deeply concerned . . . to enable them, in the current circumstances, to have some security in their relationship with the land, and, in particular, to give continuing Aboriginal groups and communities the opportunity of obtaining an appropriate title under Australian law over lands on Reserves which they are interested in to use and develop for economic and social purposes'.

McMahon's proposed form of land title was completely inadequate. Ownership of Aboriginal land clearly remained with the Crown. The title was to be in the form of a lease to be known as a 'general purpose lease' and would be provided for periods of up to fifty years 'in line with existing pastoral leases'. He said that this new form of lease would be created rather than 'attempt simply to translate the Aboriginal affinity with the land into some form of legal title right under the Australian system . . . because we concluded that to do so would introduce a new and probably confusing component, the implications of which could not clearly be foreseen and which would lead to uncertainty and possible challenge in relation to land titles elsewhere in Australia which are at present unquestioned and secure'. He also proposed new safeguards regarding mining on Aboriginal lands. The McMahon proposals for Aboriginal land reform were not implemented, as the Liberal-Country Party coalition was defeated and Labor came into power in 1972.

Labor's policy on Aboriginal land rights was spelled out at its twenty-ninth conference held in Launceston in June 1971. This conference stated that all Aboriginal lands were to be 'vested in a public trust or trusts composed of Aborigines or Islanders as appropriate. That exclusive corporate land right be granted to Aboriginal communities which retain a strong tribal structure or demonstrate a potential for corporate action in regard to land at present reserved for the use of Aborigines . . . Aboriginal land rights shall carry with them full rights to minerals in those lands. The sacred sites of the Aborigines will be mapped and protected.'

This policy was revised following a meeting between Mr Whitlam and the demonstrators at the 'Aboriginal Embassy' in Canberra on 9 February 1972. After this meeting Mr Whitlam said that the Labor Government would 'establish community ownership of land in the Northern Territory by identifiable communities or tribes by way of freehold title'. He maintained this stance in his policy speech given at Blacktown Civic Centre on 13 November 1972. He said, 'We will establish once and for all aborigines' rights to land and insist that, whatever the law of George III says, a tribe and a race with an

154

identity of centuries — of millenia — is as much entitled to own land as even a proprietary company'.

Shortly after taking office the Labor Government set in motion procedures to give Aborigines title to their land. The first move was to commission Mr Justice A.E. Woodward on 8 February 1973 to inquire into and report on the 'appropriate means to recognise and establish the traditional rights and interests of the Aborigines in and in relation to land ... ' in the Northern Territory. His mandate was quite clear. As he stated he 'was not concerned with whether Aborigines should be granted rights in land, since the government had already decided that they should'. His task was 'simply to advise on how such rights should be granted'.

Mr Justice Woodward presented two reports, the first in July 1973 and the second in April 1974. In his second report he outlined basic principles regarding the granting of Aboriginal land. He said that 'Any scheme for recognition of Aboriginal rights to land must be sufficiently flexible to allow for changing ideas and changing needs amongst Aboriginal people over a period of years'. He stated that 'Cash compensation in the pockets of this generation of Aborigines is no answer to the legitimate land claims of a people with a distinct past who want to maintain their separate identity in the future'. He maintained that it was 'important that Aboriginal communities should have as much autonomy as possible in running their own affairs', and should be free 'to follow their own traditional methods of decision-making' and 'to choose their own manner of living'.

Regarding existing Aboriginal Reserves, Mr Justice Woodward recommended that 'Aboriginal reserve lands should be owned by Aborigines in fee simple. The title in each case should be held by an Aboriginal corporation. With the consent of the responsible Minister land could be transferred from one Aboriginal corporation to another, but it could not be sold or mortgaged.

'The landholding corporation should be called Land Trusts and they should hold the land for the benefit of all those having traditional interests in it as rights over it ... Regional Land Councils should also be incorporated to direct the Land Trusts in the performance of their duties, to provide the necessary administrative services for the Trusts, to protect the interests of the traditional owners of land, to conduct negotiations concerning any proposed commercial use of the land ...

'The proclamation should describe the reserves by their boundaries which, where a coastline is involved, should include both off-shore islands and waters within two kilometres of the low tide lines ... Regional Land Councils should be primarily responsible for the Administration of leases, licenses and permits ... Apart from the matters specifically dealt with in this report, Aboriginal land should be subject to all laws normally applying to freehold land ... Entry to Aboriginal land should be regulated by a permit system to be administered by the Regional Land Councils, with provision for permits to be issued locally in some cases.'

Claims also could be made for the granting of Aboriginal title to unalienated Crown lands. Regarding pastoral properties containing traditional Aboriginal land he said that a commission under a Supreme Court Judge should be set up to inquire into the extent of such lands, and consider claims 'for the purchase or economic development of land for Aborigines. Some pastoral leases ... should be purchased as tribal lands or as economic ventures ... Compulsory acquisition of land should be considered where necessary ... It should be avoided where cattle station owners are working their own properties.'

Land set apart for Aborigines in towns 'should have the same tenure as is normal in each town'. In Darwin 'Land should be acquired for Aborigines at Kulaluk and, unless there are very strong arguments to the contrary, Railway Dam. The Bagot Reserve should be leased ...'

The establishment of land rights for Aborigines meant that a number of Aboriginal organisations would have to be established and incorporated. This would include the two regional Land Councils and Community Councils at the townships in the Reserves. Mr Justice Woodward also recommended procedures regarding government departments associated with Aborigines, tourism, conservation and sacred sites. He also made significant recommendations regarding mining on Aboriginal land. 'Minerals and petroleum on Aboriginal Lands should remain the property of the Crown ... However Aborigines should have the right to prevent exploration for them on their traditional lands ... This Aboriginal power of veto should only be over-ridden if, in the opinion of the Government the national interest requires it ... Any such decision of the Government should be subject to disallowance by either house of the Parliament ... The Land Council should conduct all negotiations, and give or refuse its consent on behalf of the traditional owners ... All royalty payments should initially be divided as follows: two tenths to each regional Land Council, three tenths to the local community or communities (if any), and the balance to the Aborigines Benefits Trust Fund.'

The recommendations of the Woodward Aboriginal Land Rights Commission were of the greatest importance for the future granting of title to Aboriginal land in the Northern Territory. They formed the basis of the future enabling legislation. In summary, Aborigines would receive community title in fee simple in perpetuity to the Reserves and to unalienated Crown land traditionally owned by Aborigines. The land would be held for the traditional land owners by a Trust. The administration of the land operations and permits would be through the Land Councils. Such councils and town councils would need to be incorporated. Mining should not take place on Aboriginal land without the owners' permission unless it was in the national interest.

On 16 October 1975 the Minister for Aboriginal Affairs introduced the Aboriginal Land (Northern Territory) Bill 1975 and the Aboriginal Councils and Associations Bill 1975 into the House of Representatives. Both Bills incorporated almost all of the recommendations of Mr Justice Woodward. The two Bills, however, were not passed owing to the historic double dissolution of the Australian Parliament. The Liberal National Country Party were subsequently elected and took office on 13 December 1975.

The Liberal National Country Party adopted in principle the main thrust of the Labor policies regarding Aboriginal advancement and land rights. On 4 June 1976 the Minister for Aboriginal Affairs Mr R.I. Viner introduced the Aboriginal Land Rights (Northern Territory) Bill 1976. Under this legislation Aborigines would receive communal freehold title to their land in perpetuity; land trusts would be the instruments for receiving the title to land; Land Councils would be set up; and a Land Commissioner would be appointed to hear claims on other unalienated Crown lands. The new Bill, however, made provision for complementary legislation to be made by the Northern Territory Legislative Assembly regarding the control and protection of sacred sites, control of entry into Aboriginal land, and access to the sea adjoining Aboriginal lands.

The provision for the Territory Assembly to pass this complementary legislation aroused widespread criticism. Many people saw this new move as a fundamental departure from the policy of complete Commonwealth control, and the possibility of a weakening of Aboriginal interests through the Country Party's domination of the Northern Territory Legislature and through the powerful mining lobby. Land Rights supporters, political, student and Church groups agitated for amendments to the Bill to assure the full protection of all aspects of Aboriginal land. The ramifications of land usage and conservation raised in the Ranger Uranium Environmental Inquiry in the Alligator Rivers' 'Uranium province' also made the issues more complex.

The large number of comments and criticisms made regarding the Land Rights Bill resulted in the appointment of Mr D.O. Hay, the Defence Force Ombudsman, to examine the objections, and to make suggestions regarding changes which ought to be made. As a result over forty amendments were made to the Bill. These concerned mining on Aboriginal land, the powers of the Land Councils, and matters associated with the powers of the Northern Territory Legislature and complementary legislation.

The House of Representatives debated the second reading of the amended Bill in November 1976. In presenting the Bill Mr Viner indicated the changes which had been made. He concluded by saying, 'I have said before that I believe that the passage of legislation to grant land rights to Aboriginals in the Northern Territory will be a most significant and progressive step in the social and political history of this country. It will, at long last, signal Australian acceptance of Aboriginals as a people having a unique and distinct culture within Australian society.'

The debate on the Bill in the Senate took place on 7, 8 and 9 December. The Bill was passed on 9 December 1976. Two other Bills were passed at the same time as the Land Rights Bill. They were the Aboriginal Councils and Associations Bill 1976 and the State Grants (Aboriginal Assistance) Bill 1976. The Bills were proclaimed on 26 January 1977.

Australia Day, 26 January, was a most fitting occasion for the proclamation of the new Land Rights Act. It was on that day in 1788 that Governor Phillip had proclaimed New South Wales, that is, the whole of Australia, to be a possession of the British Crown. This imperial deed cost Aborigines title to their land. On the same day 189 years later Territory Aborigines were given title to their traditional land in the reserves.

Speaking on the occasion of the proclamation of the new Act, Mr Viner said, 'While the Australian people have much to be proud of in the creation of a great nation in these two centuries, it should not be forgotten that the pages of our history are blotted with the stains of gross injustice, slaughter, dispersal, dispossession and finally indifference perpetrated on a unique and gentle people whose historical and spiritual link with this land extends back not 200 but 40 000 years.

'The granting of land rights to Aboriginals recognises not only the justice of prior claims to ownership, it also recognises the validity of Aboriginal traditional law and cultural values.

'What we require now is the goodwill of the people of Australia to make this legislation work. White Australians are not unaware of the strength of their own attachment to the soil, to the earth. To Aboriginals land is more. It is their very life, the source of not only their spirit but the place to which their spirit must return. They are indivisible with their land. It is life itself. It is the force that has enabled them to survive for 40 000 years. It has been the strength of their fight — now won — for their birthright'.

The Northern and Central Land Councils were also gazetted on Australia Day, with the boundaries which had been recommended by Mr Justice Woodward.

The major concern of the Northern Land Council has been the complementary or reciprocal legislation of the Northern Territory Legislative Assembly. Aborigines and their supporters objected strongly to the proposals set out in the proposed ordinance which Dr Goff Letts, the majority leader and Chief Secretary, introduced on 3 March 1977. The Northern Land Council immediately sent a telegram to the Prime Minister stating that, 'The Legislative Assembly is deciding what to do with Aboriginal Land. We have seen their Bill. They would let white men confuse our people again with words and papers that they can make work and never for us. They intend to find poor Aboriginals to stand like puppets while they speak the words and never for us. Why do we have to be the ones who have to ask all the time? Why does our word have to be questioned all the time? They will ask us to do things we know nothing of and when we fail and are ashamed we will let them have what they want. They know that. If you help us now we will go forward. If you leave us now we are finished.' The Council followed up the telegram by sending Silas Roberts and James Galarrawuy to Canberra on 10 March to request the Government to do their utmost to ensure that the Legislative Assembly legislation would be more in line with the spirit of Mr Justice Woodward's recommendations.

The Northern Land Council objected to the Bill because it treated 'Aboriginal Land as if it were still simply an Aboriginal Reserve run by the old Welfare Branch than Aboriginal-owned freehold land'; that 'rights of policemen, public servants, politicians and others in regard to freehold land were adequately covered in existing law ... that Aborigines are capable of controlling fisheries and other access to the two kilometres of sea adjoining their land ... that the traditional laws regarding the control of sacred sites should be recognised in Australian law; and that 'all the palaver concerning gazettal of permits should be deleted in favour of an internal access permission system arranged outside of law by the owners of the freehold land and the Land Councils.'

Continued criticism of the proposed reciprocal legislation resulted in the Bill's being left until after the Legislative Assembly elections on 13 August 1977.

Another Territory ordinance had aroused opposition from Aborigines. In June 1976 the Legislative Assembly passed the Territory Parks and Wildlife Conservation Ordinance 1976. A section in this ordinance precluded Aborigines from using guns or cars when hunting in these designated areas. As a result of representations by the Northern Land Council, the Legislative Assembly deleted the restrictive clause, thus enabling Aborigines to hunt with guns and vehicles. Hunting still plays an important part in the life of Aborigines and many of them still get most of their meat this way. They only kill what they need, and do not shoot animals for fun nor waste them. The Aborigines are not a threat to wild life such as feral animals like cattle, goats, cats and buffaloes

In mid-1977 Mr Justice Toohey was appointed the Aboriginal Land Commissioner in terms of the Land Rights Act. His task is to advise the Minister for Aboriginal Affairs and investigate and report on Aboriginal traditional claims to vacant Crown land in the Northern Territory. He also is to register claims to alienated Northern Territory land and inquire into the likely extent of traditional claims to such areas.

Claims of this nature had been heard by Mr Justice Ward, who had been the interim Land Commissioner since April 1975. Mr Justice Ward had handled applications and claims pending the passage of the Land Rights legislation. His sensitive handling of these claims had reassured Aborigines and other residents of the Northern Territory that justice would prevail in all recommendations made to the Minister. Mr Justice Ward's health had prevented him from continuing in the position.

Early in 1977 the Northern Land Council, acting on the instructions of the traditional Aboriginal owners, laid claim to the vacant Crown land between the Mary and the East Alligator Rivers. This included the 'uranium province' which was the subject of the Fox Uranium Environmental Inquiry. The area also included the proposed Kakadu National Park. As the Aboriginal Land claims were inseparably connected with the uranium environmental inquiry, Mr Justice Fox was appointed to hear the land claim, as well as conduct the inquiry.

As a result, Mr Justice Fox agreed to the Aboriginal claim to the Alligator Rivers region. He stated, 'We recommend that the un-alienated Crown Land referred to ... but excluding the area selected as the regional centre be granted to a Land Trust for the benefit of the groups of Aboriginals who are entitled by Aboriginal tradition to the use or occupation of that land, being the clan groups mentioned . . . above'. The Northern Land Council thus won its first land claim, and a very important one at that. Uranium mining in the area will be subject to Aboriginal permission unless the national interest overrides their decision. They will enjoy the royalties which will eventuate if uranium mining proceeds in the area. (An account of the Ranger Inquiry is given in chapter 14.)

The Land Rights legislation is for the Aborigines of the Northern Territory probably the most important event that has taken place during this century. They now have their land. They now have an identity and a dignity. A new spirit of purpose and responsibility is very evident. Councils and landowners in many places are developing their own areas. They are now very particular to whom they give permits. Anthropologists and 'other students of Aborigines' are suspect. They do not wish to be subjected to endless questioning and critical examination. They want to be themselves. They want to develop their lives as they see fit, and work out their way of life with their long cultural background, and the new non-Aboriginal ways. They want to do things for themselves, rather than be passive recipients of welfare handouts. They want Balanda only to support them, not to direct them. They want Government money for their own development and not to be manipulated.

Mr Silas Roberts, then Chairman of the Northern Land Council, expressed this very clearly in a moving statement to the Ranger Inquiry. He said, 'There are too many people who are not Aborigines who speak about us and try to tell the world what we want and what we think. It is time for us to speak out and I do so now after having thought about what I am going to say with other members of my Council who have been a great help to me.

'Aborigines have a special connection with everything that is natural. Aborigines see themselves as part of nature. We see all things natural as part of us. All the things on earth we see as part human. This is told through the idea of dreaming.

'By dreaming, we mean the belief that long ago, these creatures started human society, they made all natural things and put them down in special places. These dreaming creatures were connected to special places and special roads or tracks or paths. In many cases, the great creatures changed themselves into sites where their spirits stay. My people believe this and I believe this. Nothing anyone ever says to me will change my belief in this. This is my story as it is the story of every true Aborigine. All the land is full of signs, and what these great creatures did and what they left we see as very important. And we see this just as much as we did before.

161

'These creatures, these great creatures, are just as much alive today as they were in the beginning. They are everlasting and will never die. They are always part of the land and nature as we are. We cannot change and nor can they. Our connection to all things natural is spiritual. We worship spiritual sites today. We have songs and dances for those sites ... and we never approach without preparing ourselves properly.

'When the great creatures moved across the land they made small groups of people like me in each area. These people were given jobs to do but I cannot go any further than that here ...

'In my travels throughout Australia, I have met many Aborigines from other parts who have lost their culture. They have also lost their land and by losing their land they have lost part of themselves. By way of example they are like Christians who have lost their soul and don't know where they are — just wandering. We in the Northern Territory seem to be the only ones who have kept our culture ... We are worried that we are losing a little bit, a little bit, all the time. We keep our ceremony, our culture, but we are always worried.'

At another time Silas Roberts said 'Without land we are nothing. Without land we are a lost people.'

14
Mining cuts across
our Aboriginal traditions

'I must tell you what our relationship is with our land because the act of mining cuts across our Aboriginal traditions,' said Mr Silas Roberts to the Ranger Uranium Inquiry. 'It is true that people who belong to a particular area are really part of that area and if that area is destroyed they are also destroyed.' Silas at the time was Chairman of the Northern Land Council.

Arnhem Land Aboriginal attitudes to mining have been varied during the past fifteen years. In the earlier days many favoured mining, largely because of the high royalties which they received. Nowadays a growing number are opposing it. This is probably because they now understand more clearly the issues involved. They realise that the land is theirs through the Land Rights Act. They are aware of the complexities of the mining of uranium, whether on Aboriginal land or not.

Before the land rights legislation was passed in 1976, prospecting and mining rights on the Arnhem Land Aboriginal Reserve were the same as rights for mining anywhere else. During the past few decades companies have become increasingly interested in the minerals in the area. As a result in the 1960s and early 1970s large numbers of prospectors moved backwards and forward over parts of the reserve in four-wheel drive vehicles. The Aborigines were bewildered and annoyed as they could not check on the intruders' movements or prevent the wanton desecration of their sacred sites.

During the welfare era the Government encouraged mining on the Arnhem Land Reserve because of its policy of assimilation. The Report of the Select Committee on Grievances of Yirrkala Aborigines, Arnhem Land Reserve, stated, 'On the 13th March, 1963 an area of 140 square miles was excised from the Arnhem Land Reserve on the Gove Peninsula ... The Government's policy of assimilation assumed that the development of reserves should take place, provided that the Aborigines shared in the benefits of the development'. Aboriginal 'wards resident in the area and their rights and needs are adequately protected and catered for ... The mining operations will offer training and employment opportunities for wards in the area, which would not otherwise be forthcoming and will contribute towards their assimilation in the Australian community.'

The policy of assimilation and its implications for Aboriginal rights to their traditional land came under close scrutiny after December 1972. The Woodward Land Rights Commission was particularly concernd with mining on Aboriginal land. The subject was complex and Mr Justice Woodward said, 'Of all the questions I have had to consider, that of mineral rights has probably caused me the most difficulty and concern'.

Mr Justice Woodward recommended that 'Minerals and petroleum on Aboriginal lands should remain the property of the Crown ... However Aborigines should have the right to prevent exploration for them on their traditional lands ... This Aboriginal power of veto should only be over-ridden if, in the opinion of the Government, the national interest requires it ... The Land Council would conduct all negotiations, and give or refuse its consent on behalf of the traditional owners and any communities likely to be affected by the application, as well as having its own power of veto in the matter.' He also made recommendations regarding protection of sacred sites, negotiations with new mining ventures on Aboriginal land, and the payment of royalties.

These recommendations are reflected in the Aboriginal Land Rights (Northern Territory) Act 1976. Though couched in rather complicated legal language the provisions are quite specific: a mining interest in respect of Aboriginal land shall not be granted unless the traditional land-owner through the Land Council for the area has consented, or 'the Governor-General has, by Proclamation, declared that the national interest requires that the grant be made'. Such a Proclamation must be laid before each House of Parliament, which may disapprove the declaration made in the Proclamation.

Under this legislation the Land Council negotiates payments in respect of the granting of the mining interests, such as rents and royalties. Objections by mining interests to decisions made by a Land Council may be heard by an impartial Arbitrator. If the Minister is satisfied that the Land Council has not acted fairly then

Aerial view of the stockpile and shiploading area located near the township of Alyangula. The first shipment of manganese ore left here in March 1966

Beulah Lowe teaching a Sunday school class at Milingimbi, 1954 (*Photo Richard Harrington, Canada*)

the Minister may enter into an agreement with mining interests instead of the Land Council. Existing leases are allowed to remain, but the payments for rents and royalties may be subject to renegotiation.

The Australian Mining Council has understandably reacted adversely to this legislation discriminating in favour of Aborigines. In a widely publicised advertisement in 1977 the Council stated, 'In opposing this veto power, the industry is not advocating a free hand for mining companies on Aboriginal land. Australian mining laws provide that minerals in their natural state belong to all Australians and not to the owners of the land. A decision on whether mining should or should not proceed in the Territory is therefore the proper responsibility of the elected government.' The Government, however, is adamant that Aborigines must have the final say.

Many non-Aborigines other than mining interests question this decision and consider it to be unjust. 'There is one rule for whites, and a favoured rule for blacks,' they say. The justice of the legislation stems from the deep spiritual association that the Aborigines have with their land. If land ownership had the same spiritual significance over the same long period of time for non-Aborigines, then doubtless common justice would demand a similar law for all.

The first mining of any significance in Arnhem Land took place on Elcho Island. In 1921 the Elcho Island Naptha Petroleum Company Ltd obtained a mineral lease and began drilling alongside the newly-formed Methodist Mission there. Friction between the mining company and the Aborigines soon developed and the Mission moved to Milingimbi, about eighty kilometres away.

The Elcho Island Naptha Petroleum Company Ltd continued its drilling operations until March 1926. In November of that year the company went into liquidation. No oil had been found, and the first contact of outside mining interests with the Arnhem Land Aborigines had been characterised by mistrust and friction.

Almost forty years were to elapse before mining once again started in Arnhem Land. This time it took place on quite a large scale on Groote Eylandt on the east Arnhem Land coast. Mining on Groote was followed soon afterwards by the large mining venture on the Gove Peninsula, not far from Yirrkala, on the north-eastern tip of Arnhem Land. Then in 1977 the Government approved the mining of uranium in the large 'uranium province' on the border of the western Arnhem Land Reserve. The Arnhem Land Aborigines have now come face-to-face with three major mining ventures and the accompanying cultural upheavals of large non-Aboriginal communities living among them.

Mining on Groote Eylandt is undertaken by the Groote Eylandt Mining Company Pty Ltd (GEMCo), a wholly-owned subsidiary of the Australian Broken Hill Pty Co. Ltd (BHP). The manganese mined there is an important raw material used in steel production. It is added to the steel in the form of an alloy, ferro-manganese to improve the toughness, hardness and tensile strength of the products.

In 1963 GEMCo purchased from the Church Missionary Society (CMS) its permits to prospect on the island. The CMS, which had been on the island since 1921, had obtained these permits on behalf of the Aboriginal community there in 1961. In return GEMCo undertook to pay to the Aborigines an annual sum of $10 000 and a royalty of 1.25 per cent of the worth of all ore shipped in excess of 100 000 tons in any year. These royalties are paid into the Groote Eylandt Aboriginal Trust Fund for Aboriginal community purposes on the island. The fund is administered by seven Aboriginal trustees and four non-Aboriginal advisers. Additional royalties are paid under the Northern Territory Mining Ordinance to the Aboriginal Benefits Trust Fund (ABTF), ten per cent going to the Groote Eylandt communities.

By August 1977 GEMCo had paid $2 567 708 in royalties to the Groote Eylandt Aboriginal Trust Fund, and $6 021 188 to the ABTF. These moneys have been used by the Groote Eylandt Aborigines in various ways, including the construction of community halls at Angurugu and Umbakumba, the provision of Toyota Land cruisers for each of the clans to move to and from their traditional areas, a bakery, a school bus, school fencing, fares for Aborigines to different places for traditional dances and so on.

On 25 July 1964 GEMCo was granted special mining leases totalling 33 square kilometres. These were for a period of twenty-one years with the right of renewal for at least a further twenty-one years. They allow for the movement of Aborigines over the leased land.

On 13 May 1965 the Commonwealth Government and BHP executed an agreement by which BHP would consult with the Groote Eylandt Aborigines before applying for further mineral leases. On 30 May 1966 GEMCo was granted special purposes leases for the wharf, town site, industrial site and green belt for a period of 99 years.

The black manganese ore is mined by the open-cut method. The area is cleared of trees and undergrowth and the overburden removed. After blasting, the ore is taken to the $20 million crusher and concentrator, which is situated about three kilometres from Angurugu. The crushed ore is transported the sixteen kilometres

166

down the macademised Rowell Highway to Alyangula. The ore is stockpiled there and taken by large ore-carriers to BHP's ferro alloy plant at Bell Bay, Tasmania, or overseas. The first shipment of manganese ore left Alyangula for Tasmania on 17 March 1966.

GEMCo is committed to restore the mined land to its original state, or to plant trees requested by the local Aborigines. The company is experimenting with different trees and restoring large areas in this environmental rehabilitation program.

Between thirty and sixty Aborigines, mainly from Angurugu, work with GEMCo, on equal terms with non-Aborigines doing the same work, as plant operators, drivers, store assistants, nursing orderlies, general laboratory assistants and labourers. The work force tends to fluctuate, but an average of about thirty Aborigines have usually been employed at any one time over the past few years. GEMCo has also initiated training programs for young Aboriginal men and women. Several Aboriginal families live at Alyangula. Those employed by GEMCo can attend the club at Alyangula and drink there.

GEMCo's delightful mining town, Alyangula, is situated at Milner Bay on the north-western tip of Groote. Alyangula has modern cyclone-resistant housing for married and single employees, a recreation club, a community hall, a swimming pool, tennis courts, a cinema and video-tape television facilities, which serve the present population of about one thousand. The up-to-date Alyangula Area School provides educational facilities up to Standard 12, the matriculation year. A small number of Aboriginal and non-Aboriginal children from Angurugu commute daily.

From the outset the most cordial relations have existed between GEMCo and the Angurugu community, and the Company has done everything in its power to help the Aborigines meet the challenge of the new industrial era which has come to the island. At the same time the effect of this high-powered technology, economic affluence, and completely different social norms have had a most dramatic effect on the Groote Eylandters and their traditional life-styles.

Several years ago Mr Najiwarra Amagula spoke of the way he, as an Aboriginal, saw the affect of mining on the island. 'In some ways it is good that white people have come. We can get good wages working with BHP. We can have things we never had before like wirelesses, bicycles and trucks. Many of us live in good houses, with electricity and water laid on. All different kinds of vehicles have come here, and we see planes arriving all the time. Our children have a good school now with plenty of teachers these days, instead of just a few teachers as we used to have.

167

'I think it is good in one way, but in another way it is not good at all. The first white people who came to our island brought us good news. These other white people who came later looking for manganese have brought some good things as I have said, but they have brought bad things as well. They have brought strong drink, and this has spoiled my people. I don't drink myself, but I see my people drinking, even some of the older men, and my people never did this in the old days. Drink has brought us a lot of trouble ... They don't give their wives money for food and they don't look after their children. Their money goes on drink and gambling. This is what I mean when I said that there are two sides to this coming of white people to our island. They have brought both good and bad.'

The second and larger mining venture in Arnhem Land is being undertaken by the North Australian Bauxite and Alumina Company Pty Ltd (Nabalco) on the Gove Peninsula on the north-eastern tip of Arnhem Land. This enormous $300 million project requiring a mining town of 3500 people is another focal point of Aboriginal and non-Aboriginal contact.

Nabalco is a joint venture in which Swiss Aluminium Australia Ltd, a subsidiary of Alusuisse, has a seventy per cent interest and the Australian partner, Gove Alumina Ltd, has thirty per cent. The Australian consortium consists of Peko-Wallsend Ltd, the AMP Society, the MLC Assurance Co. Ltd, the Bank of NSW, the Commerical Banking Company of Sydney Ltd and Elder Smith Goldsborough Mort Ltd.

Nabalco was granted a forty-two year lease to mine the massive 250-million tonne bauxite deposit, which is one of the largest deposits of its kind in the world. Bauxite is the ore from which alumina or aluminium oxide and then aluminium is processed. Aluminium is an important light-weight, corrosion-resistant metal used extensively in the aircraft, boatbuilding and coach-making industries. Aluminium foil and cans are familiar in a wide range of food and drink packaging. Kitchenware and electrical goods extensively using aluminium continue to be major consumers.

After a million-dollar, two-year feasibility study, Nabalco and the Commonwealth Government entered into an agreement on 22 February 1968, which was approved and incorporated by the Mining (Gove Peninsula Nabalco Agreement) Ordinance 1968. On 30 May 1969 Nabalco assigned its interests in the agreement to Swiss Aluminium Australia Ltd and to Gove Alumina Ltd. On the same day Nabalco was granted a special forty-two year mineral lease with the right of renewal for a further forty-two years. This lease covered an area of 20 000 hectares. A number of special purpose leases were also granted, covering a total area of about 1 800 hectares, including 650 hectares for the town site of Nhulunbuy. The mineral lease specified the right of Aborigines to move across the land covered by it. It also provided for the calculation of royalties and a review of these payments every seven years.

Once approval had been given, Nabalco commenced building operations. The cargo jetty and ten-megawatt diesel power station were completed by August 1970, the overland conveyor, reclaimer and shiploader by June 1971, and the full power station and the town by December 1972. Production started in 1973. In order to help Australians finance their share the Government relaxed its ban on the export of untreated bauxite and permitted Gove Alumina to export up to forty million tonnes on its own account during its first twenty years of operation.

Bauxite occurs in commercial quantities mainly in the tropical and sub-tropical zones of the world. The bauxite at Gove is readily accessible. It is from three to four metres thick and is in the three forms: loose pisolitic-round, pea-sized grains loosely cemented in a fine grained matrix; cemented pisolitic, where the grains are firmly cemented into a fine grained material; and tubular, a continuous massive structure full of irregular tubular cavities. Bauxite is red-brown in colour, and this colour is a feature of the mining area, on unsealed roads, the stockpiles, the slurridge swamps and the dust covering the plant machinery and the workers.

The bauxite deposits at Gove are mined by the simple procedure of removing the topsoil or overburden which is on average about one metre thick. It is loosened in the ground by ripping or blasting and then excavated by front-end loaders into fifty-tonne capacity trucks which carry it to the crusher. After crushing the bauxite is loaded on to one of the longest overland belt conveyors in the world, which carries it 18.7 kilometres to the stockpile in a journey of about one and a half hours. On arrival at the stock pile it is automatically stacked to await reclamation, either as feed for the alumina plant or to travel to the export wharf for loading into bulk carriers. About 4.5 million tonnes of bauxite is mined and stockpiled each year. Approximately 2 million tonnes are exported each year to other alumina producers in Japan, Europe and the USA. Ships of up to 100 000 tonnes can be berthed at the export wharf.

As well as exporting bauxite Nabalco produces alumina, the half-way stage in the production of aluminium, from its ore. The plant at Gove is one of the world's big alumina producers, with a capacity of a million tonnes a year. Alumina at Gove ready for export is stored in three concrete silos, two holding 50 000 tonnes and one, the largest alumina silo in the world, holding 100 000 tonnes.

In accordance with the terms of the lease, Nabalco conducts a major conservation and rehabilitation program. Once an area has been mined the overburden is replaced and the land is planted with native seeds, trees and plants. Further attention is being given to the disposal of the waste red mud. This mud has been washed free of caustic soda, used in the production of alumina, and is pumped into special ponds.

The Gove airport and Gove Peninsula are named after Flying Officer William Gove who was killed on active service in the Northern Territory during World War II. The mining town is called Nhulunbuy, the Aboriginal name for Mt Saunders, under which the town nestles. Mount Saunders, Melville Bay and Mount Dundas were given these names by Captain Matthew Flinders when he charted the area in the *Investigator* on his historic voyage in 1802 and 1803.

Nhulunbuy is a delightful town built down to the edge of the Arafura Sea. It is about twenty kilometres from the airport, which in turn is 650 kilometres by air from Darwin. The town was carefully planned for about 5000 inhabitants. It is necessarily self-contained with a sixty-four bed hospital, a community health centre, a dental clinic, an area school taking pupils up to standard twelve, a pre-school, a post office, swimming and recreation centres, a sports oval, a town hall, a fire station, churches, a courthouse, a police station and motor registry, and a modern air-conditioned shopping complex. Nhulunbuy has an automatic telephone exchange, and is linked by a radio troposcatter system to Darwin and other Australian and international telecommunications networks.

Yachting, four-wheel drive excursions, bowls, tennis, swimming and cricket are all very popular. The town also has a variety of clubs and other organisations. Nhulunbuy has a tropical climate like the rest of Arnhem Land and is subject to cyclones. The warm climate, the easy-going life style, the proximity to the sea, modern buildings, picturesque surroundings and conveniences of running water, electricity, refrigeration and air conditioning provides magnificent living conditions here as in many other centres of the Top End.

Before the Nabalco plant and Nhulunbuy had been built three other projects had begun to change the timeless character of north-eastern Arnhem Land and its dreamtime people.

The first had been the establishment of the Methodist mission at Yirrkala about twenty kilometres to the east in 1934, to which reference has already been made.

The second had been the construction of a military airstrip at the present Gove airport during World War II, and its occupation by some 5000 members of the Royal Australian Air Force.

The third had been the construction of ELDO, the European Launcher Development Organisation Down Range Tracking Station, situated twelve kilometres south of Gove airport. ELDO's function was to trace guided missiles launched from Woomera in South Australia.

ELDO's highly complex electronic devices, computers, radar screens and intricate scientific equipment were in direct contrast with the timeless atmosphere which had returned to Gove when the RAAF withdrew. ELDO greatly assisted Nabalco in its early construction stages especially by enabling the company to tie into its radio link, thereby enabling direct telephone calls to be made between the Nabalco and its offices in Sydney and Darwin. When ELDO closed its operations the buildings were taken over by the newly formed Dhupuma Aboriginal transitional college.

Since Nabalco started, care has been taken to try to preserve the several Aboriginal sacred sites in the Gove Peninsula. The first, on the cliff face and seaward summit of Mount Dundas, is the home of the Thunderman dreaming. The four significant rocks on the beach at the foot of Mount Dundas are connected with the Turtle Hunter dreaming. The second site is a clear area about 130 metres by 500 metres connected with the Morning Star dreaming. The Macassar Beach site is a 'prescribed area' where Aborigines used stones to record and to pass on to future generations the important aspects of Macassan culture. The township of Yirrkala, except where Aboriginal artifacts are sold, is out of bounds, as is also land outside the mining leases except by permission.

The mining and export of bauxite and alumina is of great importance to Australia and to the Territory as it approaches statehood. The initial construction of the project and town provided a large number of jobs for non-Aborigines. Nabalco at the present time employs almost a thousand people. The annual royalties of about $1 million are of great benefit to the Aborigines throughout the Territory and to those at Yirrkala. But the whole operation is on traditional Aboriginal land to which Aborigines have now been given freehold title. The large enclave of non-Aborigines has inevitably heightened tension with Aborigines. The bark petition by the Yirrkala people to the House of Representatives in 1963 and the subsequent Gove Land case before Mr Justice Blackburn have already been noted.

Mr Justice Woodward recorded that the Yirrkala community in

171

submission had 'said that leases to the mining company were granted without the consent of the Aboriginal community and that in future there should be real consultation between the community and the company.' He said that because of the huge sums involved 'it is obviously not possible to retrace many of the steps already taken ... this is yet another case where companies and the local Aborigines will have to live together for many years and the new land-owning status of Aborigines must, in my opinion, be brought into account ...' He recommended that 'the existing special purposes leases should be rescinded in favour of similar leases granted by the Aboriginal land owners', and that rents be renegotiated, especially for any additional land required for the disposal of the 'deadly' red mud effluent from the alumina works.

Mr Justice Woodward was critical of the lack of employment opportunities for Aborigines offered by Nabalco. He said, 'I draw attention to the fact that the company, apparently as a matter of policy, employs and trains practically no Aborigines ... the company does offer contracts to Aboriginal groups to provide goods and services of various types and I agree that this is often the best way of providing work opportunities for Aborigines. But if the local community wishes to raise questions of training and employment, Nabalco should give them close consideration.'

Nabalco's policy regarding the employment of Aborigines is different from that of GEMCo. The latter has consistently tried to employ Aborigines in the general work force. Nabalco has adopted the policy of getting Aborigines to provide goods and services on a contract basis rather than try to train them for the general work force.

The third major mining venture in Arnhem Land is the proposed mining in the 'uranium province' in western Arnhem Land. As in the other two places, uranium mining here is taking place on Aboriginal land. This area contains many sacred sites, cave paintings and archaeological sites. Western Arnhem Land is also noted for its scenic beauty and abundant wildlife. Environmentally it is unique, and is to be proclaimed a national park.

There are four main centres at which it is planned to mine uranium ore and to convert it into uranium oxide or yellow cake. One is at Jabiru, and is run by the Ranger Uranium Mines Pty Ltd, a joint venture involving the Commonwealth Government through the Australian Atomic Energy Commission (AAEC), Peko Mines Ltd and Electrolytic Zinc Company.

The three other sites are Jabiluka, Koongarra and Nabarlek. Jabiluka is just off the road to the East Alligator about twenty-four kilometres to the north of Jabiru, and the exploration licence is held by Pancontinental Mining Ltd. Koongarra is about twenty-four kilometres south of Jabiru, the exploration licence being held by Noranda Australia Ltd. Nabarlek lies about sixty-five kilometres to the north-east in the Arnhem Land Aboriginal Reserve, and the licence is held by Queensland Mines Ltd. These four deposits in this small area account for most of Australia's known uranium supplies.

In 1967 Peko Mines and Electrolyte Zinc jointly started an exploration program of the Ranger area. In June 1970 an aerial survey detected radiation anomalies there. In June 1971 the two companies formed the Ranger Uranium Mines to manage the development of the project. By 1976 Ranger had spent almost $6 million on their operations. Ranger plan to produce 3000 tonnes of yellow-cake a year, rising to 6000 tonnes. The company estimates that the mining operation will take from between twenty to thirty years.

As three, or perhaps all four, projects have been given the green light, it is thought that Jabiru, or the large mining town built in its environs serving the whole province, will need to accommodate from 4000 to 5000 people. This town will probably be similar in size to Nhulunbuy. A town of this size can be expected to have a similar influence on the Aborigines of the area as have had the towns on Groote and at Gove.

Because of the impact of uranium mining on the Aborigines and on the environment, on 16 July 1975 the Prime Minister, Mr Gough Whitlam, directed that an inquiry be conducted 'in relation to the proposal for the development by the Australian Atomic Energy Commission in association with Ranger Uranium Mines Pty Ltd of uranium deposits in the Northern Territory of Australia'. Mr Justice R.W. Fox, the Senior Judge of the Australian Capital Territory Supreme Court; Mr G.G. Kelleher, a civil engineer and Hearings Commissioner; and Professor C.B. Kerr, Professor of Preventive and Social Medicine at the University of Sydney, were appointed a Commission to conduct the enquiry.

The Fox Commission was required to inquire 'In respect of all environmental aspects of: (a) the formulation of proposals; (b) the carrying out of works and other projects; (c) the negotiation, operation and enforcement of agreements and arrangements; (d) the making of, or the participation in the making of, decisions and recommendations; and (e) the incurring of expenditure, by, or on behalf of the Australian Government and the Australian Atomic Energy Commission ... in relation to the development by the Australian Atomic Energy Commission in association with Ranger

Uranium Mines Pty Ltd of uranium deposits in the Northern Territory of Australia'. The Environment Protection (Impact of Proposals) Act 1974 defines environment to include 'all aspects of the surroundings of man, whether affecting him as an individual or in his social groupings'.

The Commission commenced public hearings in Sydney on 9 September 1975. Subsequent hearings were held in Sydney, Darwin, Mudginberri, Gove, Brisbane, Adelaide and Melbourne. Arrangements were made for witnesses from Tasmania, Western Australia and the Australian Capital Territory to testify either in person or by statutory declaration. A total of 281 persons including a number of Aborigines gave evidence, and 354 documentary exhibits were received in evidence. The Commission made a two-week visit to England and the Federal Republic of Germany to see nuclear plant and facilities in operation. Public hearings concluded in Sydney on 12 August 1976.

The Fox Commission issued two reports under the title of *Ranger Uranium Environmental Inquiry*. The first report was dated 28 October 1976 and the second 17 May 1977. The first report stated that the 'hazards of mining and milling uranium if those activities are properly regulated and controlled, are not such as to justify a decision not to develop Australian uranium mines' and that 'the hazards involved in the ordinary operations of nuclear power reactors, if those operations are properly regulated and controlled, are not such as to justify a decision not to mine and sell Australian uranium'. The first report also stated that the 'nuclear power industry is unintentionally contributing to an increased risk of nuclear war', and recommended safeguards regarding export and use of uranium.

The second report was more extensive, covering the impact of the Ranger proposals on the Aborigines and the natural features of the region. Recommendations were made concerning technical aspects of the Ranger mining and possible changes in their proposals. The Commissioners also recommended that the 'constructions of the mines in the Region be commenced sequentially at appropriate intervals'; that 'a major national park be established in the region' in accordance with Mr Justice Woodward's recommendations; that 'a large or sudden influx of tourists be prevented'.

The Commissioners made a number of recommendations regarding Aborigines in the region. They said that 'Aboriginal title should be granted, the national park established ...', and that Aborigines be employed as rangers, health workers, and workers at the mines. The land on which the town would be built should 'not become Aboriginal land but become part of the national park'; that 'Mudginberri and Munmarlary pastoral leases be resumed, and that opportunity be given for Aboriginal land claims to be made and determined in respect of these areas'.

In their conclusion they stated that the Ranger project should proceed only subject to their recommendations; that the Noranda mine (Koongarra) should not be developed, at least for the time being; and that 'if the Ranger proposal is allowed to proceed no other mining, with the possibility of that proposed by Pancontinental, be allowed in the Region west of the Arnhem Land Reserve for the time being at least'.

On 25 August 1977 the Commonwealth Government gave approval for the mining of Australia's uranium reserves. The mining and export of uranium would be strictly controlled. When making the announcement, the Prime Minister, Mr Malcolm Fraser, said that almost all of the conditions recommended by the Ranger Uranium Environmental Inquiry had been followed. The notable exception was the rejection of the proposed sequential development, that is, mining in different areas would commence in sequence and not start at the same time. This recommendation was rejected.

Mr Fraser said that the Government had decided to act after an exhaustive consideration of the evidence. The Government had a high sense of responsibility to all Australians and the community of nations. He said that there were four fundamental considerations in the proposal: they were the need to reduce the risk of nuclear proliferation; the need to supply essential sources of energy to an energy-deficient world; the need to protect effectively the environment; and the need to ensure that proper provisions were made to protect the welfare and interests of the Aboriginal people in the region.

The Prime Minister said that if Australia had not proceeded with uranium mining it would have denied the country an effective voice in strengthening safeguards, non-proliferation measures, and moves towards a plutonium economy. It would have denied Australia significant economic benefits and abandoned the world's energy-poor countries. The nuclear debate had now started in earnest.

The proposed uranium mining by Queensland Mines Ltd at Nabarlek in the Arnhem Land Reserve about thirty kilometres east of Oenpelli has had an unfortunate history. Relations between the company and the Aboriginal traditional land owners have been strained. The Aborigines have complained that there was insufficient consultation in the first place, followed by the desecration of the Green Ant sacred site by the company.

Queensland Mines Ltd entered into agreement with Mrs G.D. Stevens on 23 December 1969 to prospect the Nabarlek area for which she had an authority. As a result, Queensland Mines discovered a rich uranium deposit in 1970. During this period the Aboriginal land owners at Oenpelli raised objections to activity in the sacred sites near the Nabarlek hills. The objections were withdrawn and a payment of $5000 made to the community as a goodwill gesture.

On 22 December 1971 a mineral lease was granted to Mrs Stevens and subsequently transferred to Queensland Mines under agreement. In May the Superintendent of Oenpelli informed the Secretary of the Department of the Northern Territory that 'doubts were expressed as to the accuracy of the stated facts which led to the withdrawal of the Aborigines' objection to mining lease applications'. The Oenpelli Aborigines formally objected to the Administrator in a letter dated 22 June 1972.

On 26 July 1973 Queensland Mines made the Aborigines another offer which, Mr Justice Woodward stated, 'I can only describe as contemptuous, which amounted to arranging the sale to them of 173 040 shares in the company at the then full market price of $1.70 per share. This offer was rejected by the Nabarlek Aborigines who reiterated their opposition to any further exploration or mining development at Nabarlek ... In a letter of 22 February 1974, Queensland Mines made a new offer to the Nabarlek group of a lump sum payment of $600 000, and an extra royalty.' The Nabarlek Aborigines also rejected this offer and indicated that their objection to the mining development would be maintained.

In his recommendations Mr Justice Woodward said, 'I have no hesitation in recommending that this is a case in which the Aboriginal view should prevail'. His final recommendations regarding the whole of mining concludes 'Queensland Mines Limited should not be permitted to develop mineral deposits in the Nabarlek area without Aboriginal consent'.

The First Aboriginal Mining Company (FAMCo) has been an attempt by Aborigines and their advisers to engage in mineral exploration on their own land. On 29 October 1970 Aborigines representative of various tribes and groups of people who have traditional claim and title to this area applied for authorities to prospect. The representatives were from Oenpelli, Croker Island, Goulburn Island, Milingimbi and Maningrida. The Goulburn Island Progress Association, Maningrida Progress Association, and Murgwangi Community Association were also involved.

Between April and July 1971 agreements were made between Ocean Resources and FAMCo whereby Ocean Resources would act for FAMCo. Later Canadian Superior Mining (Aust.) Pty Ltd, Consolidated Gold Fields Australia Ltd and Pancontinental Mining Ltd were associated with the venture.

Various meetings were held from 1971 until 1976 but no positive action was taken. In November 1976 the Registrar-General commenced de-registration action as no financial returns and minutes had been filed since the formation of FAMCo. Later that month FAMCo's solicitor requested deferment of de-registration action so that financial statements could be made and forwarded. On 29 March 1977 the parties executed a deed regularising previous agreements.

The whole operation has been complicated and complex. Nothing may come of the agreements. On the other hand they indicate that Aborigines are interested in mining on their own terms and in their own way. FAMCo may be the forerunner of a number of similar Aboriginal companies in the future.

The mining of manganese and bauxite in Australia's tropical north is of importance for the maintenance of generally accepted standards demanded by a Western technologically-based society such as Australia. The mining of uranium is a much more contentious issue but could be of great importance as a source of energy in an energy hungry world. The mining of Australian uranium and the control of the Western world's supply may be a very effective means for the prevention of indiscriminate proliferation although this too is debatable. The fundamental problem of the disposal of highly toxic radioactive waste has yet to be solved.

The exploitation of these minerals on Aboriginal land in the Top End is a potential source of high income for Aborigines. The double royalty payment ensures a lucrative return to them, either directly or through the activities of the Northern Land Council and the ABTF. This has been very marked on Groote Eylandt. The figure of $600 000 together with additional royalties, which was rejected by the Nabarlek Aborigines, indicates the amounts which mining companies are prepared to pay. The Aborigines as on Groote have excellent opportunities for employment by the mining company on high rates of pay.

Mining also brings Aborigines and non-Aborigines together in advantageous circumstances. Aborigines can meet other races on their own ground, and generally speaking, on their own terms. They remain in their own homes and meet non-Aborigines who are foreigners. This was the basis of the encouragement to mining as an important feature of assimilation in the welfare era. This is the exact reverse to the situation in Darwin and elsewhere. Here Aborigines

177

are transients or living outside their traditional homelands in the middle of large numbers of urbanised people. They are not at home and are seen to be not at home, but to be fringe dwellers and outcastes.

Yet when all this has been said and the advantages which they receive from mining ventures in Arnhem Land have been seen, Aborigines are more and more opposing mining on their land. They are aware of the benefits and are quick to take advantage of them. If mining has been established then they make the most out of it. They can be unassumingly skilful bargainers! At the same time they would prefer to have no mining. They now have the power of veto on new mining projects. Their attitudes expressed at the Fox Ranger Inquiry and their flat refusal to negotiate with Queensland Mines indicate their feelings. Their views may, and probably will, change. But new mining on their land at the present time is not favoured.

Aborigines have a number of reasons. First and foremost are the deep emotional ties which they have with the land. The land forms their link with the eternity of their dreaming. Their totems or ancestor-heroes are one with them and with the land. If mining damages the land and desecrates their sacred sites, then their link with the timeless past is broken and could be destroyed forever.

Mining also brings large numbers of white people with their vehicles and roads, their shops and their alcohol, and their soliciting of Aboriginal girls. Aborigines resent white attitudes of superiority. They retreat from complex situations and do not try to fight them. Their retreat is to their land, their country and their home. If this place of retreat is cut off then they have nowhere to go. They feel defeated and depressed. They become people without a soul.

Then for all Australians, white or black, there is always the danger of the destruction of the remarkable and unique ecology of Arnhem Land.

The mining companies at Groote and Gove are committed to the restoration of the land as they complete sections of mining. This they are doing and there is no reason to doubt they will continue to do, and to do well. But uranium mining is different. Radio-active tailings from the Ranger project could contaminate the Magela flood plains and drainage. The waters of Van Diemen Gulf could be infected despite the best efforts of the mining companies to prevent it. Pollution has occurred in many parts of the world despite stringent safeguards. The Government claims that it can provide the necessary protection. Only time can tell. Human tragedy of the greatest magnitude will be the devastating result if the Government has made a wrong judgment.

15

We have to look
two ways with education

'We have to look two ways,' said Jaboni Lalara when talking about education. 'I have to look two ways. I have to look your way and I have to look my way ... Most of us don't worry about that (houses, cars, money, clothes) much. If I have got my boat and my land and my house, so long as we have two ways we learn my way and your way.'

Jaboni Lalara from Groote Eylandt had only three years of education at the mission school at Angurugu. Even then his school hours were limited. 'We had our school hours in the afternoon because we were two groups of children, the girls and the boys. The boys had to go in the afternoon, which meant we had to work in the morning and go to school in the afternoon.'

After leaving school, Jaboni worked at the mission and then with the Groote Eylandt Mining Company as a driver on one of the big ore crushers. His workmanship was of a very high order, and GEMCo greatly appreciated his services.

Jaboni has high hopes for the education of his three children. He also knows what he wants from their education. 'I understand myself', he said, 'just as white people or anybody likes to get better schooling: not only the white people, but we also want to see our children go to better schools so they can have the qualifications for their job and get better experience ...

'There are two ways. The Aboriginal people, like my people on the Island, they want to try to learn what the European people are doing. They try to get their qualifications all right. But on the other side we have a very important thing too. They have to think about the tribal way and ceremony way to teach the young people. That is the main thing. So that is up to the older people to teach the younger people, but not my age group, we only know a little about the tribal way...

'I don't like my boys to fall in the European way too much. I like to get my boys back to the tribal ways. Not for always like the men of olden days because he has to stand for the life of the Aboriginal people, because he has to stand to a certain law for himself too, because he has to look back to hold that law. This is what we are working on now so that we can try to get all young people to be involved in the ceremonies and things like that.'

Both Governments and missions took far too long to realise their obligations to teach or to allow for the teaching of the 'two ways' in Aboriginal education. Missions started schools as part of their program of evangelisation and civilisation. Government entered the field of education to promote their policy of assimilation. Only recently has there been a realisation of the need and the obligation for Aboriginal groups to have an educational system which can accommodate their own ways together with the ways of the larger white society.

That the Commonwealth Government did not undertake any responsibility for the education of full-blood Aboriginal children in the Northern Territory before 1950 was a scandal. Proposals had been made in the McEwen Memorandum of 1939, but nothing had been done. The War had been one reason for the delay. So also had been bureaucratic lethargy and public indifference. The expulsion of seven full-blood Aboriginal children from the Darwin School in February 1949 was a catalyst which made the Government move quickly. So also was the blistering speech regarding Australia's treatment of her Aborigines made by the USSR Ambassador Molotov at the United Nations in reply to Dr Evatt's charges of Russian denial of civil liberties to her people.

Christian missions had undertaken Aboriginal education during the preceding sixty years. They had restricted finance, inadequate facilities and limited personnel. Their methods were sometimes unimaginative, but their motives were the highest. For them education was the handmaid of evangelisation. Literate Aborigines would be able to read the Bible and other Christian literature. Education would also bring them a wider understanding of the Western world and they would be able to cope with white man's ways more easily. They would be strengthened in their Christian life and would understand more of the 'civilising influences' of Western culture.

The Jesuits started the first Aboriginal school at Rapid Creek, Darwin, in 1883. Attendance at the school was erratic, because of

At the opening of Dhupuma College, Gove Peninsula, 1972 (*Photo Australian News and Information Bureau*)

Kormilda College, a transitional school at Berrimah, south of Darwin

the nomadic habits of the pupils' parents. In 1890 the Jesuits transferred the Rapid Creek Mission to Daly River, which had been started four years earlier. Schooling continued there, and in 1897 about fifty children were on the roll. In 1901, however, the Jesuits closed their Daly River Mission, and yet another Territory project was abandoned after great toil and sacrifice.

The Anglican CMS started schools in the missions which they established, at Roper River (1908), Groote Eylandt (1921) and Oenpelli (1925). In 1948 Mr P.W. Beckenham of the Australian Council for Educational Research wrote, 'Remembering that the children of these missions are myalls whose manner of living for years to come will be along the simplest lines, the Society aims at an all round development of the physical, and intellectual conditions of the respective tribes, retaining what is best in their customs, and fitting the individuals for a worthy part in the communal life of the tribe as a step towards the ultimate opportunity of entering the larger national life.'

Beckenham also stated that the CMS did not consider Aboriginal teacher training as essential at that time. Rather, he reported them as saying, 'skill acquired incidentally is regarded as sufficient training for missionary teaching'.

The Methodist Overseas Missions (MOM) in Arnhem Land also started schools soon after the establishment of their stations at Goulburn Island (1916), Elcho Island (1921-1922, 1942), Milingimbi (1922), Yirrkala (1935), and Croker Island for half-castes (1940). The MOM Report of 1937 reflected the mission's attitude to education and the problems of the time. 'The school is one of the most important parts of our work, and it is greatly regretted that owing to shortage of staff and pressure of other duties, the school has had to suffer so much broken time.'

By 1950 there were about four hundred children on the rolls of the seven CMS and MOM Aboriginal missions in Arnhem Land. Each school usually had only one teacher, often untrained, who normally could only give part of his or her time to teaching. Senior Aboriginal children sometimes assisted as pupil teachers. School buildings were usually inadequate and equipment was the barest minimum. There was no common curriculum for the seven centres, and the teachers usually followed syllabuses to which they had been accustomed in the South.

The 'dormitory system' was adopted by these two mission authorities during part of this time. By this means the missionaries tried to isolate children from the 'degradation' of camp life, and the nomadic habits of the parents. Boys and girls were housed in separate dormitories, where they were taught Western-style hygiene, eating habits, dress, and general way of life.

A number of people have bitterly attacked missions for their efforts to control Aboriginal life-styles through the dormitory system. They say that the children were divorced, not only from their family life, but also from their traditional culture. They claim that it was a deliberate attempt to break down Aboriginal ways of life and supplant them with Western culture. Whatever the rights and wrongs of the dormitory system, one thing is apparent. The more stable, well-spoken and understanding of the older Aboriginal men and women today, at least by European standards, are those who grew up and were educated through the dormitory system.

The first move to establish Government-provided education for Territory Aborigines was made in 1940 by Mr E.W.P. Chinnery, who had been appointed Director of Native Affairs in the Northern Territory, and Commonwealth Adviser on Native Affairs. He planned that each settlement in the Reserves would be a focal centre for education, health, industry and general welfare. He was unable to implement his scheme because of the War.

As the numbers of the defence forces in Darwin and the Top End escalated with the threat of Japanese invasion in the early 1940s, the Army employed several hundred Aboriginal men as menials. They were housed, many with their families, in residential compounds. Their education and general welfare immediately became a matter for concern for the authorities.

Following discussions between Chinnery and the Army, Major W. C. Groves of Army Education was appointed in 1943 to outline proposals for the education and welfare of Aborigines employed in the Army. In his report issued in 1944, Groves advocated the establishment of regional 'settlements' for single men, for married men, their wives and their families, and for wives and families of Army personnel in other areas.

Groves outlined a suitable curriculum for Aboriginal education. He said also, 'The future development of the natives of the Territory will demand more native leaders; it may be taken for granted that any plan for their development will make provision for the natives themselves to participate on reasonable terms in the economic life of the Territory and in the service of the government — medical, clerical, teaching and the like.' The conclusion of the War and demobilisation of Aboriginal Army personnel prevented the implementation of Groves' recommendations.

In 1948 the proposal that the Commonwealth should take over from the States the responsibility for Aboriginal welfare throughout the whole country was not accepted. Instead the State Premiers arranged for a conference of Commonwealth and State Aboriginal Welfare authorities to be held in Canberra in February. This conference was the forerunner of similar welfare conferences. Mr F.H. Moy, Director of Native Affairs in the Northern Territory, and Professor A.P. Elkin, Vice-Chairman of the Aborigines Welfare Board of NSW, were among those present.

The conference devoted much of its time to Aboriginal education. It resolved that a Consultant in Native Education should be appointed, and that the Commonwealth Office of Education should conduct a survey of needs, prepare a standard curriculum, provide Government schools, and put pressure on missions to accept the standard curriculum and to staff their schools with trained teachers. If missions undertook these responsibilities then they should be subsidised by Government funds.

The Government was forced to implement these proposals quickly. In January 1949 seven full-blood Aboriginal children, aged between five and nine years, who had attended the Darwin School for most of the preceding year, were refused admission. They were told that they would have to go to a proposed new school to be opened in the Bagot compound instead.

Reporting this incident on 11 February 1949, *The Sydney Morning Herald* stated, 'The Administrator, Mr A.R. Driver, said today it was Government policy that full-blooded aborigines should not attend main State schools, but should be educated in their own establishments. The children had been enrolled last year through a mistake of the headmaster.' As a result the Bagot School started on 4 February 1949 with an enrolment of sixteen children.

This unhappy incident accelerated Government action. In 1949 Mr (later Professor) H.W.S. Philp and Dr T.L. Robertson made a quick survey of the educational needs of Aborigines in the Territory. This survey was followed by a Conference on the Education of Aboriginal children in Sydney from 28 to 30 September 1949. Acting on the Philp Report and the Conference recommendations, the Commonwealth Office of Education drew up a series of proposals for Government Aboriginal schools in the Territory. Final agreements were made in March 1950.

Under these arrangements, the Commonwealth Government accepted direct responsibility for the provision of Aboriginal education in the Territory; administration would be through the Commonwealth Office of Education; the Government would seek the co-operation of missions in education with the promise of financial assistance; Government schools would 'first be established in areas

183

where natives are in contact with white culture'; and the language of instruction would be English 'except where local conditions render bi-lingual instruction desirable'. Provision was also made for buildings, equipment, and the recruitment and training of teachers. Teacher training would include one- to three-year courses, 'heavily laden with Anthropology and other specialised studies'.

The Commonwealth Office of Education (COE) administered Government-sponsored Aboriginal education in the Territory from 1950 until 1955. Four schools were opened in 1950, including the Bagot School. By the end of 1955 there were eleven. Teachers employed rose from five to twenty-one, and enrolments from 153 in 1950 to 563 in 1955. Expenditure increased from £20 794 in July 1952 to £37 147 in June 1955. No new Government schools were opened in Arnhem Land during these six years as all centres at that time were under mission control.

The COE during this period experienced all the traumas of a new venture. In 1950 there were no buildings, teachers' residences or equipment. Teachers were recruited hurriedly and were often inexperienced. Adequate finance was not forthcoming. Clashes between teachers and Native Affairs Branch personnel were frequent. On the other hand the Government had made a start in the field of Aboriginal education. The Commonwealth was now committed to an ongoing program. Mission schools in Arnhem Land and elsewhere throughout the Territory were now assured of a much better deal through the 1953 Missions-Administration Conference. At the same time they were required to raise their teaching standards.

The administration of Aboriginal education was transferred from the Commonwealth Office of Education to the Welfare Branch of the Northern Territory Administration on 1 January 1956. The Welfare Director put forward a number of reasons for the transfer. Among other things he maintained that education was an important part, but only a part, of the overall program for Aboriginal welfare and assimilation. All areas of welfare should be controlled by the one agency. Under the new scheme there would be only one authority on Government settlements, instead of the two that currently existed. He said that Welfare Branch staff and teachers would now belong to the same organisation and would be part of the same team. The construction of all buildings, for education and for other purposes, would also be controlled by the one authority.

The Welfare Branch continued to administer Aboriginal education until the dramatic changes brought about by the new Labor Government in December 1972. On 13 February 1973 responsibility for Aboriginal education was transferred from the newly-formed Department of Aboriginal Affairs to the Northern Territory Division of the Department of Education. This new Education Department was independent of the Education Department of South Australia, and was required to develop an integrated educational policy for the whole of the Territory.

Official educational policy of the Welfare Branch had been that of assimilation, in line with the other Government activities in Aboriginal welfare during these two decades. One typical Annual Report, that of 1957-8, stated that 'the special aboriginal schools are regarded as an interim measure, designed to bring the children to a level where they will be able to attend the same schools as other children in the Territory'. Education was part of the overall policy for Government and mission settlements. The purpose of these communities was to provide centres for 'education and training; to provide those facilities and care necessary for good health; to provide welfare services fitted to the needs of the people'; and 'to teach Aboriginals the habits and skills of living in a wider community'.

The number of schools and pupils enrolled rose dramatically during the two decades of the 'welfare era'. The twenty-seven Government and mission schools throughout the Territory in 1956 increased to thirty-one in 1960, forty-two in 1965 and sixty-three in 1973. In 1956, 1633 children were enrolled in these schools; in 1960, 2175; in 1965, 3398; in 1973, 6087. The number of teachers increased during this time from 52 in 1956 to 67 in 1960, 112 in 1965 and 313 in 1970. Proportionate growth took place in the Arnhem Land schools. There were 603 children enrolled in 1956, 718 in 1960, 1024 in 1965, and 1923 in 1973.

In the mid-1960s the missions in Arnhem Land realised that they could not adequately staff the rapidly expanding schools, and began handing over their management to the Welfare Branch. In 1964 the school at Goulburn Island was transferred to Government; in 1966 those at Yirrkala, Umbakumba and Angurugu; in 1967 that at Roper River; in 1969 those at Milingimbi and Numbulwar; and that at Oenpelli in 1970. The last to be handed over was Shepherdson College at Elcho Island in 1975.

During this period of transition a number of mission teachers were teaching alongside Welfare teachers at the same school. Finally almost all the mission teachers became Commonwealth officers, receiving much larger salaries than the mission allowances to which they had been accustomed. Some maintained their mission connections and handed their extra income back to the missions.

In 1962 the Minister for Territories, Mr (later Sir) Paul Hasluck, introduced a plan to provide facilities so that there could be a 100 per cent attendance of Aboriginal children at school during the next four years. These goals have not been reached, even by 1977, for a variety of reasons. In the 1960s some Aboriginal groups were still semi-nomadic. This made systematic schooling for the children very difficult. In the 1970s parents still tended to move fairly frequently between the settlements, missions, Darwin and the outcentres during the Dry, causing attendance in some areas to be very erratic. Moreover parents often did not see the purpose in sending their children to school. Parents and children also interpreted the self-determination policies of 1973 onwards as freedom for children to absent themselves from school. School attendance in many places in Arnhem Land still leaves much to be desired.

Staffing has often been a problem. Difficult climatic conditions, isolation and culture conflict often made recruitment difficult and wastage high in mission and Welfare schools. Welfare schools were much better off. Staff enjoyed comparatively good housing, and their salary rates at the time were the highest in Australia. They also had a very generous staff/student ratio, certainly the lowest in Australia. The mission staff were not so well off, and the missions wisely handed over their responsibilities during the 1960s.

The Watts-Gallacher Report of 1963 in the curriculum and teaching methods in Territory Aboriginal schools had far-reaching affects for the next decade. Miss B.H. Watts was a Lecturer in Education at the University of Queensland. Mr J.D. Gallacher had had a long and varied experience in Aboriginal education.

Following the recomendations of the Watts-Gallacher Report, from the beginning of 1964, children were enrolled in pre-schools, provided they reached the age of at least four years before the end of June of the year of enrolment. The minimum age was reduced in 1970 to three years. In their fifth year of age, the children moved from the pre-school into an ungraded infant school. After three years here they moved into either an 'academic' or a 'general' stream in the primary school. Students in the 'academic' stream progressed through grades 3 to 6, following the South Australian curriculum. After successfully completing Grade 6, they took Grade 7 in a 'transitional' school in a town centre. Here they were able to complete their primary school education, and also engage in extra-curricular activity to prepare them for life in a non-Aboriginal environment as well as their own. At the age of fourteen or more they had the opportunity of continuing their education in one of the high schools.

Students in the 'general' stream in the primary school spent five years in ungraded groups. They had a set curriculum and minimum essential goals were set for each level. They were encouraged to develop desirable behavioural attitudes and to gain the skills necessary for living and earning a living. In the better schools a sound course was designed to meet the needs of the community and to prepare the students for further education at the post-primary level.

In 1964 the Welfare Branch appointed an officer to publish material for schools and adult education classes. During the next two years he was able to import useful educational material from Papua New Guinea and the Australian States. He also began the audio-visual section of the Branch. School broadcasts were taped and sent off in the same way as the complete migrant English series were sent to schools.

In the mid 1960s the need arose for the provision of a new style of school, in order to introduce tribal children going on to high school to Western educational patterns and life-styles. As a result Welfare established a transitional school called Kormilda College at Berrimah, about fifteen kilometres south of Darwin. The first classes started in September 1967. Since then suitable students from Arnhem Land and elsewhere are chosen at the end of Grade 6 to complete their final year of primary education at Kormilda. During this year they are introduced to non-Aboriginal ways of life, and whenever possible meet with non-Aboriginal people.

The growth of Kormilda has been very rapid. In 1968 only six boys and three girls were studying in the transitional classes. By 1977 there were 175, forty-six of whom were doing the high school course. There was about an equal number of boys and girls.

Two other transitional schools have now been opened. One is Dhupuma College, situated near the large mining town of Nhulunbuy on the north-eastern tip of Arnhem Land. Students who successfully complete Grade 7 here continue their studies at the Nhulunbuy Area School. Numbers at Dhupuma have fluctuated, and doubt exists regardings its future. The other transitional school is known as Yirara College and was built near Alice Springs in 1973.

In the 1960s the Welfare Branch became concerned for adequate curricula for all aspects of Aboriginal education.In 1963 the Branch appointed an Inspector of Curriculum, and during the next decade a great deal of work was done. Much of this found its way into Welfare Branch schools on a more or less prescriptive basis, and into mission schools in the form of recommendations. From about 1964 onwards there had been specialist teachers in art, music and physical education. Welfare also set up triennial conferences which formed an integral part of forward planning. Inspectors and specialist teachers conducted the courses in central locations and at larger schools.

The Government also set up a Survey of Educational Buildings on Aboriginal Communities (SEBAC). This survey was most comprehensive and formed the basis for forward planning and the provision of suitable school buildings on missions, settlements, and cattle stations.

The growth and development of educational policy and practice for Aboriginal children during the welfare period was very impressive. The Annual Report of the Welfare Branch for 1971-72 indicated this. 'During the year ended 30 June 1972, all aspects of the education programme ran at record or near-record levels. The following figures are worth noting: 6181 children attended special schools, leaving only a small number of children on some pastoral properties without access to an educational facility. There were 1101 children of pre-school age attending pre-school centres on settlements, missions and pastoral properties. This figure represented approximately 70% of all children eligible and compared favourably with the Australian average of 30%. There were also 128 teachers in training at ten teacher-training establishments throughout Australia and a full complement of head office professional staff ensured full contact with teachers in the field.'

The Report indicated that various building programs had been completed or initiated, and went on to state, 'For the first time, Aboriginal teaching officers who have successfully completed a two-year course at Kormilda College have been appointed as Commonwealth public servants in the Fourth Division.' These five officers took up appointments, two at Oenpelli, one at Maningrida, one at Croker Island and one at Warrabri. It is significant that four out of five of these teachers came from Arnhem Land.

The survey indicated that special schools for Aboriginal children were now organised along the lines set out in the Watts-Gallacher Report. There are now fifty-six schools operated by the Welfare Division and nine by missions throughout the Territory. In addition there were 485 Aboriginal children enrolled at schools conducted by the Department of Education and Science. At 30 June, 222 teachers were employed at Government schools on settlements, missions and pastoral properties. In addition fourteen technical instructors were employed at these schools and sixteen untrained teachers assisted in pre-school centres. Schools operated by mission authorities employed fifty-two teachers and two technical instructors.

Development also continued to take place in the special services of art, music, physical education, manual training, domestic science, adult education, pre-school and deaf education. The year 1971-72 was one of 'developing, compiling and implementing a new curriculum for Aboriginal traditional arts and crafts'. Special activities in music included the 1971 Eisteddfod, attended by fifteen schools from all over the Territory, and the second annual Areyonga festival. Aboriginal schools had been popular performers at eisteddfods over a number of years. A new curriculum for physical education was adopted. Sports days were held in almost every school. Eight manual arts centres operated during the year, eleven being situated in the Top End. A new curriculum for pre-schools was formulated. Of the eighteen schools having domestic science classes, seventeen had trained teachers in charge.

Educational excursions provided Aboriginal children in remote areas with the opportunity to broaden both the social and educational horizons beyond the immediate environment in which they lived. In the year 1971/72, 136 children from thirteen schools went on interstate excursions; 146 children from four schools visited places within the Territory; 953 children from thirty-six schools went to central area sports; and 546 children from nineteen schools visited other schools for combined activites.

This review indicates the phenomenal development in educational programs for Aboriginal children that had taken place during Welfare's administration. Yet despite this obvious growth and progress, there were three major areas of concern. They were the continued control of education by the Welfare Division, the lack of teaching in Aboriginal languages, and the fact that educational principles and practice were based on Government assimilation policies.

The question of the control of Aboriginal education by Welfare had been the subject of debate during the previous decade. The Legislative Assembly's 'Select Committee on the Education Needs of the People of the Northern Territory' of 1962 recommended the establishment of an Education Branch which would include Aboriginal education. Ten years later the Australian Council for Educational Research recommended the same. Despite these recommendations no changes were made.

The absence of teaching in Aboriginal languages was the second area of concern. Even though Aboriginal culture was now taught in primary schools, the Branch insisted on teaching in English from the earliest grades. Their preoccupation with English negatived experimentation with early education in both Aboriginal and

English, even though many countries with underprivileged minorities were following this program. Bilingual education was not seen to be a viable exercise.

The third and most contentious area of concern was the role which education played in the Government's policy of assimilation. The ultimate goal of education was seen to be a particular form of social change. This change was directed towards the assimilation of Aborigines into white society. Authorities acknowledged that there was a place for Aboriginal culture in the curriculum. It was claimed nevertheless that this was becoming so fragmented that its major significance would soon be lost. There was only one way left, and that was the white man's way. Aboriginal children should be prepared for this through education.

During the past decade, however, a number of people began questioning the assumption on which assimilationist policies were based. They saw that Aboriginal culture in many places had not been lost, just as Aboriginal people were not dying out. Aborigines were now being given back their land. They demanded that their education should be preparation for life in both societies, rather than for just the one.

Aborigines themselves realise that they have to follow two ways in education. They accept that they are living with a larger, more numerous white society. They acknowledge that they are under the legal, social and economic constraints of a wider society. But at the same time they are Aborigines. They insist on the right to remain as Aborigines and to be taught as Aborigines. They also have to follow the Aboriginal way.

The policy changes of 1973 were dramatic and decisive. Assimilation was thrown out and self-determination brought in. Aborigines now were not to be changed, but would themselves determine what changes they wanted to make at their own pace in their own time. They could now choose their own life-styles, and work out their attitudes to both cultures.

The implementation of this policy meant that Aboriginal education was taken out of the hands of the Welfare Division and incorporated into the Department of Education. Bilingual education was introduced and provision made for schooling in the homeland centres which were being encouraged. A new age had dawned.

How Aboriginal education will fare in this new age is almost impossible to predict. The first few years have been difficult and have provoked numerous criticisms. The homeland movement has seriously disrupted children's education, despite efforts to provide limited facilities in many of the places. Truancy in many of the settled communities has become commonplace, and is the direct result of a mistaken understanding of the meaning of self-determination. The bilingual education program has started, but how far can it be effective in places where sometimes more than ten different languages are spoken?

These are some of the criticisms which are being levelled at educators at the present time. Yet despite these difficulties one dominant feature of the new age must be emphasised. Educational policy is now directed towards helping Aborigines retain their Aboriginality, while at the same time providing them with opportunities for meeting the challenges and complexities of cross-cultural living in a wider Australian society.

Bilingual education is an important feature of the new educational plan. This method aims at fostering greater efficiency in school work by the use of Aboriginal languages, and developing a more healthy concept in each child through their use as a means of instruction. The program seeks competency in reading and writing in Aboriginal languages as well as in English, and by this means tries to develop closer communication, involvement and mutual understanding between the school and the community. It is hoped that it will develop and maintain the children's self-esteem and legitimate pride in both cultures.

Of the five Territory schools that started the bilingual program in 1973, three were in Arnhem Land. They were at Angurugu on Groote Eylandt, where the vernacular is Anindilyaugwa, at Goulburn Island, where the language is Maung, and at Milingimbi where the main language is Gupapuyngu. Six additional schools in Arnhem Land started the program in 1974 and 1975. They were Elcho Island (Gupapuyngu), Yirrkala (Gumatj), Oenpelli (Gunwinjgu), Numbulwar (Nunggubuyu), Umbakumba (Anindilyaugwa) and Roper River (Roper Creole). By 1977 about 1800 Aboriginal children in the Territory were being taught in bilingual classes.

Bilingual education is now widely accepted throughout the Territory. In a recent Aboriginal Adult Educators' Conference, Mr D.J. Raff stated, 'For the first time in Aboriginal schools the bilingual program has enabled Aboriginal teachers to play the major role in teaching and to have an increasingly greater influence on curriculum design and school organisation ... From the children who have been through the program and made a successful transfer to literacy in English, we have learned there is no need for special bridging materials. All that is required is instruction in the idiosyncrasies of the English orthography, and reading material to suit the interest and age level of the children.'

The bilingual program to be effective needs a large number of Aboriginal teachers. At present the number is low; but many Aboriginal teaching assistants have expressed a desire for further training in the Territory, mainly at Batchelor. The Education Department also plans to extend to three other centres the external training program, which has had a two-year trial period at Yirrkala. The number of Aboriginal teachers should then increase substantially.

The Aboriginal secondary grants scheme greatly helps Aboriginal children in secondary schools. In order to get the assistance, children must be enrolled in secondary schools, go to school regularly, maintain reasonable progress in their studies and be under twenty-one years of age. Students in the lower forms of secondary school obtain $250 a year or $300 a year for books and school clothing. Parents of children in lower secondary forms receive $14 a fortnight to help to keep the children at school, or if the student is in the last two years of secondary school, $20. Parents are also assisted with boarding costs if children have to live away from home to attend school. Children receive $3 in the lower forms or $6 in the last two years each fortnight for pocket money. The Government also pays for school, sports, library and teaching fees at Government schools, and at non-Government schools in approved cases. Government also pays a child's fares if he has to go away to school.

These payments are made to ensure that Aboriginal children are not handicapped financially as they continue with secondary education. Some non-Aborigines have been highly critical of this form of discrimination favouring Aborigines. They are quick to point out that often these moneys are either wasted in gambling, or spent on grog, or used for purposes other than that for which money is given; but the same could apply to family endowment or other Government assistance to any community. The least any Government can do is to make quite sure that underprivileged members of the community are given every opportunity of furthering their education and developing themselves and their communities in the best way possible.

Welfare had been responsible for adult education during its two decades' administration. There were centralised courses in leadership and later in literacy. Courses were also conducted for those adult education instructors who had no formal teaching qualifications. Supervised homework classes were the responsibility of this section, as was the organisation of the traditional classes taken by Aboriginal men and women either during or after school hours.

192

When the Adult Education Section was enlarged to include Adult Educators, Aboriginal Adult Education Assistants and Programmers, the basic concept remained the same: to meet the needs of the Aboriginal communities. The Aboriginal Assistant had a key role to play, not only in assisting to identify needs, but also in encouraging adults to take part.

After 1973 the Education Department started a program of Aboriginal adult education with a changed basic philosophy. The role of the Territory adult educators was now seen to be similar to that of adult educators in developing countries. President Nyerere of Tanzania had spelt out this role in 1976 as 'the liberation of man' and 'helping people work out what kind of change they want and how to create it'.

In 1977 the Aboriginal Adult Education scheme of the Department of Education had a senior adviser and sixteen field educators, eight of whom were in Arnhem Land. Sixteen Aboriginal Adult Education Assistants also were employed. They were backed up by three programmers who supplied their needs for materials. The Department planned to increase the number of adult educators in the future and to establish regional advisers at Gove, Alice Springs and Katherine as well as at Darwin. The Department also saw the need for Aboriginal educators, either full or part time.

Aboriginal Adult Education is run in conjunction with the school in each place. The Principal of the school has the responsibility of the oversight of the education of adults as well as that of the children in that community. The management of adult education is carried out by objectives, which are drawn up after consultation with other Government departments and interested bodies. Field adult educators draw up their own more specific objectives in conjunction with the community decision makers.

Meaningful education of children and adults is of the greatest importance for Aboriginal welfare and advancement. Mission, Welfare and Education Department teachers have given dedicated service in many cases over a number of years. Policies have changed as Aborigines have developed. Government is now providing facilities and staff on a greater scale than ever before. Curricula are being adapted to meet their changing needs. Aboriginal people now have an unprecedented opportunity to better themselves.

The initiative to grasp these opportunities to a very large extent now lies with them. Parents and children need a greater commitment to schooling, especially in the higher grades. At the same time schooling must be seen by them to be relevant and leading to meaningful employment. More will need to offer and train to become teaching officers, although the non-Aboriginal teacher will always be necessary for bilingual and bicultural education. Right motivation, true application, and dedicated service can mean that Aboriginal people, as never before, will be able with pride to take their place as true Aborigines, and to provide their contribution in the complex society of all Australians. They can now fulfil their wish to have the two ways in education which they desire.

16
We look at work differently

Aborigines from Arnhem Land and elsewhere in the Territory often say that their attitude to work is different from that of the Balanda or white man. They point out that in former days they hunted and gathered their food, had their ceremonies, and went out to fight, but had no formal work as white people have. Their material possessions were few and confined to what they could carry. They had a limited trade, but only in essentials such as ochre, spears, baskets, stone knives and the like. Nowadays they usually work only if they have certain goals in mind. They need food, and want vehicles, boats, transistors and similar goods. They use money to travel or charter aircraft for their ceremonies. When they have achieved their goals they see no reason to work, provided they have sufficient money for food. This can be covered through social security. So they say, 'We look at work differently'.

Non-Aboriginal attitudes to Aboriginal labour normally have been very negative. There has been, and still is, a definite prejudice on the part of many private employers against Aborigines. Employers say that they are lazy and irresponsible, have no initiative and are unreliable. There are nevertheless some notable exceptions in Arnhem Land, on some of the nearby cattle stations, and in mining on Groote Eylandt.

In the Report of the Senate Select Committee on Aborigines and Torres Strait Islanders of August 1976, Dr Frank Stevens referred to white attitudes in the pastoral industry in the Territory. He said, '... there are theories which hold amongst managerial people that whites will not work under blacks. This effectively precludes them from gaining leadership or an authoritarian role and status. This

195

could possible be correct, but the question whether Aborigines have leadership capacity and the psychological cohesion to give leadership in a cross cultural sense rests on the reservations which have been built up in the minds of whites about their ability.'

Dr Stevens continued, 'There are lots of situations where Aborigines apply themselves among themselves and even in mixed race cattle camps where the proficiency and physical abilities of Aborigines are recognised, but in fact they are rarely rewarded because you have this economic restraint and leadership restraint arising out of a European situation and not the Aboriginal situation itself.'

Aborigines often have little incentive to 'get on'. Their relationship to life is one of 'being' rather than 'doing'. Work is of secondary importance to being able to live as they want to. There is little motivation to work to attain European life-styles, which many of them have rejected or adapted to suit their own situation.

Aborigines on the Arnhem Land coast worked for Macassans in order to get rice, metal-ware, cloth and, most important of all, alcohol. They enjoyed fishing and gathering trepang in the shallow bays along the coast. They offered their services and sometimes their womenfolk for the rewards which were for them, rich. They received knives and axes to make spears and dugout canoes, and Dutch gin, for which they had a great partiality. The work they did was very similar to their normal hunting and gathering and was no great burden to them.

Work on the missions and settlements was quite different. They now dug the ground, planted crops, chopped down trees and sawed them up, built timber houses, and made roads and primitive airstrips. They sailed the small boats bringing stores from Darwin across the Arafura Sea. Women and girls worked as domestics, and then in the hospital and the school. Wages did not exist as the missions were so poor. They received food, usually in the form of flour, tea and sugar, and vegetables and fruit from the garden when these were available. They also received tobacco. This was the great prize, especially as the missions did not deal in alcohol.

A stick of chewing tobacco was the yardstick for wage calculation for the Groote Eylandters for a number of years. The missionaries would draw a stick of tobacco on a piece of paper or wood, and fill in an inch for each day's work. The workman would watch the drawing day by day until it was completely filled up. Then they would get the greatly desired reward for which they had spent so much time doing such uninteresting things.

By the 1950s when Welfare came on to the scene the missions in Arnhem Land had become established communities. Government

One of the projects of the Umbakumba Housing Association

Aboriginal workers at the manganese mining operations on Groote Eylandt and missions considered these communities as 'focal points' and 'key instruments' for its policy of assimilation. Thus the Annual Report of the Welfare Branch for 1961-2 stated that it was 'Government policy to establish settlements — operated either by the Government or by Christian Missions — to serve as training centres in social change for aboriginals'. Sedentary Aborigines would now be trained for employment.

Welfare planned that assimilation would take place in three stages. During the first stage, nomadic Aborigines would be encouraged to live in settled communities, where they would have their first introduction to white civilisation. In the second stage they would periodically move out of the community within a circumscribed white environment for work training. In the third phase Aborigines would move freely into the white community as fully trained workers, following their own vocation, and doing their work alongside their white colleagues. 'Employed side by side with other Australian workmates to whom he is now a true competitor for all benefits offered within the wider society, he will come to experience the full impact of competitive society.'

Vocational training in the communities was therefore a most important aspect in the outworking of the policy. Missions and settlements were to educate children and provide basic vocational training for them. They were to 'introduce to all members of the group the general concept of work as a worthwhile aim in life'. They were to 'prepare the younger age groups for a wider life outside the settlement and tribal community'. The 'settlements are training centres where work and living habits and attitudes will be developed, skills taught, education and health services provided.' This will enable Aborigines to bridge the gap between their present standards 'and those which they will necessarily have to attain to be acceptable in the community'.

Despite these high ideals and the dedicated service of Government and mission personnel during the two decades of the welfare era, the scheme did not progress very far beyond stage one. Even by the early 1970s there was little indication that it would progress, even tentatively, into phase two. Nomadic Aborigines in Arnhem Land were now settled in communities. Government had provided schools, health services, vocational training and employment in these towns. A small number spent a short time in Darwin on health or education courses. But the communities were becoming static. The people were there to stay or they went back to their homeland centres. Only a handful of full-blood Aborigines moved out, and then for short periods only, into the wider white community to be 'employed side

197

by side with other Australian workmates'. The three-phase policy of assimilation of Aborigines into the outside life and work force was a failure.

This does not mean to say that not much had been accomplished during those twenty years. Many Aborigines had been trained, and a growing number were working in their communities or nearby. But they refused to leave their communities and their land. They did not want to be swamped by the wider Australian society.

The employment, wage rates, training, feeding, clothing and housing of Aborigines in Arnhem Land was covered by the Wards' Employment Ordinance. The purpose of the Ordinance was 'to facilitate the emergence of wards as self-sustaining units in our economic structure'. The provisions of the Ordinance, however were guidelines rather than legal requirements. The two employers of Aboriginal labour in the reserves were the Government, through the Welfare Branch, and the missions. Neither felt constrained to abide by its provisions. The Welfare Branch maintained that it was not bound by the legislation, unless the legislation specifically mentioned Welfare. The missions rightly claimed that they just did not have the financial resources necessary to fulfil the conditions of the legislation. The Wards' Employment Ordinance was thus applied to the pastoral industry only.

Welfare and other Government agencies frequently discussed Aboriginal employment through the Employment Advisory Board, which was created under Section 13 of the Wards' Employment Ordinance. This Board advised the Administrator on all matters relating to the training and employment of wards. The main problem which the Board saw was the lack of opportunities for the gainful employment of Aborigines on the settlements and missions. Another problem arose from differences of interpretation of the Government policy of assimilation. Government and mission superintendents were not sure whether they should see the communities as temporary, transition camps preparing Aborigines for the future life in the wider Australian community, or whether they should view them as being more or less permanent.

Despite these difficulties, training programs were provided for nursing assistants, hospital and hygiene assistants, hygiene workers, teaching assistants, home management, patrol assistants, forestry, butchering, baking and cooking, for work in the communities.

During the first decade of the welfare era, there was no fixed wage for those employed in the various centres in Arnhem Land. The Methodist stations were the only ones who laid down a uniform employment and wage policy. Later all areas came under a set training allowance which was provided for missions through the Government assistance plan for subsidies.

After reviewing the employment of Aborigines on settlements and missions, Dr Colin Tatz wrote in 1964, 'Few, if any of the original policy aims have been achieved ... Employment on settlements and missions is rarely productive. It is not gainful employment ... Vocational education may lead to Aborigines being accepted as "qualified" in their segregated communities, but it does not enable them to move out into ordinary communities, as policy implies, there to sell their labour "under the same conditions as other Australians for work of a similar class".'

The same observation was equally valid in 1972. Again this does not mean to say that training had not been undertaken or that Aborigines had not been usefully employed within their own communities. What it does mean is that, in general terms, by 1972 Aborigines had not yet reached the stage where they were able to compete on the open market. There was no indication that they would, or wanted to do so in the foreseeable future.

Bearing in mind this very great limitation for the assimilation of Aborigines into the overall Australian workforce, the vocational training and employment outlined in the 1971-2 Welfare Report is very comprehensive. 'Under the main schemes at present operating in the Northern Territory, about 4000 Aborigines are receiving on-the-job training at settlements, missions and other locations. Additionally, some 335 of the trainees attended formal training courses in 1971/72 ranging from several weeks to almost a year in duration.' To understand correctly the 4000 trainees mentioned above, it should be realised that the 'trainees' in most cases were the employees of missions and welfare in the communities, doing the various communal, health, and educational tasks, but classed as trainees under a training allowance.

The Report continued, 'Courses offered range through areas such as pottery, carpentry and joinery, bricklaying, plumbing and welding to training as tourist guides, office assistants, hygiene and nursing and teaching assistants. The courses are residential and generally are conducted at a number of venues in Darwin with hostel accommodation provided for trainees...

'Increases in the number undertaking courses and the lack of a central large vocational training complex have caused difficulties in the administration, implementation and development of training programmes in recent years. To help overcome these difficulties, a vocational training centre is being developed at Batchelor, some 60 miles from Darwin, using the residential and messing facilities taken over from the Australian Atomic Energy Commission following the cessation of uranium mining and processing in the area.' This was at Rum Jungle.

The Report spoke of the training allowance scheme on settlements and missions. 'Prior to 1969, a "cash-and-kind" payment system operated for Aborigines working on settlements and missions. The cash component commenced from $7.20 for adult males and $4.60 for adult females and higher rates were paid for certain categories of workers. In addition, food, some other items and accommodation were provided without cost.' Following surveys conducted in 1967, 1968 and 1969 the 'training allowance scheme for Aborigines' undertaking on-the-job training at Aboriginal centres as well as those receiving formal vocational training was instituted. The Aboriginal worker was now responsible for the purchase of food, clothing and domestic requirements and for accommodation and service charges for himself and his dependants.

The allowances under the training scheme ranged between $25 and $36 each week for adult males and $18.75 and $27.00 for adult females. To meet increasing living costs, the allowances were to be raised to between $28.75 and $41.40 each week for adult males and between $24.50 and $35.25 for adult females, these rates being effective from 1 July 1972. The Report added, 'Aborigines working under this scheme receive on-the-job training in up to 240 categories associated with the maintenance and development of settlements, missions and reserves. There are now 3353 training positions available ... Already 15 Aborigines occupy staff positions on settlements and are paid the same wages and enjoy the same conditions of employment as other staff.' The other staff were non-Aboriginal.

Several aspects of the training allowance scheme ought again to be mentioned. The finance needed to pay for this scheme, and later to pay award wages, was not generated within the community at all; it came from massive Government subventions. The training allow-ances stabilised the 'wage' policy throughout the communities in Arnhem Land and elsewhere, clothing and rations being abandoned in favour of a lump sum approach, which was a major move forward in the right direction. At the same time the 'training positions' were in reality work positions in the various communities, usually under the supervision of non-Aboriginal staff members, Government or mission, paid through Welfare.

The Report stated that despite the incentives offered by the Welfare Division, and the sympathetic attitude of some employers, 'relatively few Aborigines seek permanent employment in the town areas. One of the main reasons for this is unsatisfactory supervision on the part of some employers.' The overriding reason however, was that the greater proportion of Aborigines did not want to live permanently away from their communities. They lived in Darwin and elsewhere away from home for only short periods of time.

The Report spoke of employment in the pastoral industry, where the payment of award wages had been in force since December 1968. 'The application of award-level wages to Aborigines did not (as was expected in some quarters) lead to widespread disemployment on pastoral properties. Nevertheless, a number of station managements did become more selective . . .

'Rapid expansion of the mining industry over the last five years, particularly at Groote Eylandt and Gove, has resulted in the employment of a sizeable number of Aborigines . . .' This statement was true of Groote but incorrect regarding Gove. Here Aborigines were not employed by Nabalco, but undertook contract work.

'Maritime industries such as fishing, prawning and pearl culture are employing other groups of Aborigines. For example, up to thirty women have been employed on piece-work rates during the prawning season as process workers in the prawning factory on Groote Eylandt.'

The Report also mentioned that a few Aborigines occupied positions in Government departments in Darwin, but that six teaching officers had been appointed in 1972. Some Aborigines in the communities engaged in their own business enterprises, often with assistance from the Aboriginal Benefits Trust Fund and the Groote Eylandt Aboriginal Trust Fund. 'Projects financed wholly or in part from these sources have been mainly in the fields of market gardening, animal husbandry, fishing, mining and prospecting, brick making, bread making, garbage collection services and a variety of tourist services.' These ventures, though highly commendable, were very small, employing only a few workers, and unfortunately did not last long.

A number of Aborigines in coastal areas continued hunting, fishing, crabbing, crocodile shooting, making artifacts and bark painting. The Report continued: 'Individuals and groups of Aborigines are often employed on short-term contractive-type employment in the pastoral industry, e.g. fencing and mustering, and in the performance of municipal/domestic-type duties in urban areas.'

This was the way in which the Welfare Division saw Aboriginal employment not long before its policies were so dramatically changed. Large numbers of Aboriginal men and women were being employed in the communities by Government or by missions entirely from massive grants through Welfare. Welfare classed them as trainees, as they had had no formal training. They received therefore training allowances. Almost all were employed within the communities for communal needs. Very few went to Darwin, and if they did, they did not stay long. Stable outside employment came for those at Angurugu with the Groote Eylandt Mining Company and at the prawning factory. These places, however, were within fifteen kilometres of home. Training to be 'employed side by side with other Australian workmates . . . within the wider society' just did not take place.

While full-blood Aborigines of Arnhem Land rarely stayed away from their communities for employment for any great length of time, the part-Aboriginal folk did. Almost all of those who grew up on Groote Eylandt or Croker Island found employment, married and settled outside the Reserve. Their numbers were much smaller, their training for employment was more intense, and they were more readily accepted by non-Aborigines in Darwin and elsewhere throughout Australia.

The provision of social service benefits for Aborigines was another feature of the welfare era. As Aborigines were being assimilated into white Australia, it was agreed that they should receive the same benefits as were provided by the Department of Social Services for other Australians. These benefits included age, invalid, dependent wives' and widows' pensions, child endowment, maternity allowance and sickness benefits.

The Welfare Conference in 1951 therefore requested the Commonwealth Government to pay these benefits to Aborigines. By 1960 the Commonwealth Department of Social Services stated that 'Aboriginal natives, other than those who are nomadic or primitive are eligible [for the appropriate benefits] on the same conditions as other members of the community'. The Department stated that an Aboriginal would 'not be regarded as nomadic or primitive so long as he remains within the sphere of influence of that mission, station or settlement'. Prior to 1959 Aborigines were eligible only for child endowment and sickness benefits. On 2 February 1960 they became eligible to receive all benefits provided by the Department of Social Services except unemployment benefits.

In 1960 the Director-General of Social Services stated regarding Aborigines that the guiding principle would be that,' wherever possible, payment will be made to the individual concerned'. If recipients can demonstrate that they 'are able to manage their own affairs', then they will receive the benefits personally. Where Aborigines were on missions or settlements 'part of the pension is paid to the Aboriginal for his own personal use and the rest is paid to the authority controlling the community for the pensioner's maintenance . . . on the same basis as residents in benevolent homes'.

During the greater part of the welfare era social service moneys for Aborigines living in the towns were paid to the people concerned. For those living in Arnhem Land, and on other reserves, the moneys were paid directly to Welfare or to the missions. These agencies gave out pocket money, but kept the remainder for general welfare, including communal feeding, clothing and other essential services. The common practice of the Arnhem Land missions seems to have been that all social service moneys were added to other subsidies, and the total was used for general welfare for all Aborigines.

The bulk-funding of Welfare and missions was made in this way because of the assumption that Aborigines living on settlements and missions were not capable of managing their own affairs. At this time many could not, but there were those who could. Missions and Welfare also maintained that they were able to spread benefits over a much wider group when they received bulk-funding. They said that the health of children and old people improved with regular, well-balanced meals. They insisted that the money would go where it was most needed and not be gambled or frittered away.

The bulk-funding of social service benefits came under increasing criticism as being protectionist and paternalistic, and that those for whom public money was provided were not receiving their entitlement. The system was abolished in the late 1960s and social security payments were made directly to the individuals concerned. This did not apply to unemployment benefits, for which Aborigines in the reserves at the time were not eligible.

Clearly a number of Aborigines do not use the social security benefits in the way intended. The same thing could be said about all people throughout Australia who are receiving benefits. The main objection to bulk-funding lay in the principle involved. Moneys are given for specific purposes to named individuals. They are the ones who should receive the money. They are the ones who should be responsible for what use they make of it. For far too long those concerned — and deeply concerned as they were — for Aborigines and their advancement and welfare, have adopted paternalistic attitudes towards them. They did things for Aborigines instead of allowing Aborigines themselves, even through their mistakes, and by trial and error, to learn to do things for themselves.

When the Department of Aboriginal Affairs superseded the activities of the Welfare Division of the Northern Territory Administration in December 1972, the responsibility for the employment of

Aborigines was transferred to the Department of Labor. Responsibility for most of the vocational training was transferred to the Department of Labor and Immigration from the following year. The Department of Aboriginal Affairs, however, still maintained an interest in vocational training. These included projects such as community development programs at Nungalinya College and language workshops run by the Summer Institute of Linguistics. The Department of Aboriginal Affairs is also working in conjunction with the Department of Employment and Industrial Relations and the Department of Education on schemes to provide adequate vocational training for Aborigines.

In April 1973 Aborigines living in communities in the reserves became eligible for unemployment benefits. Before this, only Aborigines living outside the reserves had been eligible. Now Aborigines in Arnhem Land qualified for these benefits, and a suitable 'work rule' formula was evolved to ascertain whether they were eligible in their particular circumstances.

In the meantime the Employment Training Scheme for Aboriginals administered by the Commonwealth Employment Service continued. This scheme had been commenced in 1969. It was designed to encourage the employment of Aborigines and to facilitate their movement to areas where they could obtain regular and a wider range of employment. They were paid living-away-from-home allowances, and employers received subsidies. From July 1969 until July 1973, 262 placements had been made under the scheme. In the year ending July 1973, 192 placements had been made but only twenty-nine living-away-from-home allowances were given throughout the whole of the Territory. This indicates that the scheme was not very effective.

The continued chronic state of Aboriginal employment during the next four years was a cause of great concern for the Government. An issue such as this is of international as well as of national significance. Deprivation, ill-health, child morbidity and mortality, and unemployment amongst minority coloured groups within dominant white societies is frequently the subject of scrutiny and comment by world organisations. For this and for other reasons Governments are very sensitive about these problems.

In a statement made in the House of Representatives on 26 May 1977, the Minister for Aboriginal Affairs, Mr R.I. Viner, outlined new initiatives to be made by his Department and that of Employment and Industrial Relations to deal with the problems of Aboriginal unemployment. He pointed out that at the end of February 1977 there were 12 218 Aborigines registered for employment with the

Commonwealth Employment Service. This figure was for the whole of Australia and included non-tribal Aborigines. He said that this number represented more than one-third of the estimated Aboriginal labour force. It was more than six times the unemployment rate for Australia as a whole.

Mr Viner also stated that about fifty per cent of the Aboriginal labour force did not, or were unable to, register with the Commonwealth Employment Service. He said that the Commonwealth Employment Service placed 6600 Aborigines in employment during 1976, but that the total number registered as unemployed rose by 1800 during that period.

He went on to say that these statistics 'do not reveal the full effects of unemployment upon Aboriginal citizens. Unemployment to this excessive extent, through its inter-relationship with health, housing, education and community development generally is severely undermining the progress in Aboriginal affairs made by successive governments at considerable public expense since the 1967 referendum.'

He pointed out that some Aborigines had chosen to return to their traditional life-styles. Others had not. 'In most areas where Aboriginal communities now reside this lifestyle is no longer possible ... Because of this, Aboriginals have become accustomed to food supplied through stores on settlements. Consequently, they have required a cash income. Unemployment benefits have been available to Aboriginals as to other Australians unable to obtain work. In some cases ... the lack of activity when combined with unemployment benefit has produced serious social problems such as alcoholism and other health hazards.'

Mr Viner said that initiatives to be taken in these communities consist of Community Development Employment Projects (CEDPs) which would provide work for all Aborigines in a particular community who wished to work. Finance for the CEDPs would be provided to individual Aboriginal Councils to enable the Council to pay for work performed by individual community members.

He continued: 'As a positive demonstration of the Government's policy of encouraging Aboriginals to manage their own affairs, the Aboriginal Councils will be able to determine the projects it undertakes and how it allocates its labour. However, to assist in the elimination of social problems within communities, my Department will encourage the inclusion of projects such as youth activities and alcohol rehabilitation measures ... Also ... special training will be provided for Aboriginals who wish to acquire or upgrade their skills to equip them to either take over skilled jobs within their community now undertaken by non-Aboriginals, or, if they so desire, leave the community to join the open labour market.'

Mr Viner concluded by saying, 'Fundamental to any long term improvement in the employment status of Aboriginals both in remote communities and in the open labour market is an improvement in the levels of educational attainment by Aboriginal students. My colleague, the Minister for Education, in consultation with the Minister for Employment and Industrial Relations and myself, will promote a redirection of education programs to prepare Aboriginals for a work environment or for specific job training.'

These initiatives outlined by Mr Viner are undoubtedly a sincere effort to alleviate the problems caused by Aboriginal unemployment in the reserves as elsewhere. They allow Aborigines themselves to determine the projects and to provide jobs for all who want them. Unfortunately the answer to Aboriginal employment is not quite so simple. Cross-cultural factors are of the greatest importance. The problem of Aborigines living in non-productive areas is another.

One main issue concerns Aboriginal attitudes to non-Aboriginal-style work patterns. For many years Aborigines have sat back or have taken only a minor role, while non-Aborigines worked for them. This has created a very bad precedent. Moreover Aborigines in their former hunting, foraging, food-gathering economy had to be constantly active to survive. But they were in their own environment, moving in the areas which they knew, fishing and hunting in places which they believed had been given to them and to their great totem heroes. They were at home at work.

Today, Aborigines are not at home in their work, even though their work may be in their home communities. They have set hours of teaching, working in the hospital, shop, office or garage or on the roads. They are expected to do the same work day after day, week after week, and year after year. The same applies to work outside the community at mining projects such as GEMCo on Groote. Many Aborigines have expressed the view that they want jobs because they want the money, and they want the goods the money can buy. But they do not want to be tied down. Once they have worked for a while, or gained the amount of money that they planned, they want to relax and to 'do their own thing.' They want time for their ceremonies, to visit their relations, and to return to their country.

Aborigines working away from their home communities comprise another issue. They are now much more aware of their identity through the granting of land rights. The land is now theirs, and they wish to enjoy their heritage. A number of Aborigines are turning away from the disturbing life of the disparate communities and returning to live permanently or temporarily in their own country. Work patterns here are quite different. They usually return to their hunting and food-gathering economy, supplementing bush food with cash items from the store. The money comes from community work projects or from the sale of artifacts.

The third issue is closely related to the second. Land rights, the homeland movement, and a new awareness of identity are tending to draw Aborigines away from any desire to live away from their homes, to compete in the open work force, and to face up to pressures of multiracial living. They don't want to leave their country just for the sake of work. A self-imposed form of separate development is a natural complement to any policy of self-determination.

This raises the fundamental dilemma. Work and welfare services in the communities in the reserves can be undertaken only from finance from massive Government grants. The communities are in no way viable economic groups. They do not and cannot generate any form of capital or productivity. Municipal taxes and rates if applied would only meet a fraction of the cost of running these centres. Aboriginal communities are still the recipients of a gigantic welfare operation, even though opportunity and encouragement for employment is given for all engaged in the operation.

This feature also has significance for training of Aborigines to take over jobs from non-Aborigines in the communities. Aboriginalisation is an essential complement to self-management. But the fact still remains that communities, even when run by Aborigines or by a Department of Aboriginal Affairs conducted as an Aboriginal Congress, could still only survive through ever-increasing Government funding.

A postscript needs to be added on an Aboriginal understanding of the usage of money. Some people say that Aborigines are unaware of the value of money and how to use it. This is not true. Aborigines certainly know what money is and how to use it. This is no more evident than when one stands around a ring of gamblers, usually women, and sees how they are gripped with the game and hear what they say they are going to do when they win. And speaking of women gambling, what other exciting thing can many of them do? If they have houses, they do not use them the same way as non-Aborigines, and need to spend little time in them. If they have no jobs and do not want to go fishing or hunting, then what else do many do, but spend many hours of the day, and sometimes of the night, in gambling?

Aborigines certainly understand what money is. They may often have different priorities. Some prefer to spend their money on alcohol, vehicles, boats, transistors, expensive toys, and trips by charter aeroplane, instead of on basic things such as food and clothing. Education in child-care, diatetics, the abuses of alcohol and general money usage has been given to children and to adults over a number of years. More education is still needed. But experience can be a good educator. Unfortunately to be hungry because of bad stewardship and bad housekeeping can often be a better stimulus to future responsible action than abstract talk.

Aborigines are not lazy, irresponsible and unreliable when they are doing the things that they want to do and approximate to their culture. The tracker will travel for days with little sleep or food to find the missing person. The hunter will spend long hours carefully searching out and stalking his prey. Women will spend all day on the beach and in the billabongs gathering bush foods. It is when they see no need for work or the work is so foreign to their background and life-style that they work badly, are unreliable or opt out. Unfortunately socio-economic pressures on them are such that in the process of time many will become more disadvantaged and become encapsulated in perpetual poverty. For Aborigines look at work quite differently from the mass of grasping society around them.

17
Black men, white laws

For many years the Aborigines of Arnhem Land did not receive justice at the hands of white men. In many cases they were not even treated as human beings. They were shot and poisoned and deprived of their land. When brought before the courts they were tried by white men's laws which they did not understand. They were judged by European legislation which did not take into account their own complex culture and law. Until recently they were not 'equal before the law' and did not receive 'equal protection of the law' as stipulated in Article 7 of the Universal Declaration of Human Rights.

The South Australian Government did little for the welfare of Aborigines during its administration of the Territory between 1863 and 1911. Instead there had been gross injustice when the northern frontiers of white expansionism extended into Arnhem Land. Killings by whites led to retaliatory spearings by blacks. These in turn led to punitive expeditions and massacres. There was no justice. When they could not retaliate with spears they retreated into the bush or adopted the role of parasites. They had few rights and little protection from the law.

Commonwealth policy relating to Aborigines during the first years of its administration from 1911 was more enlightened and humane. Aborigines were thought of as a dying race, so they had to be protected and given a decent burial. The Government created reserves, controlled their movement, and legislated for their welfare. They gave missions leases and encouraged them to care for what they thought were the last stages of a dying race.

The first stage in law reform relating to the Aborigines came as the direct result of the injustices arising from three trials of Aborigines from eastern Arnhem Land in 1934. The circumstances were these.

On 17 September 1932 Caledon Bay Aborigines killed five Japanese and looted their vessel. A sixth Japanese and the European skipper escaped. These killings were made in retaliation for alleged interference with Aboriginal women, and insufficient payment to those who prostituted them. Later two white beachcombers, F. Traynor and W. Fagan, were killed on Woodah Island, also for alleged misuse of Aboriginal women. On 1 August 1933, Constable McColl, one of the police party sent to investigate the killings, was speared to death at Woodah Island. When these killings became known, there was an immediate outcry among the white residents of Darwin and the Territory, and the demand for a punitive expedition to go and teach the Caledon Bay Aborigines a lesson. 'You cannot kill a policeman and get away with it,' was the common sentiment.

The possibility of such a punitive action by the police aroused strong protests from among many church people and organisations in the South. The knowledge of the horror of such inhumane actions in the past, and the thought of a further mass killing of men, women and children aroused widespread revulsion. As the Anglican CMS was working at Roper River and on Groote Eylandt, close to the area of the killings, this Society persuaded the Government to allow them to send a 'peace expedition' there. The expedition consisted of three men, the Reverends H.E. Warren and A.J. Dyer and Mr Donald Fowler, a former RAN wireless operator. Fowler had witnessed a similar massacre in the South Sea islands and wanted to do his utmost to prevent the repetition of such a tragedy. The peace party was to go unarmed, was in no way to attempt the job of the police and arrest the killers, but to try to establish peaceful relations with them. The party was to suggest that the killers give themselves up in order to prevent the police killing their whole clan.

During the stormy wet season between December 1933 and March 1934 these three men with their Aboriginal assistants made various trips to Caledon Bay and to the eastern coast of Arnhem Land in the mission lugger *Holly*. They found the remains of Constable McColl, which they brought back to Groote and buried. They recovered the remains of one man, either Traynor or Fagan, which they buried on Woodah. They made contact with the killers of the Japanese, the two whites and Constable McColl, and persuaded them to go to Darwin and face the charges there, for the sake of their people.

The self-confessed killers were taken to Darwin by the Reverend A.J. Dyer in the *Oituli* of the trepanger, Mr Fred Gray. Shortly after their arrival in Darwin they were arrested by the police and clapped in irons. This was contrary to the agreement which the Government made with the missionaries. The authorities had stated that they would not apprehend the Aborigines until they had laid proper charges.

An account of the trials of these Caledon Bay killers can be found in the Commonwealth Law Reports. In summary, the three Aborigines were found guilty of killing the Japanese and were given twenty years with hard labour. Two, Tukiar and Merara, were surprisingly acquitted of the murder of Fagan and Traynor through lack of evidence. On 6 August 1934 Tukiar was found guilty of the murder of Constable McColl, and was sentenced to death.

This decision, together with the severe sentence passed on the self-confessed killers of the Japanese, aroused a storm of protest throughout Australia and Britain. Feeling ran high. The adequacy of white man's law to achieve full justice for the Aborigines was seriously questioned. Court procedures and white prejudices in Tukiar's case immediately set in motion an appeal to the High Court of Australia. As a result of the appeal, the conviction was quashed and Tukiar was discharged.

In delivering judgment, Mr Justice Starke stated, 'It is manifest that the trial of the prisoner was attended with grave difficulties, and indeed was almost impossible. He lived under the protection of the law in force in Australia, but had no conception of its standards. Yet by that law he had to be tried. He understood little or nothing of the proceedings or of their consequences to him and had the misfortune to place the counsel assigned to him "in the worst predicament that he had encountered in all his legal career".' He went on to say that the 'Chief Protector of Aboriginals for the Northern Territory informs us that "the conditions of interpreting the statements of aboriginals through other aboriginals, especially during the formal proceedings of the Court, make it difficult and almost impossible to get more than an approximation of the truth". Yet the learned Judge in his charge to the jury passes by all these difficulties and dangers. But, worse still, he wholly fails to suggest for the consideration of the jury the possible effect upon uncivilised aboriginals of a police party capturing their lubras, and apparently endeavouring to capture the aboriginals as well.'

Judge Starke continued, 'It was, no doubt, necessary for the police to capture and handcuff lubras if they were to achieve the object of their expedition, but the rules of English law cannot be cited in support of their action. To uncivilised aboriginals, however, and particularly to the prisoner, the conduct of the police party may well have appeared as an attack upon the lubras and themselves and provoked or led to the attack upon the police in their own defence. A finding of not guilty, or of manslaughter was quite open to the jury on evidence. Yet the learned Judge is silent upon this important aspect of the case, and practically invites the jury to find the verdict of guilty ...'

Mr Justice Starke concluded: 'The trial of the prisoner seriously miscarried, but the reasons for this conclusion go deeper, to my mind, than the irregularities just referred to. Indeed, these latter do not seem to have been the subject of any objection on the part of counsel who appeared for the prisoner. But the conduct of the case by counsel is not above criticism.' Mr Justice Starke then indicated that Counsel for the defence had made a public announcement after the prisoner had been convicted in order to clear the name of Constable McColl. For this he said, 'Comment is needless ... The result is that the prisoner's conviction should be quashed, and his discharge ordered.'

When the authorities freed Tukiar they took him to Bagot to await repatriation to eastern Arnhem Land. After a few days he disappeared. Why he did so and where he had gone, no one knows from that day to this. No trace of him has been found either in Darwin or in his own country. Common Darwin rumour among Aborigines at the time said that the police murdered him in retaliation for the killing of a mate. One of the Caledon Bay police party, Vic Hall, in a book written many years later called *Dreamtime Justice* has a fanciful story of his fight with the black tracker Pat. Pat tracked and killed him because, he claims, Tukiar had killed his boss.

Tukiar agreed voluntarily to go to Darwin to tell his story in order to save his people from destruction. His trial was a sad miscarriage of justice. He was freed but he was never seen again. He died, but the tragedy and pathos of his story brought the plight of his people before the white people of Australia in a way which could not have been done, except through his death. His trial brought clearly to their notice the inadequacy of legal procedures in cases involving illiterate Aborigines from remote areas.

Because of the unsatisfactory trial of Tukiar in Darwin, Professor Elkin advocated that all cases should be tried in the district where the offences occurred. Special courts should be created for cases in which Aborigines were involved. In the meantime in April 1933 a panel of sixty jurors petitioned Acting Judge Sharwood in the Supreme Court in Darwin that Aborigines be tried in accordance with their own tribal customs, and not under the present criminal code, 'on charges of murder, manslaughter and other acts of

Aboriginal traditional painting depicting Christianity, Maningrida Church

TOP: Non-European Uniting Church ministers working in North Australia.
BOTTOM: Bishop K. B. Mason after the ordination of Reverend Michael Gumbuli,
4 November 1973

violence, when the offences are known or are proved to be of a purely tribal nature'. The jurors stated that 'It is known that if one Aboriginal unlawfully and violently injures another, his tribe will see to his proper punishment irrespective of what the white man does to him. It is strongly urged that the whole question should be investigated and reported to the Government by men who have lived amongst the natives and have knowledge of their codes ... Leaving the matter in the hands of those who have no knowledge of the Aboriginal would only result in a remedy worse than the disease.'

On 24 May 1933 the Government passed the Criminal Procedure Ordinance abolishing the use of juries in the Northern Territory in cases involving Aborigines, except in trial on indictment of offences punishable by death. On 2 May 1934 the Crimes Act and Ordinance added the important proviso that where 'an Aboriginal native is convicted of murder, the Court shall not be obliged to pronounce sentence of death; but, in lieu hereof, may impose such penalty as, having regard to all the circumstances of the case, appears to the Court to be just and proper ... For the purpose of determining the nature and extent of the penalty to be imposed where an Aboriginal native is convicted of murder, the Court shall receive and consider any evidence which may be tendered as to any relevant native law or custom and its application to the facts of the case and any evidence which may be tendered in mitigation of penalty.'

Legal authorities, humanitarian bodies and missionary societies continued to hold meetings and to draw up reports and recommendations about adequate legal reform. The press gave the matter much publicity. In December 1933 the National Missionary Council arranged a Conference with specialists in law and anthropology which recommended that in all cases of breaches of the law in which Aborigines were concerned 'full consideration should be given to tribal traditions and customs, in order that full justice may be done'.

After discussion and debate the various groups in 1934 advocated a positive Aboriginal policy including the appointment of an administrator 'chosen for his knowledge of the problems of racial contact and clash'; a 'Department of Native Affairs to deal with the education, health and employment of Aborigines'; and a 'Department of Native Justice'. The Department of Native Justice should have a judge with special knowledge of Aboriginal anthropology, who would hold his court in various places in the Territory. He should be assisted by six magistrates also trained in anthropology. Nothing came of these suggestions.

As nothing was done, concerned people continued to press for law reform in cases involving Aborigines. In 1936 T.G. Strehlow pointed out difficulties relating to Aboriginal evidence. The examples are taken from Central Australia, but applied equally well to Arnhem Land. He said that Aborigines will normally give evasive or untrue replies if they think that the interrogating white men are either unsympathetic or antagonistic. Aborigines undoubtedly know the difference between truth and lies. They will lie to a white man to gain some advantage or escape from impending trouble. Again Aborigines normally brand a man a liar even though he is unable to fulfil his promise because of normally accepted excuses. Strehlow concluded his observations by stating that if an Aboriginal 'is confronted suddenly with a direct accusation of crime of a serious nature, his first reaction will be to deny it in the most emphatic way ... If the man putting the questions is a white man who does not possess either the esteem or the respect of the native who is being questioned, the latter will probably persist with his denial ... If the man putting the questions is a white man who does possess the esteem ... the latter may and usually will admit his guilt ...'

Ten years later Professor Elkin raised problems regarding Aboriginal evidence and justice in North Australia. He pointed out that the Aborigines were an invaded and subject people living in a condition of parasitism. Because of this background their evidence was frequently unsatisfactory when given before white people and judged by white values. Professor Elkin gave as an example of the 'fear' or 'worry' factor in the Tukiar case. Tukiar gave two differing statements regarding the killing of Constable McColl. In one the motive was the suspicion and fear aroused by the seizure of his wives by the white men. In the other, McColl's adultery with one of his women was the motive. After being found guilty in questioning he informed his counsel that the first account was true and that he had told the other story because he was 'too much worried'. There is every reason to believe he denied the second account because he wanted to say the right thing and obtain that fair treatment of which Warren had assured him.

In the course of his careful review Elkin pointed out the obvious: that the usual mechanisms of court procedure were unsatisfactory when Aborigines were involved. Evidence under oath or unsworn testimony allowed by the Northern Territory Evidence Ordinance (No 2) 1939 was not significant in the social context of Aborigines. The hearing of Aboriginal cases by local Justices of the Peace who had typical racist attitudes was unjust. In criminal cases in the Northern Territory where indictable offences punishable by death necessitated juries, the juries were white people who would find it very difficult to be impartial.

214

Professor Elkin suggested that in the Northern Territory all cases involving Aborigines should be removed from the jurisdiction of Justices of the Peace and from trial by jury. He quoted Judge D.J.D. Bevan of the Northern Territory who had written, 'Speaking generally I do not hesitate to say that where a European is charged with an offence against a coloured man, no matter what the evidence may be, the matter is decided on the question of colour ... My experience for the last two years has been such as to lead me to the conclusion that the jury system in criminal cases in the Northern Territory is quite unsuited to the administration of justice, and has led me to recommend strongly the abolition of trial by jury, and the institution of a trial by a judge and two assessors.'

In the meantime Mr E.W.P. Chinnery had been appointed Director of Native Affairs in 1939. Shortly after taking up office he drew up a new plan of administration and recommended the provision of Courts for Native Affairs. The Native Administration Ordinance of 21 August 1940 authorised the Administrator to appoint magistrates for native affairs, to establish and abolish courts for the same in different places, and to appoint the Supreme Court a court of appeal from native courts. The Ordinance limited the jurisdiction of a court for native matters to cases between Aborigines.

Laws relating to Aborigines during the two decades of the welfare era from 1953 to 1973 reflected the prevailing policy of assimilation. Welfare legislation usually discriminated in favour of Aborigines. Some of the regulations, though aimed at protection, nevertheless infringed on Aboriginal rights. One such piece of legislation concerned the power of the Director of Welfare regarding the movements of a ward where he considered that it was 'in the best interests of the ward'. Prior to 1961 the Director, under section 17 (1) of the Welfare Ordinance could take the ward into custody; authorise a person to take the ward into custody on behalf of the Director; order that the ward be removed to, and kept within, a reserve or institution; order that the ward be kept within a reserve or institution; and order that the ward be removed from one reserve or institution to another reserve or institution. The Director could not act in this way if a child under fourteen years would be thus removed from his parents, or a parent removed from his children, unless the Administrator so authorised him.

Although the 'committal order' for this procedure was used only as a last resort after persuasion to take a 'holiday' elsewhere had been refused, the Legislative Council and other interested people considered that the Director's powers in this regard were excessive.

As a result the Ordinance was amended in 1961 so that the Director or welfare officer had to apply to a Court of Summary Jurisdiction for a removal order where he considered it 'in the interest of a particular ward or in the interest of wards in a particular place or in the public interest'.

The application of the amended section 17 did not apply where the ward voluntarily sought asylum in another community. This came about in instances involving breaches of tribal law. The offender then was usually only too pleased to be allowed to go elsewhere. Recourse to section 17 was made only in cases involving infringement of the liquor laws.

The authority to direct and the power of arrest by a superintendent or a welfare officer was another questionable aspect of the Welfare Ordinance. Under a new section 61 introduced when the Ordinance was amended in 1961, 'the superintendent of a reserve or an institution ... may, for the purpose of controlling the management of or maintaining order in the reserve or institution, give orders and directions to a ward who is on a reserve or institution'. He also 'may arrest without warrant a ward whom he believes on reasonable grounds to have committed an offence against the last preceding subsection'.

When presenting the Welfare Amendment Bill in 1961 the Director said that section 61 should be regarded as a temporary measure until police could be stationed on or near the Aboriginal communities. The provision of police in communities has taken a long time. Only several Arnhem Land communities had resident police even by 1977. In the meantime, until the abolition of the Welfare Ordinance in 1973, superintendents or their representatives had powers exceeding those of citizens at common law or of police officers in the course of their duties.

Disciplinary action on missions and the penalties proposed by the Welfare Branch were also suspect in law. The rules were set out in a document entitled 'Discipline on Mission Stations and Government Settlements' at a Missions-Administration Conference held in Darwin in July 1961. The document stated that the superintendent had no jurisdiction in respect of tribal disputes or the contravention of Aboriginal law. But he did have 'full jurisdiction over all residents as civic leader, in respect of breaches of settlement rules'. He also had qualified jurisdiction in respect of breaches of church laws and rules.

The need for such guidelines arose out of the practical circumstances of life on the missions and settlements. It was obvious that from time to time offenders must be dealt with. The questions were

'How?' and 'By what means?' Further questions needed to be asked: 'On what authority?' or 'Is this or that action legal?'

The normal disciplinary action used by superintendents was to deprive people of food; but this contravened section 71 of the Welfare Ordinance. Superintendents could send offenders on 'walkabout'; but this contravened section 17 of the Ordinance. The acceptance of church laws such as monogamy and Sunday observance for qualification for food and residence was highly irregular and inexcusable.

Sections 61 to 70 of the 1953 Welfare Ordinance made provision for the protection of Aboriginal women. Under section 61 a person could not 'habitually live with a ward unless he is a ward or a relation of the ward'. Under section 62 the Director could order a ward or relative of a ward not to live with another ward. Under section 64 'a male person, other than a ward' might not 'habitually live with a female ward to whom he was not married; habitually consort with a female ward to whom he was not married; between the hours of sunset and sunrise be in the company of a female ward to whom he was not married, except with lawful excuse; cohabit with, have or attempt to have sexual intercourse with, a ward to whom he was not married'. The purpose of those provisions was to prevent exploitation — the immoral exploitation, if you like — of persons who were not able fully to look after themselves.

Sections 61 to 70 were repeated when the Welfare Ordinance was amended in November 1961, and some of its provisions were covered by the Police and Police Offences Ordinances. As a result section 45C stated that a 'person shall not habitually live with a ward unless he is a ward or a relation of the ward', and under section 45D the Director could order a ward or a relative not to live with another ward. The provisions still took protectionism far too far. Even though the legislation was for 'the good of the wards', the sexual life of consenting adults is an individual matter and was far beyond the legal authority of the Government or any other welfare agency.

The law relating to Aborigines and liquor was of great importance. Section 141 of the Licensing Ordinance 1939-1962 stated that a person 'shall not sell, give or supply liquor, or permit liquor to be sold, given or supplied, to a person who is a ward within the meaning of the Welfare Ordinance 1953-1961'. Section 142 stated 'A person who is a ward ... and who is found drinking liquor to have been drinking liquor or in possession of liquor is guilty of an offence'. Under the Justices Ordinance 1928-1961 a special magistrate had to hear proceedings under this Ordinance.

The 1959 Report of the Select Committee of the Legislative

217

Council stated that the reasons for the prohibition of alcohol for Aborigines stemmed from the 'belief in the inability of the aboriginal race to consume liquor without deleterious effects'. In the Legislative Council debate on the report, the Director of Welfare said, 'I consider that I would be renegade to the responsibilities of the position that I hold if I did not speak in the strongest terms against the proposal that is at present being considered. The supply of liquor to wards is a vicious practice which leads to debauchery and prostitution ... it leads to most serious crimes against the person by Aborigines against Aborigines in some cases.'

In 1964 legislation was passed enabling Aborigines outside the reserves to purchase and consume alcohol. Welfare and missions continued to prevent Aborigines bringing liquor in to the Reserve communities. Later Maningrida, Umbakumba, and Roper River had 'wet' canteens. Aborigines from other areas went to Darwin to get drunk, or to bring back illicit supplies to the communities. Further aspects of Aborigines and alcohol are considered in a subsequent chapter.

During the first decade of the welfare era the Director or a Welfare Officer was required to provide adequate legal counsel for a ward or Aboriginal appearing in the courts. The usual practice of Welfare was to engage legal counsel for all criminal and indictable cases, while Welfare Officers appeared as counsel in summary and non-indictable cases. The latter procedure could sometimes be unsatisfactory because of the lack of training and competence of Welfare Officers, conflicting interests between the client and the Welfare Branch, or the authoritarian relationship between the Welfare Officer and the Aboriginal.

In 1962 the Legislative Assembly repealed clauses (b) and (c) Section 82 (4) of Welfare Ordinance in order to ease the 'intolerable burden' being placed on the welfare staff. Under this legislation a ward could not admit guilt except on the advice of his counsel, the Director, or the Welfare Officer appearing for him, and that a statement by a ward was not admissable in evidence unless his counsel, the Director or a Welfare Officer was present. These provisions were made to protect the Aborigines being charged, but had been very difficult to administer and were sometimes very hard on the Welfare Officer concerned.

In 1960 Mr Justice Kriewaldt in an article on 'The Application of the Criminal Law to the Aborigines of the Northern Territory of Australia' strongly urged that juries should be abolished when the accused was an Aboriginal. He pointed out that trials by jury from 1944 to 1956 had resulted in verdicts of manslaughter and acquittal in a large percentage of cases. There had been the difficulties encountered by juries in understanding and valuing evidence given by Aborigines, and 'the attitude many white citizens of the Northern Territory hold towards the application of criminal law to Aborigines'.

Mr Justice Kriewaldt also claimed that the law now protected Aborigines. He said that 'by and large, Aborigines enjoy the protection of the law to the fullest extent in their dealings with whites'. This claim was still open to doubt, even though some progress had been made in law reform. At that time cases were not heard in the remote communities such as those in Arnhem Land. Judge Kriewaldt admitted that cases involving Aborigines took place 'as if the accused were not present'. The Aboriginal still did not know what court procedure was. He often could not understand basic English, let alone the complexities and nuances of legal jargon. He still stood in mortal fear of the police.

Judge Kriewaldt added, 'I can see no possible way by which this difficulty can be overcome. It matters not what changes may be made in the composition of the tribunal before which Aborigines are tried, or what alterations are affected in the rules of procedure regulating trials, the fundamental fact that most accused Aborigines do not understand the proceedings will not be affected for many years to come. There is no solution. If the criminal law is to be applied at all to Aborigines, it must simply be accepted that, for some years yet, many aborigines will not understand, even to a limited extent, the method whereby it is decided whether they be guilty or not.'

In 1977 the relationship between white and Aboriginal customary law has been the subject considered by the Australian Law Reform Commission. On 9 February 1977 Mr Ellicott, the then Attorney-General, after consulting with Mr Viner, the Minister of Aboriginal Affairs, directed the Commission to report on matters concerning the application of Aboriginal customary law.

In the week of 13 June 1977 a number of members of the Commission, including the Chairman, Mr Justice Kirby, visited the Territory and consulted with interested groups in Alice Springs and in Darwin. The purpose of the visit was to obtain advice from Aborigines and other interested members of the community concerning the issues raised by the terms of reference and the methods which the commission should employ in the future.

Among the many issues raised was the difficulty of communication arising out of courtroom procedures and pre-trial investigations by police. In an Interim Report No 2 the Commission drew attention to the submission made by Mr Jim Lester for a conference organised by the International Commission of Jurists in 1973. At this conference Mr Lester said, 'Aboriginal people have many difficulties in understanding and coping with the courts. First is the language problem. People don't understand court language and procedures, and they make mistakes and have to be corrected, which then makes them embarrassed. I have heard the magistrate say, "Take your hat off when you come into the court". The people then become confused and afraid.'

Jim Lester, who has had a lot of experience in helping Aborigines in court continued. 'Aboriginal people are severely limited in their understanding of English. Court language is hard to understand, and most of the people don't understand the charges against them. Sometimes it is hard for the interpreter to put into the Aboriginal language. The same problem applies in the police station.

'Aboriginal languages are very different from English. This makes it very hard for the people to understand the English. They use the negative differently. If they are asked, "Did you or did you not do that?" they will say, "Yes", meaning, "Yes, I did not do it."

'Then there is the fear of the court situation. There are so many uniformed police and figures of authority in the court ... Many of the people when asked why they say "Guilty", will reply "The policeman told me when I go in court I have to say, 'Guilty'". The authority of the policeman, and their fear, would make them do as they are told.

'Cross-questioning confuses the people, especially about details of time and place. They can't understand the importance of such things. They think, "Why are they asking me all this?" They then become afraid, and they might agree with anything, or forget what they have just said.

'Fear of payback also affects people in court. In their own culture anyone who tells tales is likely to get into trouble ... This makes the people afraid sometimes to be a witness against another man. In court it might make them afraid to tell of any wrong treatment by a policeman, for fear that a policeman gets back at them sometime.

'People who are frightened in court will often plead guilty, even when they are innocent, so as to get finished and out of court. They can also plead guilty because they don't know what is going on.

'Aborigines have a different culture, and different ideas about crime ... Aboriginal people can't understand why they should be arrested for fighting, even if injury is done ... The people don't understand either the English, or the charge of "disorderly behaviour". There is no such thing in Aboriginal society. If a person is upset with a person or group, he may shout or swear or threaten them. The other people ignore him and let him get it out of his system . . .'

The Commission Report also drew attention to the fear of authority which Aborigines experience. This was highlighted by the Reverend Jim Downing of the Institute for Aboriginal Development in Alice Springs, who stated, 'If an authority figure — and this does not mean only police — says "You don't have to answer me", and then proceeds to ask questions, the very weight of his authority dictates that they must answer . . . I do not think it means anything in their understanding of their rights in this matter . . . and no matter what he may say about not having to answer, the weight of his authority dictates that if he goes on asking questions, he expects them to answer.'

Another problem arises out of the authority situation because of the Aboriginal tendency to give the answer thought to be expected, rather than that which is necessarily the case.

The main response of the Commission to the problems outlined above was a reflection on a statement made by Jim Downing. 'I think the people must be questioned in regard to crime, but I think the disadvantages are so great that the people are themselves so disadvantaged by our system of law and its application that the only safeguard that I can see is for cross-examination only to be allowed with an independent interpreter interpreting the law process to shield the person from their anxiety and weight of authority.'

The Commission also supported the use of the 'prisoner's friend'. Mr Justice Forster, the Senior Judge of the Territory, had laid down 'judge's rules' including the function of the prisoner's friend in the case of the Crown v Anunga and others in the Supreme Court of the Northern Territory on 27 August, 8 September 1975. Mr Justice Forster was joined with Justices Muirhead and Ward in stating that the guidelines were an expression of the views of the court. The 'judge's rules' state that an 'interpreter should be present to ensure complete and mutual understanding'. Where practicable, 'a prisoner's friend' should be present during the interrogation. '"The prisoner's friend" should be someone in whom the prisoner will have confidence, by whom he will feel supported.' These are but two of nine guidelines which the judges stated 'are not absolute rules, but the consequences of their non-observance may be the exclusion of statements of persons questioned. They might also provide guidance in interrogating migrants.'

One new area of great assistance for Aborigines in court has been the Aboriginal Legal Aid Service. This service was set up in 1972 and is funded, and to some extent co-ordinated, by the Department of Aboriginal Affairs. An elected all-Aboriginal Council controls its activities. The Northern Territory service, as elsewhere, employs solicitors and Aboriginal field officers, who may act for Aborigines in criminal and civil cases if requested. Aborigines are also free to engage legal counsel of their own choice if they so desire.

Since August 1975 the police are required to notify the Aboriginal Legal Aid service of all Aborigines being charged and the nature of the charge. This has enabled Aborigines to have appropriate representation in court, if they do not make their own arrangements.

The appointment of Aboriginal Justices of the Peace is a further attempt to help Aborigines have fair trials. Two such Aboriginal JPs assist the magistrates in Arnhem Land. They advise them on aspects of Aboriginal customary law relevant to the cases.

Local courts are being held in Aboriginal communities in Arnhem Land. These are held, not only in the larger centres of Nhulunbuy and Alyangula, but in rooms and buildings at Maningrida, Elcho Island and Oenpelli. The first court held at Oenpelli took place under a tree. Soon magistrates will be hearing cases, at least initially, in each of the main Arnhem Land centres.

Over the years Aborigines have been frightened of the police and do not trust them. The injustices of the past are obvious reasons for this mistrust. Residential police who will be able to know the people and their culture will do much to break down these prejudices. The possibility of Aboriginal police and Aboriginal magistrates will remove much of the existing racial bias. In the long run, so much will depend on the character of the policemen, the conditions prevailing at the time in the communities and the communities' attitudes to law and order.

The Government, judiciary, legal aid and police together with interested organisations and people are co-operating to ensure that Aborigines will be treated justly and with due respect to their cultural background and heritage. The Australian Law Reform Commission will probably continue its deliberations on Aboriginal customary law over the years and make a number of recommendations. The future holds great promise when compared with the past.

Good law is a dynamic instrument for reform and social change for the Aborigines of Arnhem Land. Good law is a means whereby all people, Aborigines and non-Aborigines, are equal, instead of being subjects of discrimination, inadequate political policies and ineffective administration. In law Aborigines are able to achieve basic human rights and maintain the dignity which they once lost.

18
Health

The health of the Arnhem Land Aborigines prior to white settlement is very hard to ascertain. As far as can be determined they were free from serious communicable diseases with the exception of yaws. The Macassans probably brought malaria. They certainly introduced Aborigines to alcohol. The population remained at a fairly low level because of their nomadic existence, inter-tribal warfare, and limited infanticide and cannibalism. Their diet of bush foods, animals and fish was constant and fairly well-balanced. They were therefore probably in reasonable health.

Their health deteriorated drastically when they came into permanent contact with whites and Asiatics. They had no immunity against the foreign diseases which the newcomers brought, and quickly succumbed to leprosy, smallpox, influenza, whooping cough and venereal disease. Those living on the beach or in shacks in Palmerston (later called Darwin) became addicted to opium and alcohol. Within the short space of two decades almost all of the Aborigines of Darwin and western Arnhem Land were badly afflicted with disease and were in the gravest danger of dying out.

Aboriginal contact with the white settlemens at Fort Dundas (1824-29), Fort Wellington (1827-29) and Port Essington (1838-49) was of short duration. With the exception of a severe influenza epidemic their health remained reasonably good. The white inhabitants, who were unable to cope with the rigours of the tropical North, had the high sickness rate.

Aboriginal health commenced to decline rapidly after 1869 when the North was permanently settled at Palmerston. Disease followed hard on the wake of the new arrivals. The construction of the

Overland Telegraph Line between 1870 and 1872 brought a number of white workers to the Territory. For a decade after 1872 white and Chinese miners flocked to the Pine Creek goldfields. Between 1886 and 1889 three thousand Chinese were indentured to form labour gangs for the first stage of the proposed overland railway from Darwin to Adelaide. By 1888 it was estimated that 6750 Chinese were mining, market gardening and rice-growing in the Territory. The European population of the Territory in that year was less than 1000.

Palmerston and the goldfield quickly became notorious for their poor sanitation and primitive buildings. The 'Northern Territory Times' in 1873 said that 'Palmerston had become unbearably dirty. The smells are strong enough to knock anyone down. The sea breeze is like the pestilential smell from a boiling down factory ...' Leprosy was found there in 1884; malaria, dysentery and beriberi were common in 1885; typhoid broke out in 1886, and smallpox in 1887. The Chinese had brought leprosy and smallpox; the Europeans venereal and other diseases.

The Chinese also brought opium to the Territory. The opium trade was at first quite open and legal. The disastrous effect of opium-smoking by Aborigines, however, caused the South Australian Government to pass the Opium Act in 1895 forbidding the supply of opium to Aborigines. Despite this legislation Aborigines continued to be debilitated by opium for a number of years. In 1872 the South Australian Government also passed legislation forbidding the supply of alcohol to Aborigines. This law, also, was frequently abused.

The deleterious effects of opium and alcohol on Aborigines continued to be a major concern for the health authorities in Palmerston during the next decade. In 1904 Dr Fulton, the Government Medical Officer, deplored their evil effects, causing them to lose what little 'morale' still remained in them. As the result of his efforts the Opium Act of 1905 was passed, which totally prohibited the importation and sale of opium except for medical purposes for all inhabitants. The result was positive and immediate. Within a year the Government Resident was able to report that the 'passage of prohibitive opium laws ... has removed one of the worst dangers threatening the Aborigines'.

Most Aborigines in the Palmerston area were infected with venereal disease during these years. Europeans and Chinese procured Aboriginal women for prostitution, and the disease soon assumed epidemic proportions. In 1906 the Government Medical Officer urged the complete segregation of all Aboriginal women, but to no effect. In 1910 he reported that 'of over 100 female Aboriginals around settled districts examined by him, only one was found to be free from traces of venereal trouble'.

The prostitution of Aboriginal women by their own husbands as well as by other races and the general condition of Aborigines continued to be a scandal. In 1909 the Protector reported that 'men of all nationalities have free use of native women ... [they] lure these women from legitimate employment ...' He went on to say that this situation would continue unless some provision was made for their protection. This special legislation took the form of the Aboriginal Act of 1910, which, as has been noted, came too late. Irreparable damage had been done.

Those Aborigines who contracted leprosy and who were unable to return to their tribal areas were incarcerated in appalling conditions on the Mud Island Leper Station. The Government started this leper colony in 1885 with virtually no facilities. It took five years to provide simple bark huts for them. Living conditions were deplorable and little attempt was made to cure those who were diseased. The island was infested with mosquitoes, and the leprosy patients soon had to contend with fever and other illnesses. Some escaped to the mainland through the help of relatives and the Chinese. In 1906 the resident doctor said that the colony was 'unsuitable for any being of the human species'.

Leprosy quickly spread to Aborigines living in the Pine Creek and Alligator River areas, and quickly decimated the tribes living there. The 1901 Health and Aboriginals Report stated that only about sixty out of the 190 who had been in the Alligator Rivers area only seven years before had survived. Most of the deaths were caused by leprosy. The Report urged that leprosy 'should be taken in hand before the disease had spread to those tribes that live in proximity to our white centres of population'. Urgent action was needed because of the threat to the European, not the Aboriginal people! Leprosy was also prevalent among the Chinese.

Aborigines were discouraged as patients at the Palmerston Hospital which was opened in Packard Street on 19 June 1874. The hospital was situated on the cliff overlooking Doctor's Gully and the Chinese garden near Peel's Well. The first record of Aboriginal patients is dated 1886, when only two of the thirty-nine patients were Aborigines. The Chinese were cared for at the Chinese Hospital which was started in 1879. Even by 1909 only seventeen of the 176 admissions for the year had been Aborigines.

From the mid-1870s Government Medical Officers at Palmerston were also the Protectors of Aboriginals. They continued this dual role until 1908 when the responsibility for Aboriginal welfare was taken over by the police. This was a very unfortunate arrangement, as police were prosecutors of Aboriginal offenders as well as being their protectors. The health authority resumed the role of protector from 1927 until 1939 when Dr Cecil Cook was the Chief Medical Officer.

Before the turn of the century, however, the overworked government doctor at Palmerston had little time for his additional work as Protector, except handing out rations, a blanket a year, and caring as best he could for the sick and diseased. In 1900 the Government Resident was able to get the South Australian Government to care for over sixty half-caste children living between Palmerston and Katherine and needing care. The doctor urged that the Government should recognise them as whites rather than Aborigines, and to remove them from Aboriginal camps 'so that ultimately they may be useful members of society'.

Aboriginal health continued to deteriorate during the first decade of the 1900s. In 1902 the Medical Officer said that 'the Aborigines here are on their way gradually to extinction'. In 1907 the Government Resident reported, 'Year after year the decrease in the numbers of aborigines in the settled districts is observable ... In addition to disease ... which is one of the causes for decrease, this result is further contributed to by the fact of so many lubras permanently leaving their camps and living openly with men of nationalities other than their own.' There was also a high incidence of sickness among Aboriginal prisoners at Fannie Bay Gaol.

Commonwealth control of the Territory from 1911 commenced the beginning of a new phase in Government attempt to care for Aborigines. Dr Herbert Basedow was appointed Chief Medical Inspector and Chief Protector of Aborigines. He had two doctors as his assistants. Dr Basedow resigned after a few months' service, and was followed by Professor Baldwin Spencer in January 1912.

Professor Baldwin Spencer immediately embarked upon a policy of protection and training of Aborigines. After his year's term he was followed by Stretton, who continued his policies. Stretton arranged for the proclamation of small reserves in the remote areas, and the Kahlin Reserve to accommodate the Aborigines in Darwin. The latter were housed in bark huts, but the compound quickly deteriorated into a third-class shanty village.

Despite these attempts, Aboriginal health in the towns and on the remote areas still continued to decline. The health survey of Aborigines of the Territory by Dr Breinl of Townsville emphasised prevalent severe morbidity and mortality resulting from introduced diseases. The 1913 Government Medical Officer's report stated,

'Where Aborigines have come into contact with whites and Asiatics certain diseases have been introduced, notably venereal disease and tuberculosis, and these have taken heavy toll. No traces of these diseases can be seen among secluded and uncivilized blacks.'

High incidence of venereal disease continued during the Commonwealth era. In 1915 health authorities estimated that thirty per cent of the men at the Pine Creek railway construction camp had some form of venereal disease. There was also a high incidence of the disease at the Kahlin Compound in Darwin, and among the Chinese and Europeans. The problem took on such grave proportions that in 1917 the Administrator proclaimed that Darwin, except the compound, was a prohibited area for Aborigines.

Leprosy continued to spread. Up to 1915 this disease was confined to the area bounded by the Alligator Rivers, Oenpelli and Croker Island. After that date the whole of Arnhem Land became an endemic area, and many Aborigines contracted the disease.

Many Chinese and Aborigines also suffered from tuberculosis. In 1913 at least thirty per cent of Chinese died from this complaint. By the 1930s, however, tuberculosis had declined among them. This was not the case with Aborigines. Cattle brought from Queensland to Oenpelli in 1914 and 1915 caused the disease to spread throughout Arnhem Land. These cattle were a potential source of infection for a number of years, largely because Aborigines usually ate the infected meat half-cooked. It was not until the Tuberculosis Act of 1945 that effective control was established. But once again the damage had been done. Many Aborigines died or suffered permanently from this disease.

Hookworm, originating from Asia, also became widespread at the Kahlin Compound and on the missions as they became established in Arnhem Land. This disease rapidly increased as Aborigines changed from their nomadic to a settled way of life. Despite a nationwide Australian Hookworm Campaign, hookworm infestation continued unabated in Arnhem Land for a number of years. Dysentery and enteritis were also commonplace.

Medical services for Aborigines greatly improved during the twelve years' energetic service of Dr Cecil E.A. Cook. He was Chief Medical Officer and Protector of Aborigines from Feburary 1927 until April 1939. His task was not made any easier by the world-wide economic depression of the early 1930s. Dr Cook had conducted an investigation into the epidemiology of leprosy in the North between 1923 and 1925. His interest in the Top End through this study eventually led to this Darwin appointment several years later.

Dr Cook was the moving force behind the formation of the North

Australia Medical Service in 1928. This was renamed the Northern Territory Medical Service (NTMS) in 1931. He tried to make the NTMS a model medical service for remote Australia. At the same time as Protector of Aboriginals he worked hard for the betterment of the Aboriginal people. He was also outspoken against Communism and a fierce defender of the White Australia policy. He greatly feared that the social and economic background of Aborigines would make them an easy prey to overtures by Communist agitators.

Dr Cook endeavoured to control Aboriginal employment and migration and to arrange for routine medical inspection and treatment. He undertook a vigorous campaign for the improvement of hygiene on missions and employment camps. He opposed any segregation of the medical services, and maintained that Aborigines should share the same staff and facilities as the rest of the population. Aborigines were treated differently only as practical necessity demanded. They were given treatment at the clinic at the Kahlin Compound, but taken to the Darwin Hospital when major surgery was involved. He insisted that the first priority for the Northern Territory Aerial Medical Service was for preventive medicine rather than just medical evacuations.

In March 1934 Dr Clyde Fenton was appointed medical officer at Katherine. He raised money to buy an aeroplane and the NT Aerial Medical Service came into being. This form of service had been pioneered by the Presbyterian Australian Inland Mission through the inspiration of the Reverend John Flynn. Dr Fenton was able to make regular inspections of remote missions, and undertake a routine weekly visit to the small hospital at Pine Creek, as well as evacuate the very sick to Darwin. In six years he logged 3000 hours flying time and travelled over half a million kilometres. The service relied on Traeger's pedal radio transceivers and the Overland Telegraph Line for its communications.

Dr Cook was instrumental in having the 1928 Northern Territory Leprosy Ordinance passed. He was able to enforce the isolation of any person suffering from leprosy. He immediately closed the iniquitous Mud Island Leper Colony. Leprosy patients were isolated at the Darwin Hospital or on missions until the new Leprosarium at Channel Island was opened in 1931. The buildings of the former quarantine station were upgraded and extended for this purpose. From that time onwards until the outbreak of war in 1939 the number of lepers resident at Channel Island remained constant at about sixty. During this time ten Europeans also were admitted to the Leprosarium.

The Administrator, Hon. F. Chaney, presenting Roy Marika with M.B.E.

TOP LEFT: Rachel Malangura, Oenpelli, 1978. TOP RIGHT: Djawa, Milingimbi, 1978.
BOTTOM LEFT: Phillip Roberts of Roper River, the subject of the book *I, the Aboriginal*
by Douglas Lockwood. BOTTOM RIGHT: Gula, a tribal elder on Groote Eylandt

In 1933 the training of half-caste girls as nursing assistants at Aboriginal hospitals was commenced at the Darwin Hospital. The girls were given the same training as their European counterparts, but could not sit for the nurses' registration examinations because they lacked the necessary preliminary educational qualifications. In 1933 the first dispenser-dresser at the hospital was appointed. He was Xavier Herbert, the author of the well-known book, *Capricornia*. He also became manager/superintendent of the Kahlin Compound which provided such realistic material for the tragic characters of his book.

Work on the construction of the ninety-eight-bed Darwin Hospital was started in 1939 after several unnecessary and costly delays. The new hospital was built on the site of the Kahlin Aboriginal Compound at Myilly Point. This compound was transferred to Bagot in 1938 to make way for the new hospital. Prior to this Dr Cook had converted some disused government stables at Myilly Point for use as an Aboriginal clinic. Here regular inspections for venereal disease, tuberculosis, leprosy and hookworm were undertaken. This clinic was transferred to Bagot along with the compound.

Dr Cook tried to assimilate Aborigines into the white community. He said that his ultimate aim was 'the conversion of the detribalized Aboriginal in town districts from a social incubus to a civil unit of economic value, and in the country districts from an unproductive nomad to a self-supporting peasant'. To this end he tried to provide Aborigines with opportunities for education and training, and improve their health and social status. He introduced legislation for their control, segregation and protection. He prevented them entering Darwin's China Town or visiting areas infected with communicable diseases. He acquired the Bagot Reserve in 1936 in order to enable detribalised Aborigines to have facilities for a planned community and to help in their assimilation into European society. His attempts to make Bagot into a model town were frustrated when the Army took over the compound shortly after the transfer from Kahlin in 1938.

Dr Cook also tried to assimilate part Aborigines into white society. In the 1930s he removed them from Aboriginal camps and reserves. He placed the girls in selected European homes for domestic training and gave the boys technical training. He encouraged them to marry among themselves or to approved white people. He built and furnished homes for them under a self-aid housing scheme.

In 1939 a Native Affairs Branch was created and the administration of Aboriginal welfare reorganised. The office of Protector of

Aboriginals was separated from that of the Chief Medical Officer. At the same time the Commonwealth Department of Health took over the responsibility of health services in the Northern Territory. As his powers as Protector of Aboriginals had been taken from him Dr Cook resigned.

During the War years the Army controlled the Darwin Hospital and all Territory medical services. From December 1940 they took over the Bagot Reserve where they established the 19th Australian General Hospital. Aborigines from Bagot were either repatriated to the reserves or transferred to Berrimah. The NT Aerial Medical Service also ceased functioning during the War. The RAAF and Army were able to maintain supplies and give medical assistance to the Arnhem Land missions.

Leprosy control broke down completely during the War. With the imminent invasion of Darwin by the Japanese in 1942, the Channel Island Leprosarium was closed. The Aboriginal patients were left to fend for themselves. They crossed to the mainland at low tide, and most of them made their way back to their tribal areas. Here they were allowed to mix freely with their relatives and soon a number of these became infected. Leprosy once again assumed epidemic proportions in the Arnhem Land communities.

In June 1951 the Deputy Director of Health in Darwin reported 201 full-blood and thirty-four mixed blood leprosy patients in institutions or at missions in the Territory. Others had been hidden by relatives to avoid being sent into permanent exile at a leprosarium. Surveys started in 1952 showed that the total number of cases in the Northern Territory exceeded 400, an average of 56 per 1000 persons, which was one of the highest incidences of the disease in the world. At the same time the number of Europeans in the Territory tracing infection with leprosy to exposure to Aborigines or part-Aborigines was about twenty. Fortunately those infected with leprosy usually responded well to sulphetrone therapy, reducing quite dramatically the numbers of infective cases needed to be isolated.

The separation of health services and Aboriginal welfare between 1939 and 1954 did not appear to work very well in practice. A serious lack of co-ordination between the Native Affairs Branch and the Department of Health was evident. Each blamed the other for its shortcomings. The Health Department said that Aboriginal health could not improve until living conditions were made better. The Native Affairs Branch often ignored the professional advice given to it.

The provision of health services for Aborigines during the welfare era was divided between the Department of Health and the Welfare Branch. The Health Department was responsible for the hospitals in Darwin (Bagot from 1957) and elsewhere outside the reserves, together with laboratory services, the East Arm Leprosarium, the aerial medical service, school medical services, dental services, quarantine, and health surveys and inspections. The Welfare Branch was responsible for general health care, infant welfare hospitals and dispensaries, nursing staff, hospital assistants, hygiene, housing and water reticulation at missions and settlements in the reserves.

Health, hygiene and housing were major areas of concern for the Welfare Branch, committed as it was to a policy of assimilation. Aboriginal health had to reach acceptable standards to enable Aborigines to mix freely with non-Aborigines throughout Australia. Adequate housing was a necessary adjunct to good health and also for training in social standards acceptable by all races.

Health services for Aborigines provided by both Government departments expanded greatly from 1954 until 1972. Hospitals were upgraded or rebuilt, nursing sisters provided, hospital assistants trained, hygiene standards raised, and a determined effort made to provide more houses. The water supply in most cases was improved and water-borne sanitation provided in some communities. Numerous surveys were undertaken by the Health Department including those for hookworm, tuberculosis, leprosy and other diseases.

Daily outpatient attendance of Aborigines at the local clinic or hospital in each of the Arnhem Land communities has always been very high, usually about six per hundred. This is a daily average. The Sisters and their Aboriginal assistants attend to cuts, bruises, aches, pains and minor illnesses. Major illnesses are hospitalised, and if necessary patients are evacuated by plane to Darwin or Gove. Ante-natal and post-natal clinics are held, and uncomplicated deliveries undertaken. When Sisters have problems of diagnosis and treatment they often frequently seek the doctor's advice by radio 'sked'. Since the early 1970s Aborigines of Arnhem Land have had access to medical services in their communities and Darwin, equal to and sometimes better than any other community in the Top End.

From about 1955 to 1965 most Arnhem Land communities had a form of communal feeding. This was started in order to give everyone a balanced diet. Finance for food and staff came mainly from child endowment and pension moneys. While the scheme had its merits, it was seen by many to be too paternalistic. Those entitled to government moneys were entitled to receive the money. Improved dietary standards should come through the educational programs and the normal growth in living standards, rather than controlled feeding. As a result the scheme was abandoned.

An example of health services provided for Arnhem Land Aborigines comes from the 1970-71 Annual Report of the Welfare Division. The place was Oenpelli. 'A programme of Community Health Education was carried out giving instruction in simple first aid, health and hygiene principles, mother and child welfare and nutrition. Elementary training of junior hospital staff was also carried out in the hospital. Considerable time has been devoted to Occupational Therapy with those efforts mainly directed towards people handicapped with leprosy deformities. A chest X-ray survey was carried out, and a six-monthly mass-treatment for hookworm. All normal immunisations and vaccinations were carried out. Number of births 28; deaths 9; inpatients 436; outpatients 10 250; leprosy and physiotherapy clinics 4800; child welfare clinics 1800; school children clinics 3500.' The population of Oenpelli at the time was only 269 adults and 237 children, making a total of 506.

The provision of housing for every Aboriginal family in the Arnhem Land communities has been the aim of the Government and missions since the early 1950s. Only very limited Aboriginal housing was available before that time. Experiments with different styles and forms of construction have been undertaken in various places. The number of houses built has depended on mission or Government finance available. In the earlier days houses were built by Aborigines under mission or government supervision as part of the training program. Since the early 1970s, the construction of houses has usually been undertaken by Housing Associations or under contract with outside firms.

Opinion varies considerably among Aborigines and their European advisers regarding the most suitable types of housing. Aborigines generally do not use their houses in the same way as non-Aborigines. They normally prefer to cook, eat and (in the Dry) sleep out-of-doors. The house then becomes the place to store things and to sleep on cold or wet nights.

Some Aborigines have said that they prefer a European-type house, possibly because they do not wish to have a different or inferior house to European staff. Others just built their corrugated iron humpy on the sand dunes or on the beach. Most seem to prefer ground-level houses, of strong construction, with plenty of ventilation. Experiments have been made at Oenpelli and elsewhere with concrete style houses with a large, covered sand area for cooking and general living. Whatever the style, housing normally is made strong and durable, as wear and tear is often great.

During the past twenty years a greater number of Aborigines have been housed and they are looking after their homes much better. This is the result of teaching and living in schools and colleges. A number have stayed in transit in houses and hotels throughout Australia and in different countries in the world. They are now becoming accustomed to this life-style, and are trying to adapt it to their home situations. Better housing, a greater care of the houses, inside running water and water-borne sanitation, the use of washing machines, and education in hygiene are all making for better living and health standards within these communities. Much, however, still remains to be done.

On 1 January 1973 the Northern Territory Medical Service, a division of the Commonwealth Department of Health, assumed responsibility for all health services to Aborigines in Arnhem Land and throughout the Northern Territory. This included the provision of care for the Arnhem Land homeland centres. The emphasis was now on training in preventive health rather than on the clinical activities of the past.

By 1976, however, despite past efforts and achievements since the 1950s, Aboriginal health left much to be desired. In the introduction to the 1975-76 Annual Report of its Northern Territory Division, the Department of Health stated, 'The standard of health as measured by the usual parameters continues to improve, but these standards among the Aboriginal section of the community continue to lag far behind those of the rest of the community. This is largely due to the appalling environmental conditions under which Aboriginals live, so that progress in health standards will be slow until such times as Aboriginals are reasonably housed and provided with individual water supplies and safe sanitation. Equally important is to provide them with employment opportunities and to encourage and to assist their own initiatives, hopefully to break the vicious cycle of boredom leading to alcoholism and despair.'

The Report later stated, 'The living conditions of Aboriginals in the Northern Territory leave much to be desired. Environmental conditions are particularly poor. Many people still live in tin shanties or humpies without reticulated water supplies or satisfactory sanitation, and infants are brought up in appalling conditions which are reflected in their levels of morbidity and mortality ... Fortunately there are signs that education and social conditions are improving and we can expect better health standards to accompany this renaissance of the Aboriginal people.'

The Report stated also that 'special mention should be made of the Aboriginal infant mortality rate which is often misquoted and

233

frequently described in such superlatives as the highest in the world. The rate this decade has decreased significantly in all three regions and again fell during the calendar year 1975 to an average for the Territory of 50·1/1000 live births which, although far from creditable, is well within the medium range for such rates in world tables.' The fall in Aboriginal infant mortality is reflected in the following figures which show 142·7 per 1000 in 1965 and 50·1 per 1000 in 1975. The Australian average in 1974 was 16·1 per 1000 live births.

The number of Aboriginal births continue at a high level. In 1972 there were 874 or 36·84 per 1000 in the Territory, and in 1975, 899 or 35·72 per 1000. This rate is high when compared with the 1974 Australian average of 18·33 per 1000.

Of the 899 Aboriginal births in 1975, about 500 were delivered in hospital and about 275 took place at rural health centres. Half of the remainder were attended by trained staff. As the 1975-76 Report stated, 'Up until recently the trend has been for more and more Aboriginal women to elect to deliver their babies in hospital. There is some indication that this trend is being reversed. Although most of the women who do not deliver in hospital are attended by trained staff in health centres, there is a growing number returning to outstations for delivery. The Aboriginal health training programme is giving some attention to this problem.'

At the present time, while tuberculosis and leprosy are declining, rheumatic fever, meningitis, typhoid fever, and venereal disease among Arnhem Land Aborigines are still a cause for concern. Typhoid fever has been endemic in the Northern Territory for many years. Over the past decade there have been outbreaks at Oenpelli and Elcho Island. The Department of Health continues to encourage all people living in coastal communities in the Top End to maintain up-to-date immunisation.

The incidence of venereal disease is increasing among all races in the Territory. Gonorrhoea notifications by Aborigines rose from 87 in 1971 to 124 in 1975. Non-Aboriginal notifications in the same period rose from 5·2 per 1000 to 5·8 per 1000. Syphilis notifications for Aborigines rose from 2 in 1971 to 346, or 13·8 per 1000, in 1975. Non-Aboriginal notifications rose from 0.3 per 1000 to 1.5 per 1000 in the same period.

While the incidence of leprosy has declined in the Territory the East Arm Hospital and the Repatriation Artificial Limb and Appliance Centre continue their programs for rehabilitation and support. Also, even though the number suffering from tuberculosis is falling due to the BCG vaccination program, the disease is still

234

endemic in the Territory, and its incidence greatest among Aboriginal people.

Generally speaking younger Aboriginal people have very bad teeth. This is largely due to the change in diet from bush foods to refined foods such as sugar, biscuits and flour. General dental services are available in Darwin and Gove, although these are sometimes restricted because of staff shortages. Peridontal surveys have been undertaken in some of the Arnhem Land Aboriginal communities.

The NT Aerial Medical Services continue their fine work in emergency ambulance support and the performance of routine medical visits to Aboriginal communities. In the 1975-76 year throughout the Territory there were 654 routine flights, 330 emergency flights, 67 inter-hospital transfers. The service flew almost 800 000 kilometres in 3672 flying hours, made 3182 landings, carried 2724 patients and made 3715 radio medical consultations. The greater proportion of this service was devoted to Aboriginal health and care.

During the past few years the Department of Health in the Northern Territory has initiated promising programs for training Aboriginal health workers. The main task of these health workers is to motivate their own people to observe and to maintain better health standards in their own communities. The pilot scheme took the form of a Basic Skills Health Course held at Hooker Creek. By September 1977, 152 had been trained at forty centres.

Dr F.S. Soong, the Health Education Specialist in Darwin, is the co-ordinator of this new venture. In health education programs he favours adopting a 'human and community development model' rather than the authoritarian approach in giving information and orders. Aborigines are now involved in solving problems in partnership with health staff, instead of being told what to do. This usually involves the whole community instead of a series of individuals. An informal, non-directive approach to learning involving community discussion and decision is adopted.

After several years' experimentation, Dr Soong said that there were some basic principles which he and his health team had learned in the Health Worker training program. He said, 'The only people who can solve the Aboriginals problems, including health problems, are the Aboriginals themselves'. In doing this 'efforts need to be directed towards strengthening Aboriginal leadership. Through the training and employment of Aboriginal people, executive responsibility for education, health and welfare work in Aboriginal communities can be transferred from European workers. Non-

Aboriginal people who work in Aboriginal communities should regard themselves as resource people and not decision makers for Aboriginal people. By regarding ourselves as resource people, we are acting as friends, guests or servants to the Aboriginal communities.'

Dr Soong then said, 'As we see it, the role of the educator is to raise the level of health knowledge of the people so that they can make their own decisions about the practices that are meaningful to them. As a priority, ways have to be found so that certain basic health behaviour (such as use of the toilet, washing of hands before eating food, cleaning the eyes and seeking treatment for certain medical conditions) can be facilitated and practised by most people.

'We should ensure that certain options remain open. The result may be a synthesis of Aboriginal and European ways or adoption or rejection of European ways ... The concepts of synthesis, adoption and rejection are dynamic rather than static ...'

The possibility of linking Aboriginal and European medicine is also being discussed at the present time. Forty years of Western medicine has not resulted in the disappearance of the traditional Aboriginal medical practitioners. A number of Aborigines still consult them, often after going to the dispensary.

Dr H. Eastwell, formerly Senior Specialist in Psychiatry to the Northern Territory Medical Service has outlined two ways of involving the tribal practitioner in health care. The emphasis on the first method is modifying the traditional healer's practice. 'It envisages paying him as a health worker, utilizing his talents in the domiciliary situation and giving him a base in the bush hospital. It conceives of a close working relationship between the nurse and the tribal healer who acts as an intermediary between herself and the community.'

The emphasis of the second scheme 'is on *rapprochment* between Western health personnel and their Aboriginal counterparts. Coexistence of the systems is accepted but the utilization of the tribal healer in the general health programme is restricted ...' Dr Eastwell concludes, 'If the two systems cooperate rather than conflict, the limitations of both can be minimized. The limitations of Aboriginal medicine lie in the technical sphere, while it is strong in the social and psychological aspects of medicine ... The limitations of Western medicine lie in its insensitivity to the patient in his social role ... If a *rapprochment* can be made between the two systems, individual Aboriginals will have the benefit of both ...'

Despite past difficulties and present deficiencies Aboriginal health has improved dramatically in the past sixty years. Aboriginal people are no longer dying out as the result of imported diseases. They are increasing fairly rapidly. The delivery of health care for Arnhem Land Aborigines is as good as, or even better than, that of any other community in the Territory. Basic environmental problems such as insufficiency of housing, water and sanitation remain. Personal hygiene, balanced diet, and general health care are often lacking among individuals and groups.

Lack of sufficient housing, water reticulation and adequate sanitation may be the result of inadequate Government funding. They may also be the result of the expressed wish of Arnhem Land Aborigines to return to a different style of life, especially in the homeland centres. Aboriginal health standards may also be the result of their own self-determined way of life.

One thing is clear. Aboriginal health programs in the foreseeable future must emphasise prevention rather than cure. Facilities for curative medicine are now readily available. Aboriginal people themselves must through their own efforts as well as those of the nurses, educators and their own leaders, find ways of healthy living within their own self-determining life-styles. They must learn to care adequately for themselves to supplement what sometimes has been very inadequate caring of them by others.

19
'We are killing ourselves with grog'

Darwin has the reputation of having the highest consumption of alcohol in the world. The city certainly spends more on grog per head of population than anywhere else in Australia. The figures in 1973 were $133 per person throughout Australia, and $198 per person for Darwin. The 1973 figure of $198 would be much higher now.

There are various reasons for the high consumption of alcohol in this home of the beer can regatta. They range from the heat and humidity of the capital, the traditional Territory 'way of life', the free and easy life-style of the people, the imbalance of males to females in the population, the lack of alternative recreational opportunities, and the social tensions resulting from *de facto* relationships in an isolated, artificial environment.

The consumption of alcohol by Aborigines in Darwin and in many Arnhem Land communities is very high. Aboriginal alcoholism has reached epidemic proportions. Alcohol abuse has become the greatest threat to Aborigines throughout the Territory, and unless a change comes about they could destroy themselves. They themselves say, 'We are killing ourselves with grog'.

Aboriginal offenders comprise the greater proportion of convictions arising from drunkenness in Darwin and Territory towns. The numbers are increasing as police stations are being established in or near Aboriginal communities. Unofficial statistics provided by the Department of Aboriginal Affairs to the 1973 Liquor Inquiry (Adams Report) have shown that 'the majority of offences in the Northern Territory, such as being drunk and disorderly, are committed by Aboriginal Australians and that drinking offences per head of the Aboriginal population are much higher than the corresponding ratio for the rest of the population'.

Some people have suggested that more Aborigines appear to be drunkards because they are more conspicuous than others, or remain drunk in public places whereas non-Aborigines are more discreet. Others say that the police persecute Aborigines and arrest them in circumstances in which they would not arrest non-Aborigines. This may be so in some cases. But nowadays every Aboriginal offender is defended in court by the Aboriginal Legal Aid Service, and it is hard to imagine that allegations of police persecution would not immediately be investigated by the defending lawyers. The unfortunate fact is that even though drunkenness has been decriminalised, statistics show that a large number of Aboriginal people are convicted for offences arising from alcohol abuse. They have a problem of the gravest magnitude.

Disturbances caused by excessive drinking in Arnhem Land communities have been frightening. Aborigines living at Oenpelli, Yirrkala, Angurugu and Ngukurr (Roper River), which are situated close to liquor stores just over the border or at mining towns, have suffered very bady. The worst place has been Oenpelli where several hundred drunk men and women have sometimes been on rampage. Aborigines living at Maningrida and Umbakumba, which have 'wet' canteens, have had their difficult times. So also have the former mission 'dry' communities where Aborigines have chartered aircraft and brought in large quantities of alcohol, often against the express wish and direction of the Aboriginal Town Council.

The devastating effect of widespread drunkenness in the communities was graphically described in the Adams Report. 'It was not uncommon for people to be injured in drunken brawls, and even murders had been committed by men inflamed with liquor. Often people were terrorised and women and children, fearing for their safety, sought refuge with neighbours or the white staff or fled to the bush for the week.' I well recall on one occasion speaking with a group of Aboriginal people in one of the communities, when the drone of an aircraft was heard crossing the airstrip before landing. 'Charter', cried several of the women. They ran off, quickly grabbed some of their children and cleared out into the bush. They knew only too well what was going to happen, when the grog arrived and the men got drunk.

The Adams Report also stated, 'In some places the police had been confronted and menaced by drunken Aborigines and serious situations had resulted. At one place a party of Aborigines had broken into licensed premises and stolen a large quantity of spirits, after which they rioted in their own village and so menaced the white staff that they left the village. The white teachers subsequently refused to return and the school had to be closed.'

In 1973 and 1974 the Chaplain at Umbakumba frequently drew the attention of the public, Church bodies, Government departments and the police to the traumatic effects that drinking was having at that small Government settlement on Groote Eylandt. He said, 'It is my opinion that unless strong measures are taken to control drink at Umbakumba, then despite every well intentioned effort by the government aided by the provision of very large government spending and that of Groote Eylandt Mining Trust funds, then all this effort may be written off as futile. The Aboriginal population together with any supporting funds, will gradually disappear amid scenes of miserable degredation and squalor.'

The Adams Report indicated that drinkers are usually in the minority and that on a settlement of say 900 people thirty of the men were regular drinkers, another seventy men drank occasionally, and the rest hardly or never touch alcohol. Usually it was found that of every thirty drinkers, only about ten formed the hard core of 'binge' drinkers or 'problem' drinkers who cause most of the trouble. This statement would not have been accurate for a number of the other Arnhem Land communities in 1973. By 1977 the situation had become much worse. At the same time there are encouraging signs that some have won their way through drinking, having realised that they were 'killing themselves with grog'.

Excessive alcoholism in Arnhem Land Aboriginal communities has caused the breakdown of traditional Aboriginal society; fighting and brawling, frequently resulting in severe physical injuries; wife beating, rape, promiscuity and prostitution and the destruction of houses; and serious problems for children's education, health and welfare. A number of cases of hunger, poverty and malnutrition in women and children have been the direct result of the family's economic resources being used to buy liquor.

The 1976 Interim Report of the House of Representatives Standing Committee on Aboriginal Affairs on 'Alcohol problems of Aborigines' stated that, 'Information given to the Committee suggests that the population could be declining in those Aboriginal communities which have serious alcohol problems. In Snake Bay the number of deaths in 1975 and the first half of 1976 was approximately twice the number of births. In addition, the situation at Oenpelli in 1976 appears to have deteriorated since 1975 with the number of births and deaths being equal as at 30 June 1976. The

240

Committee was also informed that at Snake Bay, Garden Point and Oenpelli the number of women pregnant at present is well below normal.' This contrasts significantly with the rising Aboriginal birthrate outlined in the last chapter.

There is a high incidence of petrol sniffing among young Aborigines in Arnhem Land communities, especially at Elcho Island, Croker Island, Maningrida, Milingimbi and Yirrkala. The children are usually between ten and fifteen years old, although in some cases the ages range from five to twenty-five years. The greater majority are boys, although girls sometimes engage in the practice.

Mild petrol sniffing causes disorientation and hallucination. When taken in large amounts the respiratory system becomes depressed and sudden death may occur. The hydrocarbons in the petrol are toxic to the brain, liver, kidneys, adrenals and peripheral nerves. Lead poisoning or deafness may occur.

When young Aborigines are 'high' on petrol they often commit senseless acts of vandalism. Sometimes they have interfered with graves, for the cemetery is a frequent meeting place. They frequently break into shops and steal or go for rides in stolen vehicles.

Participants are mostly those who do not do well at school, even though they may be very intelligent. They are frequently haphazard in attendance and attention. They normally do not eat for long periods, are sleepy and withdrawn in class and around the camp.

Different theories have been suggested regarding causes for petrol sniffing. There may be some connection with tobacco use, which is widespread among Aborigines. Young people may feel socially excluded and frustrated, especially when they see older people monopolising alcohol and women. Adolescents may feel lost between the two cultures, have nothing to do and nowhere to go. Instead of drowning their sorrows in drink they get high on petrol. Whatever the causes, solutions can be found by providing the necessary motivation and meaningful employment.

Aboriginal alcoholism in Darwin is a very great problem. In 1976 and 1977 Dr Basil Sansom spent fifteen months studying the social life of city fringe dwellers. Dr Sansom wrote, 'The people of the Darwin fringe camp in which I have just passed some fifteen months are apt fortnightly to announce that: "Here we all live longa grog." And indeed they do. The camp is a place where drinking is an everyday and, on some days and for some people, an all day activity. The consequence is that the allocation of grog, the management of drinking, and the control of the drinkers are made the everyday concerns of every person.'

Dr Sansom pointed out that the Aborigines there have sustained a 'patterned, rule-governed and, therefore, socially acceptable form of behaviour'; otherwise the camp would be what 'its Darwin critics already hold it to be — a place of orgiastic anarchy'. This fringe community is an interesting and important example of Aboriginal self-determination for the purpose for which it has been established. Itinerants from all over the Territory have their own informal Darwin hotel where they can 'sit down longa plagen [flagon]'.

The full-time residents of the fringe camp call all non-drinkers, whether they be black or white, male or female, 'missionaries'. All such people have no place in the camp. The use of the word indicates the complete rejection of the 'externally imposed ideologies and instruments of social control' by missions and settlements. They can now do what they want, go where they wish and have as many cans each day as they feel like, in contrast to the unwarranted control in all areas of their life which had been placed upon them for so long. 'We got no missionary here,' they say.

They also say that since citizenship 'things have been different', and tap their beer cans. In 1964 the Government lifted its restriction on Aborigines' drinking. For the people of this camp, they now have their 'citizenship'! They can sit down without interference, they do not have to work, and they can drink as they wish.

There are two types of residents at the fringe settlement. The first are the permanents, who consider that Darwin is their home. They live with their families, and have responsibilities towards the visitors. They are the ceremony men of the camp. The second group are the visitors, who, as Dr Sansom says, have 'come to town to "hit the piss"'. These stay 'on the piss' for as long as funds will allow.

The visitor is expected to drink convivially and to share around the drink he buys. 'A visitor with $400 can easily spend this sum before a week is out, but he might be able to stretch his $400 to last a fortnight. For the time that the visitor is "on the piss", he (or she) will be roaringly sometimes aggressively, and more often helplessly drunk. When his monied phase of heavy drinking is over, the visitor tends to stay on to share in the drinking bouts financed by others. Many visitors leave only when they have wholly exhausted their credit and taxed the tolerance of the locals to the limit. Often, at this point, they are sent home, that is, forcibly ejected.'

Dr Sansom's insights into the functioning of this community highlight one major reason for Aboriginal alcohol abuse at the present time. Aborigines are reacting vocally and visibly against the controls under which they had to live for many years. They were unable to move without permission, they were not allowed to drink alcohol, they were not permitted to practice polygamy, and their lives were dictated to in such a way, that all authorities are now termed 'missionary'. They now feel that they are experiencing the new freedom of 'citizenship'.

Dr Sansom gives some statistics to show that Aborigines drank in the prohibition days before 1964. He wrote, 'In 1939, 313 Aboriginal offenders before the Darwin courts, were prosecuted for infringement of restrictive grogging laws. Later in 1959 in the district of Leichhardt which includes Darwin, the figure was 216 and liquor charges accounted for 89% of all offences ... Buying drink and then consuming it unsecretly are the two everyday things that the legislation of the 60's released Aborigines novelly to do.'

A second major reason for excessive Aboriginal alcoholism at the present time comes from intolerable pressures which many Aborigines are experiencing living in a cross-cultural situation. They feel that their traditional culture is under grave threat. Some think that it cannot survive the onslaught of the Western, technological, consumer society. They see no future for themselves. They have no hope, the tensions are too great. So they get drunk. This feeling has been expressed so clearly by an old American Indian Chief, seeing the same thing happening with his own people. 'I was born in the age that loved the things of nature. And then ... like a crushing, rushing wave they came, hurling the years aside and suddenly I found myself a young man in the midst of the twentieth century. I found myself and my people adrift in the new ocean but not part of it ... I knew my people when they lived the old style ... when there was still a dignity in their outlook ... Do you know what it is to feel that you are of no value to society and those around you ... know that you are belittled ... a burden to the country? ... Do you know what it's like getting drunk and for a few moments escaping from ugly reality and feeling a sense of importance. It is worst of all waking up to the guilt of it all next morning, for the alcohol did not kill the emptiness, but only dug it deeper.'

These thoughts are expressed formally in the Adams Report: 'Aboriginals may have a deeply ingrained feeling of not being wanted in their own country and feeling a race apart in that they may be socially, mentally and physically confined to Reserve or relegated to the outskirts of towns. Some Aboriginals may see alcohol as a way of being accepted by both whites and their own people and as a means of overcoming fear arising from racial tension. Excessive drinking may be due to aimlessness on the part of Aboriginals and a desire to forget depressing circumstances and low social status.'

There are other reasons why Aborigines drink to excess. They sometimes want to copy the white men of the early days of Territory settlement, who often spent their savings in a pub having a 'binge'. Then the pub or club or swill under a tree are social centres of importance where they are uninhibited. The Darwin fringe community is a clear example of this.

Most Aboriginal drinkers drink to get drunk. There is widespread agreement amongst Aboriginal people that it is extremely difficult to be a 'social drinker' without being a drunkard. One reason for this may be the fact that in traditional times families continued to eat an animal before it went bad in the tropical heat. In the same way Aborigines follow their normal eating habits by continuing to drink while grog is available. The Adams Report stated that the 'tradition of eating and drinking while you have it and everybody share no doubt worked well in the traditional way of life but it has proved itself far from a good system when dealing with alcoholic liquor. To drink everything in sight while it is there and the money lasts, and to obligate relations to do likewise is not the best way to handle liquor. Events have shown that the results have been disastrous to the Aboriginal people.'

The Adams Report also drew attention to the fact that Aborigines had no knowledge of alcohol until the Macassans arrived two hundred years earlier. 'It is not surprising therefore to find that the Aboriginal people, after less than two hundred years experience of exposure to alcohol, have greater difficulty in handling alcoholic liquor.'

Suggestions have also been made that certain genetic characteristics in their physical structure make Aborigines more susceptible to alcohol. There is no medical evidence to support this view.

The payment of award wages, increased employment opportunities, improved social security payments such as unemployment benefits and child endowment now provide Aborigines with large sums of money. They all now have surprisingly large amounts, and this money frequently is used in gambling or spent on drink. Some people suggest that Aborigines are new to money and do not know how to handle it. This is not so, at least amongst most Arnhem Land Aborigines. They know what money is, how to use it, and what they want to do with it. Their priorities may not be those of the average non-Aboriginal urban dweller.

Another important cause of Aboriginal alcoholism concerns their attitude to law. In traditional times the ancient Aboriginal Law forbade anything which attacked the Law to destroy it. The Law had nothing to say about alcohol, or who should drink it, when, how, where and how much should be drunk. There is no Law, so people don't know what to do. Moreover, drunkenness destroys the Law in the drinker's brain. In the past strong action was taken to prevent and punish those who attacked the Law in the sacred dilly bag. Communities and individuals need to see that alcohol is attacking the Law in people's brains.

There are also reasons for alcoholism such as drinking to stop a bad feeling, to forget, to 'drown one's sorrows' to appease feelings of guilt, to show off, to hide a sense of inferiority. Doubtless there are many others. The final result is the tragedy that fine Aboriginal men and women in Arnhem Land are becoming addicted or 'hooked' and are killing themselves with grog. In the process they are causing untold sorrow and injury to others and to their children.

Summarising their deliberations, the 1973 Inquiry concluded that, 'intoxicating liquor is being consumed to excess in the Northern Territory; such excessive consumption is having an adverse effect on social behaviour, law and order and the incidence of crime amongst the population generally, and in particular the health, living conditions and economic circumstances of the Aboriginal section of the population are being adversely affected by excessive consumption of intoxicating liquor'.

The Inquiry stated that contributing factors in Aboriginal alcoholism were: 'their different stages of cultural development; influences of their traditional life in which alcohol played no part; the lack in their culture of inbuilt sanctions for control of alcohol usage; their being caught up in rapid social change and subsequent social disorganisation; their lack of awareness of the harmful effects of drinking to excess; their lack of education in domestic budgeting and the proper use of money; their excessive expenditure on intoxicating liquor; and the poor conditions under which they consume intoxicating liquor'.

Recommendations made by the Inquiry were connected with legislation and education. While attempts such as these to solve the tragic problem are essential, ultimately Aborigines themselves, individually and corporately, must find the answer. In the second half of 1977 there were hopeful signs that this was happening, and many Aborigines were coming to grips with the problem.

Legislation regulating the sale and consumption of liquor is important in attempting to combat this massive Aboriginal alcoholism. The 1976 Interim Report deplored the fact that the suggested amendments to the Licensing Ordinance made in the 1973 Adams Report had not been implemented. The Committee members believed that the implementation of the following particular recommendations of the Adams Report were 'of the utmost urgency'. They were, that 'it be made illegal for liquor to be carried by ... chartered aircraft to or in the vicinity of a Mission or settlement without a permit from the licensing authority; a licensee be made fully responsible if a drunken person is found on his premises ... ; and that because the forfeiture of a licence may in certain circumstances be unduly harsh and that courts have been reluctant to invoke this section of the ordinance, that it should be changed ...' The Legislative Assembly amended the Police and Police Offences Ordinance and the Licensing Ordinance in 1976 to cover these needs.

The granting and renewal of licences for stores operating in the vicinity of Aboriginal communities have been the subject of careful consideration in the past few years. Before 1977 a ground for objection to the granting of a storekeeper's licence was that 'the quiet and good order of the neighbourhood in which such premises are situated will not be disturbed if a licence is granted'. There was no such provision for the renewal of a storekeeper's licence.

Because of this the Oenpelli Council had been unable to force the closure of the Border Store on the East Alligator River. In 1978 the Department of Aboriginal Affairs bought the Border Store on behalf of the Oenpelli community. The Oenpelli Council is new responsible for its management. The store cannot sell liquor but provides a service for the numerous visitors and campers on the west bank of the river. Oenpelli township now has its own wet canteen.

On 20 April 1976 the Licensing Magistrate refused to renew the licence of the Roper Bar Store. He ruled that 'the business has been and would continue to run without regard to the welfare of the local population'. He said also that 'the good order and discipline of a large area and an otherwise stable population would be threatened if the licence was renewed'. The Licensing Magistrate also refused the application for a liquor licence in 1977.

A significant change in legislation regarding drunkenness took place in October 1974 when the offence of drunkenness was abolished in the Northern Territory. At the same time Section 33A of the Police and Police Offences, Ordinance (Northern Territory) was inserted to ensure the safety and welfare of persons who, through drunkenness, became incapable of looking after themselves. Ambiguity in this section resulted in further amendments in February 1976. These clarified the grounds under which a Police Officer may, without warrant, apprehend and take into custody a person whom he thinks may be drunk.

Legislation like this, though essential, has only a limited affect on the overall problem of Aboriginal alcoholism. Decisions by the

Aboriginal Town Councils are more significant. Even then, such decisions have their limitations. The first need is to make sure that the decision of the Town Council reflects the true wishes of the whole community. The second need is to have the necessary power to enforce the decisions of the Aboriginal Councils. In 1977 most Arnhem Land communities did not have resident police officers. The Councils and the people had no way of enforcing the rules which they made.

Aboriginal Town Councils have two options open to them regarding the supply of liquor to their communities. They can ban it completely, or they can allow it to be brought in and try to control its sale to the community.

Town Councils in most of the former 'mission' places have banned alcohol completely. They have found great difficulty in enforcing the prohibition. Many of the local Aborigines defy the rule and bring in large quantities of alcohol by vehicle, charter aircraft, or in their own luggage. A great percentage of non-Aboriginal staff at the community do not feel that they are bound by the restriction, and demand the right to have their booze. A large number of school teachers, Government officials, and contract workers are in this category. They are able to do this through the personal liquor permit system. In some cases they sell liquor to the local Aborigines; at other times they invite Aborigines into their homes to teach them 'civilised drinking'.

Total prohibition in a community causes another problem. Those Aborigines who want to drink — and by that is meant who want to get drunk — are forced to leave home and go to Darwin or other towns. Here they become itinerant drunks, off-loaded from the 'dry' communities, who refuse to cater for them themselves.

A more reasonable approach is for Town Councils to permit alcohol to be brought into the community. Here it can be sold through a licensed club, which should hold the only liquor licence in that community. The 1976 Interim Report stated that such a club 'properly established and supervised, presents the most practical method of encouraging sensible drinking patterns'.

The Report recommended that licensed clubs be set up in this way when the community has decided to allow the consumption of alcohol; and that 'funds be made available through the Aboriginal Loans Commission of the Benefits Trust Fund for the provision of club facilities'. The Report also recommended that the personal liquor permit be abolished in these places.

During the past few years the licensing of clubs at places such as Maningrida and Umbakumba has not worked very well. The community hall at Umbakumba was badly smashed up during the first year of the club's operations. The quota of four or five cans a day did not work, as people traded in their can allowance. Widespread drunkenness occurred. Draught beer in kegs might be an answer.

Yet despite these unhappy experiences the provision of properly controlled 'wet' canteens appears to be the best solution for the communities. People do not have to resort to illegal means to get their grog. They do not have to go to Darwin to have their binge. Questions relating to the provision of draught beer to be drunk at the club, or four cans a day, either to be drunk only at the club or only at home, are matters which each community will have to work out for itself. Different places will adopt different methods if the experience of Queensland and other places is any guide. The most satisfactory solution will be when people have the facility to drink, have no restrictions, except trading times, on the way they drink, but also have a full knowledge and understanding of what they are doing and what alcohol might be doing for them.

An essential corollary to the acceptance of a 'wet' canteen is the provision of a resident police force. Such a force could be regular police, or specially trained local Aboriginal men, or both. Anything less than this would leave members of the community open to harassment and danger. The presence of the police would also be an added means in assisting Aboriginal men and women to learn to drink in moderation, and learn the consequences of harmful actions when under the influence.

The outstation or homeland movement has been one means by which Aborigines have tried to combat the disturbances caused by drunkenness. Many Aboriginal clans have moved from the mixed communities of the former missions and settlements back to their homelands. Among many reasons for this spontaneous move has been the necessity to get away from alcohol. These smaller family groups are able to cope with alcohol problems should they arise. Being smaller homogeneous groups with distinct cultural heritage, they are able to exercise greater authority among their own people.

A further means of combatting Aboriginal alcoholism is through education. The Department of Health is undertaking seminars on the use of alcohol in many major centres. These seminars are aimed at increasing the awareness and understanding of alcohol and drug problems and stimulating local action to deal with them. The use of alcohol has been incorporated as an important aspect of the Aboriginal Health Worker training program. Training workshops on health education have been held. These workshops have been attended by Aboriginal communities. The Health Department also has a working group on the development of educational material, such as films, video cassettes and so on. Nungalinya College is co-operating in this educational project. A Government film entitled 'Watch Yourself' produced with the co-operation of the Daly River community has just been released.

Massive educational programs relating to alcohol abuse should also be undertaken by the Departments of Education, Aboriginal Affairs, churches, missions and other interested people. So often so many people deplore the drunkenness and despise the drunkard, but do nothing to help in a positive way.

Educational programs have been very effective when Aborigines have realised the effects of alcohol on their traditional culture. The crisis hits home hard when they see what they are doing to their heritage, how many of the older song leaders are too besotted to sing at the ceremonies, when they cannot meet for days because leaders have been waylaid by friends on the way and become inebriated.

Educational programs are also very effective when Aborigines talk together about the implications of drunkenness on comunity projects, work and health. The sharing of their experiences in discussion often proves to be a salutary reminder of what alcohol is doing to their communities.

The most effective educational programs are those in which films show the effect of alcohol on the brain and other parts of the body. Simple, diagramatic films showing brain, liver, heart and kidney degeneration and the deterioration of the nervous system through prolonged alcoholism have been most effective in getting the message home. All Aborigines are aware of alcohol symptoms and their immediate effect on people. Most do not realise the permanent damage which this drug is causing. And Aborigines have a deep sense of themselves, their families and their clan, and are greatly upset by death. When they realise how permanent the damage is, and the way it leads ultimately to death, they become deeply shocked.

Despite the grim facts of the past and the unfortunate situation in many places at the present, there are clear signs of hope for the future. A growing number of Aboriginal men and women are genuinely trying to throw off alcohol addiction. That does not mean that they do not drink. But they are trying to drink in moderation and a number of the younger men are succeeding.

The new sense of liberation, of self-determination, of land control and of community direction are powerful factors in breaking down

249

the sense of inferiority and dependancy. This in turn removes one of the primary reasons for excessive alcoholism. Aborigines are growing in self-esteem and self-reliance. Their movements and their actions are no longer controlled by 'missionaries' and by 'welfare'. They do not have to get drunk to prove that they have 'citizenship' or equal rights with whites.

There will always be drunks in any society. There are clear indications that over a period of time there will be fewer Aboriginal drunkards than in the past two decades, even though alcohol dependance is increasing among non-Aboriginal Australians. There is great hope that they no longer will be 'killing themselves with grog'.

20
Christian
but still Aboriginal

Lazarus Lamilami said that 'a man can be a Christian and still be a proper Aboriginal man. If an Aboriginal man feels that he is being called by the Lord and wants to be a Christian, he does not have to change himself and be a Balanda or someone else. He can still be an Aboriginal and be a Christian.'

This view is shared by Aboriginal men and women who are committed Christians. They object to statements which people, usually Europeans, sometimes make that when Aborigines become Christians they cease to be true Aborigines. They deny this strongly. They say that they are not called upon to denounce their birthright or to change their clan when they are Christians. They are not asked to forget their past and to live as non-Aborigines. On the contrary, one Aboriginal person said to me on one occasion, 'I am a better Aboriginal man because I am a Christian.'

The claim that Aboriginal Christians are not true to their heritage appears to have emerged out of early mission attitudes to Aboriginal culture. Critics usually point to the fact that many early missionaries thought that Aborigines were savages and uncivilised. They say that missionaries considered that Aboriginal ceremonies were sinful and depraved. They attack early missionaries for arranging marriages of the surplus wives of polygamists, even though this enabled young men to have wives by lawful rather than unlawful means.

The relationship between Christianity and polygamy is not easy. It is true that in early mission days missionaries tried to demand certain standards of moral behaviour for all Aborigines who chose to live on the mission. They could not prevent polygamy among those who did not choose to live there. But if Aborigines at that time decided to live in a Christian place some missionaries thought that they should be taught to act as Christians and be monogamous. Missionaries and churches cannot make such demands these days. Churches and missions do not interfere with Aboriginal life-styles of non-Christians living in the community. Aborigines have the right to choose their own way of life within the parameters of their own culture and the constraints of Australian law.

At the same time the Church may require certain standards for those Aborigines who have expressed commitment to the Christian way. When an Aboriginal, who is a polygamist, voluntarily and sincerely wishes to become a Christian and to be baptised, then the Church has a right to impose its standards. This usually means that on baptism a polygamist may keep his first wife, but sends his other wives back to their relations. This may seem harsh by European standards, but there have been few problems among Aborigines because wives, especially young ones, are in great demand.

In the case where a wife who is married to a polygamous man and subsequently becomes a Christian, the Church ruling is usually different, although the Anglican and Uniting Churches have no agreed policy in the matter. It usually happens that if the polygamous man still wants a wife who has become a Christian, then she should remain with him. If the polygamous man does not want her, then she is free to leave him and to marry another. This view is taken from the Pauline attitude to marriage expressed in Chapter 7 of his letter to the Christians at Corinth. 'To the married I give charge, not I but the Lord, that the wife should not separate from her husband . . . and that the husband should not divorce his wife. To the rest I say, not in the Lord, that if any man has a wife who is an unbeliever, and she consents to live with him, he should not divorce her. If any woman has a husband who is an unbeliever, and he consents to live with her, she should not divorce him. For the unbelieving husband is consecrated through his wife, and the unbelieving wife is consecrated through her husband.'

Lamilami said that polygamy was dying out in western Arnhem Land. He said that he did not know why. One reason may be economic. There is also now not the need to have additional wives to augment the food supply, nor the need for more children to ensure protection in old age. There was at least one other reason. He continued with a characteristic chuckle, 'This is what I think myself. It is dying out because some wives are jealous of their husbands and they do not like their husbands to take any more wives. And therefore the husband is a bit frightened to take another wife.'

Lamilami then gave a hypothetical example of a man whose

252

mother-in-law had six daughters. 'This man could be right for all the daughters. They look upon him as their husband, even though he does not live with them. They can call him, "Husband", even though he does not live with them. He is able to allow them to get married to others who are in the right relationship, if he does not want them.'

The question of the brother, though married, taking his deceased brother's wife, has also presented problems for Aboriginal Christians, and for the churches to which they belong. The wisdom of this arrangement in former days is obvious. The widow usually stood in the right relationship for marriage to him. The woman and her children would have the protection of one who already has obligations to her family. The man should marry the woman and care for the children. He also had the responsibility to preserve the lineage. The custom is very similar to the Old Testament law requiring a man or close kinsman to marry, his deceased brother's wife. (The classical example of this is the delightful story of Ruth.)

Circumstances today are different. The chances of a man's death by disease, accident or fighting are not as great. Food for all is more nearly assured. Also many Aboriginal women have much more freedom. They can work and be self-supporting. This is often the case where the husband goes off to work elsewhere for long periods of time, or takes another or a *de facto* wife. When Lazarus spoke about this he had in mind all women, not just Christians. He said, 'When a man dies and his brother wants to take the dead man's wife, there can be problems. Sometimes the woman does not want to. She likes to go her own ways. When the husband dies, the whole thing is finished. She does not need to have anything to do with her brother-in-law or her relations. She can go ahead and marry someone else. These days you can see that with women. In the olden days she could not. No! She had to marry her brother-in-law. If she wanted to marry someone else she could not say it openly. She had to keep that secret, otherwise people would kill her. But these days some women can say it openly. "I want to get married to that man. I can do what I like. I can please myself." So there I can see the old way dying out.'

Other marriage customs are also changing. In many cases some of the old kinship laws are not being followed. The reasons for the changes are not the result of Christianity, but the inevitability of the influences of education and non-Aboriginal culture. Many young Aborigines say that they are not going back to their communities to marry partners who were chosen for them when they were born. A number of bright Aboriginal young women refuse to marry men old enough sometimes to be their grandfathers. They say that they are liberated, and are free to marry whom they want to.

Speaking about Christian marriage, Lazarus said, 'I do not see any problems in kinship and marriage for Christians. With kinship for a Christian Aboriginal, he can marry someone who is the right one for him to get married. That does not mean that a Christian man can marry anyone. He has to marry into his right relationship. If someone is in the straight relationship for him to get married, then he can marry and be a Christian.' Lazarus was not in favour of marriage between the races.

The relationship between Christianity and Aboriginal traditional ceremonies exercises the minds of many Aboriginal Christians. Some of them say that as Christians they should have nothing at all to do with ceremonies. They are part of the sinful past, and they have been abandoned when they became Christians. As one of them said, 'You have to cut them off like a razor.' A greater proportion of Aboriginal Christians say that there is no problem connected with some ceremonies. They say, however, that Christians should not dance parts of certain ceremonies, such as the Kunapipi.

The churches in Arnhem Land have conferences and discussions about Christianity and ceremonies from time to time. No clear answers have emerged. Most Aboriginal Christians maintain during these conferences that some ceremonies are good, and in many aspects, have implications similar to the moral teaching in the Old Testament. They also reiterate that some features of other ceremonies are not good, and that Christians should not participate in those parts.

Mortuary ceremonies, which involve all the relatives, Christian and otherwise, in the dead person's clan, are usually accepted by all. Perhaps Christian and non-Christian participants have different interpretations of what is being done. The Christians would usually say that they are singing the departed spirit to heaven. The non-Christian, on the other hand, would say that he is singing the spirit back to the dreaming home of that totem spirit. In all probability many Aboriginal Christians do not try to rationalise their feelings and motives in the same way as Europeans do.

Lamilami spoke about Christians and ceremonies. He said, 'If that ceremony is good, I think that it is not a bad thing if he is a Christian to make (that is, to participate in) a ceremony. If he wants to keep up the old traditional laws if they are good, then I think that that is good. But say new things that come in that are not very good, then I do not think that it is good for a Christian man to make that ceremony.' Lazarus often complained that a number of innovations are coming into older ceremonies, and that frequently the new versions were damaging to the earlier forms.

He continued, 'I heard someone say, "I am a Christian but I will go to this ceremony, and bring that ceremony right into the Christian life", but he never did it. It was all the other way and now he has wandered off from Christianity. But I think that good ceremonies are good for a Christian person, but a bad ceremony is not good for a Christian person. Aborigines are the ones who must decide what are good ceremonies and what are bad ceremonies. I think that the matter has to be talked about a lot more by Aborigines. Also I think that the leaders of ceremonies must understand Christian ways.'

On another occasion Lamilami said, 'The ubar was connected with creation. The kunapipi was connected with laws and a bit of creation. The ubar is all about marriage and children and things like that. The kunapipi has problems for Christian people. They can dance part of it but not all.'

Many non-Aborigines criticise the Christian churches working among Aborigines for persevering with worship which is too European and claim that there is no evidence of any form of Aboriginal theology. Such criticisms are valid, but in reply certain observations ought to be made.

The first is this. Aboriginal Christians in Arnhem Land are members of either the Anglican or the Uniting Church in Australia. They do not belong to any other church, just as the Aboriginal Christians on Bathurst Island are Roman Catholic. This is the result of mission comity, whereby mission work in Arnhem Land and the Top End initially was divided between the Anglican CMS and the Methodist MOM. Aborigines are therefore Anglican or Methodist (now the Uniting Church) not by choice but by the chance of their birth. Their form of worship, their theology, their Christian vocabulary and their hymnology all reflect the tradition of the founding mission. They are also very conservative in their faith and hold strongly to the things which the early missionaries taught them. Some of the older Christians in one Arnhem Land community resent and resist any new service form in English, saying that they know and want to continue to use the 1662 Anglican Prayer Book, though even many Europeans find difficulty in fully understanding some of the Elizabethan words and phrases.

Aboriginal forms of worship and Aboriginal theology must emerge from Aborigines themselves. Non-Aboriginal attempts to provide these have been paternalistic and abortive. On the other hand the churches should not impose structures on thought and worship which would prevent free Aboriginal expression when it wants to appear.

Indigenous worship and theology must be spontaneous if they are to be living and real. In the meantime most Aborigines understandably fall back on the way they have seen worship conducted in the past. They use the same forms which they have learned from their non-Aboriginal teachers and ministers. They often become more conservative and less open to change than many of their own non-Aboriginal colleagues. There is, nevertheless, no doubt, if the history of the Christian church in other countries is any guide, a probability that Aborigines will begin and increasingly continue to express their Christian experience in their own way in their own language.

At the same time some progress is being made to make worship more meaningful, even though it may not be truly indigenous. Services are often conducted now in the vernacular, not in English. Parts of the Bible and some of the hymns are read and sung in the local language. Services are often held under a tree, on the sand, by the river or beach, or in the camp rather than in a building, frequently situated among non-Aboriginal staff housing. Didjeridus are sometimes used, but opinions differ as to their suitability for Christian worship. Guitars are popular and are usually employed in formal and less formal services.

One of the European chaplains working in an Arnhem Land community wrote several years ago, 'I gather from conversations round about that if you rate Christian worship in terms of the numbers of enthusiastic attenders, outdoor night services are the best. That has been my own experience at Milingimbi. And if you can include a good film and a cup of tea around the camp fire, with perhaps even sharing of bush food by some of the church men and women for the purpose, even more will come.'

He continued, 'Arnhem Land has its own needs, of course, and its own emerging pattern of Christian life, not necessarily like the patterns we knew that came from outside. We who are newcomers to this ancient culture have no mandate to impose our patterns upon it, we, who after all do not fit easily into this land, and many of us "Europeans" not at all. No more can we presume to foist our western worship upon a people already reeling under the pressures and burdens our civilisation places on them.

'Sitting in a circle of music in any one of a number of ceremonies we see another life — a life without chairs, organised singing very different from anything that I have ever heard in church. People are conversing freely, passing around food, drink or the pipe from time to time during the night of singing. The people are sitting family by family, in little tribal circles; and in some ceremonies there are dances and painting of preparation of ritual emblems that help make up the whole. Everyone may participate; but not everyone must. The round of songs ends with a shout that you will not often hear in Christian gatherings.

'It is not that Christians must follow these patterns in worship. But clearly it is within these patterns that the people are attuned to listen and learn and assimilate new material . . .'

Aboriginal theology is an even more complex problem. We are probably asking too much of Aboriginal Christians if we expect them to begin formulating some kind of Aboriginal theology just at this time in their history. Within the short space of a generation these former stone-age folk have been plunged into the complexities of twentieth century Western culture. They are trying to cope with the new responsibilities of land, town councils, uranium mining, massive alcohol addiction and all the rest. Should we at the same time be saying that you must formulate your own theology and develop your own form of worship? We are asking them to do something that the Western Christian church has taken two thousand years to evolve! Are our incessant demands consistent with our repeated assertion that Aborigines are now liberated and free to choose the nature and pace of their own spiritual development? Or do they spring from our desire that we should have the means of justifying Aboriginal Christians to others? Indigenous theology will come, not because of external pressure, but from the internal desire to express their understanding of God themselves.

Those engaged in theological education among Aborigines at the present time use creation as the meeting point of Aboriginal and Christian cultures. Creation stories and the exploits of the great totem heroes of the dreamtime, clan and kinship, and the complex social structure arising out of totemism are of the greatest significance for Aboriginal people. These concepts and symbols are not dissimilar to those of creation and the calling of God's people in the Old Testament. Christians say that both religious systems require the addition of new covenant or teaching as shown in the life and death of Jesus Christ. But as the Christian Westerner uses the Hebrew Old Testament as a preparation for the New, some maintain that the Aboriginal Christian can see his traditional religion as a similar preparation. Their understanding of their past prepares them for the gospel in much the same way as the Old Testament prepares Western Christian man for his understanding of the New Testament.

Some Aborigines also speak about the Creator God in much the same way as the Christian does. Lamilami used to talk of Namumuiag. 'They don't know who Namumiag is. That is just a name. He was the one who gave us this land. He made the trees. He made the islands. He made the water. He made the grass. He made the animals. His name is Namumuiag. He is just like the creator God of the Bible. He made the heavens. He made the milky way. He made the moon and he made the sun. He made the sea. He made everything. He gave our ancestors their totems'.

The Aborigines of Arnhem Land also seem to be more conscious of the spirit world than materialistic Westerners. Their strong kinship ties bind them spiritually to their ancestors. When they die elaborate rituals ensure that the spirit returns to its place of origin. They believe spirits are good or bad. Lamilami said, 'People believed and still believe in spirits. There were good ones and there were bad ones. Bad spirits might make me sick ... Most people believe in spirits.' This consciousness of spiritual beings and forces is another way in which Christian Aborigines may be able to have a deeper understanding of Christian truths such as the Holy Spirit and good and evil spiritual powers.

The theology of liberation is becoming popular among some of the younger, more educated, Aboriginal Christians. This is not surprising, as Aborigines are a minority group struggling for identity within the larger and more powerful white society. Aboriginal Christians are reacting in much the same way as repressed minority groups in the United States and in South America. They have an affinity with the agony of the oppressed in these countries, who react with the formulation of black power and liberation theology.

The redemption of Israel from slavery in Egypt points to God's liberating power in the early history of the People of God in the Old Testament. The ministry of healing, exorcism and teaching of Jesus liberated the poor people of his day. The gospel today has the same message and the same power to liberate people from fear and repression, from guilt and sin. The gospel also speaks of justice for the exploited, and Aborigines are trying to experience this new sense of freedom and liberation through this means.

The Reverend Terry Djiniyini is one such Aboriginal Christian who is studying the theology of liberation. He said, 'I see in some aspects of liberation a relevance to the Australian Aborigine. One could see this because of his own experience. Then he is able to see clearly what kind of liberation is needed in the Australian Aboriginal community. What I am saying here is that self-liberation must be emphasised and I feel that this is needed in our community.'

This liberation must also become real for Aboriginal people. He said, 'First of all if I am speaking of spiritual things, then I would say that there are many areas in which people have to be liberated. From the power of demons, from fear, from magic that is still part of fear and from worshipping other gods that have been made by man; things made out of stone, wood and other things. Sexual liberation from using the gift of God immorally is where I see another area in which Aboriginal people need liberation.'

Djinyini then spoke about social and political liberation. 'Here I see that it is very important that Aboriginal people are to be liberated and to exercise their freedom, to emphasise their identity as people to say what they think, to see that they have a place in the community, to see themselves as persons created by God. I believe that they need to be given a place in a community. They need to be respected. They need to be seen as a fellow citizen of Australia. Not to be seen as a black or Aboriginal person, but seen as brothers, fellow citizens, living in this country of ours, Australia.'

He also spoke of the dangers of using freedom wrongly. 'This is a dangerous thing when a person has been liberated and feels free from the power that is putting the person down. What I mean here is that he rejects the traditional power structure and adopts a western culture or way of life. But I do not think so. That I know from my own experience here. I still retain my culture. I can sit with my people. I can still practise what is good in the culture of my people. And this is one of the things that I am very, very thankful to God for, because as a Christian I am able to see what is wrong in our culture, and I have tried not to practise against my Christian belief. That does not mean that I ignore my culture and say that it is not right to be involved in it. But I do not think a person as soon as he becomes liberated as a Christian should live as a European.'

Many Arnhem Land Aboriginal Christians find another form of Christian expression through the Aboriginal Evangelical Fellowship (AEF). The AEF is an Australia-wide fellowship of Aboriginal Christians which is run by the Aboriginals themselves. A large proportion of the members are part-Aboriginal people from the South. As almost all of these have lost their language and culture, their presentation of Christianity is almost identical with that of non-Aboriginal evangelicals elsewhere on the continent. The AEF is a vigorous missionary-minded group providing a focal point of identity and fellowship especially for half-castes.

Despite frequent and seemingly unjustified criticism of Aborigines becoming Christians, there is no doubt that committed Christians are usually respected by their fellow Aborigines and staff members in their communities, and also by Governments. Aboriginal Christians are frequently the leaders because they have overcome problems that they might have had with alcohol. They also have strong Christian motivation to serve their own people. This also could be said about missions and missionaries.

Lazarus Lamilami made this point clear when he said, 'The people have said that they trust the mission. "We trust the mission. That means that they can help us and that they are living with us. They help us, they live with us and we can trust them. We can trust a Government man but he has his ways. He does not let the Aboriginal see his ways. Sometimes he might not agree with the ways the Aboriginal wants." I have heard this many times. "We want the mission."'

Becoming quite animated about this Lamilami asked, 'May I go on?' to which I readily answered in the affirmative.

'On Croker Island, the Town Council now has the authority of running the town but the mission is still there. And the people say, "Even the Government has given us the responsibility of running this council . . ." But they feel, "Yes the Government is doing all this but where is the foundation? But where is the foundation of the Government?" The Church has its foundation and we can see that. The Government is giving us a lot of money which we say, is very good. But where is the foundation? The Church or the mission has this foundation.'

Lazarus felt strongly that Government policies change and their employees come and go. But the Christians were to be trusted, and the church was a continuing presence. He continued, 'The Church binds the people together . . . The missionaries live with us. The mission made mistakes about marriages, but the people are still saying, "They are the people who live with us. We can trust them."'

Despite cultural differences, problems of communication and the dramatic changes in life-styles, a large percentage of Arnhem Land Aborigines over the ages of fourteen years have been baptised, confirmed or brought into full membership of their local church. Missionaries, clergy and Aboriginal Christians have taught the way of Christ, and have invited the full commitment of their lives to him. They have then received instruction and have been baptised.

Evangelistic campaigns and missions have also called for full Christian commitment. Visiting evangelists such as the negro Dr Ralph Bell of the Billy Graham Crusade team have had a fruitful ministry in Darwin and in some of the Top End communities. The ministry of visiting Anglican East African Christians who have been touched with the Revival Movement, have also been very well received. Aborigines appear to respond more positively to non-white preachers.

Although a large number of Aboriginal people have expressed commitment to Christ and have been baptised, they often do not attend church regularly. They give various explanations. They say that they are often away hunting at the week-ends during the Dry. Some say that they find it hard to organise themselves on Sundays after being tied to the clock during the week. Some admit that they are now not interested. The form and language of worship, the predominance of white attenders in some places, the seeming irrelevance of what is said and done, must also surely be contributing factors.

The marked difference between Christian profession and practice among some Aborigines raises more serious questions, as it does among Christians of other races. Some Aboriginal Christians profess to follow Christ, but they gamble, get drunk, and commit immoral acts. They sometimes brawl and fight. Some of the young ones get caught up in the widespread petrol-sniffing and petty larceny prevalent in some communities. Drunk men, while drunk, sometimes preach excellent sermons, using word for word stock evangelistic phrases which they have heard, and in some cases, unfortunately, have used in the past when lay preachers.

The unsympathetic critic quickly concludes when he sees things like this that Aboriginal Christianity is superficial, or even does not exist. They say that the gospel cannot compete with thousands of years of traditional culture and thought patterns. Christianity is not possible for Aborigines at this stage of their development.

More thoughtful people realise that some of the seeming paradoxes are due to a variety of reasons. The influence of traditional pressures and power groups within the community, and age-old customs are hard for non-Aborigines to understand. The social pressures of communal living in tensional situations make for instability in Christian life and practice. Christian girls and young women often have to submit to advances which tribally they are unable to refuse. These and many other social and cultural problems result in what outsiders see as irrational ambivalence of conduct.

The non-Aboriginal Christian also judges by his own standards. His background, his upbringing, and his individualised way of life are far removed from the camping-style existence of most Arnhem Land Aborigines. Yet he is quick to judge and to condemn. Jesus on the other hand spoke of thoughts as well as deeds as being the means whereby we will be judged. He said to the woman taken in adultery, 'I do not condemn you; go, and do not sin again.'

Misunderstanding through language, the lack of knowledge and the use of the vernacular, and evangelistic techniques and theology based on European models are further factors which often contribute to the apparent dichotomy between Christian faith and practice among Aborigines. They often do not fully understand Biblical words and phrases. Their ideas of sin, murder, and adultery mean different things when used in an Aboriginal context. Individualised decision-making is often foreign to them. Lack of adequate follow-up teaching after evangelistic missions have caused some to fall away.

Despite these very real problems there is in every community a solid core of dedicated Christian Aboriginal men and women, who practise what they believe. They preach in church, organise its meetings, they speak to others about Christ, and they serve on parish councils and committees, and on the synods of the two churches. They often take full responsibility when the resident ministers are away. They also live lives worthy of their faith.

A feature of the homeland movement has been the demand for regular Sunday services by people who formerly did not go to church. The services are simple, in the vernacular, and usually taken by the elder who is in charge of the camp. They also request the minister in the main community to visit them regularly to take services of Holy Communion for them, and to help them with spiritual problems which some of their members may have.

Bible, worship forms, and hymns in the vernacular are essential for a better understanding of the Christian faith. Every large Arnhem Land community now has a resident linguist, who is reducing the local language into writing. This work has been basic to the bilingual program in education. This work is also invaluable for the Church. Parts of the Old and New Testament, service forms and Christian songs are now being translated by them.

The Wycliffe Bible Translators, known also as the Summer Institute of Linguistics (SIL) is one of the Christian organisations based in Darwin which employs a number of linguists and helps in Christian translation work. The SIL conducts a number of workshops and seminars enabling visiting Aborigines and non-Aborigines to be more conversant with the available aids and some of the pitfalls in the translation programs. The United Bible Societies (UBS) are also assisting with Bible translation. The UBS held its first New Testament Translators' Institute in Darwin in 1971.

SIL and UBS translators have to face a number of problems when engaged in translation. For example. how do you translate a word like circumcision (especially spiritual circumcision) when, as in the case of some tribes, women are not allowed to hear the technical term for it? Again, how do you translate 'You are the salt of the earth' for a tribe that does not use or know about salt? Again, what do you do if you want to translate 'Whoever does not receive the kingdom of God like a child will never enter into it', when, if you ask some Aborigines, they will say that children are silly, stupid or lacking in sense? These illustrate some of the difficulties which linguists face when translating the Bible.

Miss Beulah Lowe, the linguist at Milingimbi for a number of years, highlights some of the misunderstanding which she found among Aborigines when English is the medium of communication. The examples she gave are taken from hymn lines. 'Got any rivers you think are uncrossable' is thought to mean 'God's long river'; 'Got any mountains you can't tunnel through' is thought to mean 'God's high mountain'; 'God specialises in things thought impossible' is thought to mean 'God's special eyes'; 'God has blotted them out' is thought to mean 'God has blotted the mouth'; 'Turn to Isaiah and see' is thought to mean 'Turn and look at Isaiah', the informant not realising that the words meant 'open the Bible at Isaiah'; 'He took his seat above' is thought to mean 'He got a chair and took it above'; '. . . sailor trying to make the harbour' is thought to mean 'trying to build the harbour'.

Beulah Lowe then explained some of the difficulties in translating hymns. 'One obvious reason why hymns in English are so difficult is that in most cases they are not written in simple every-day English, which is the only type of English spoken and understood by the majority of our educated Aboriginal folk . . . To many people, translating consists merely of the ability to write accurately what is said by the Aboriginal helper. The translator reads a sentence, the helper says the same sentence in his own language, and the translator writes it down. If this were true, translation work would indeed proceed rapidly. Unfortunately, the ability to write what an informant says is only a part. A far more important part is acquiring from the informant an idiomatic, meaningful and accurate translation. This process is rendered more difficult by the fact that, almost without exception, informants tend to give a literal rather than idiomatic translation.' She then outlined complex principles which need to be followed when she translates hymns.

Despite these difficulties, she and others have translated hymns into a number of languages. What is more important some Aborigines are composing their own hymns, which they sing with the help of guitars. This is a good move and avoids the difficulty of translating idiomatic and metaphorical phrases from one language

263

into another. This cannot be done when translating the Bible. Progress nevertheless is being made and a number of Arnhem Land vernaculars now have basic Bible sections in their own language.

Systematic teaching of the faith is a great need for Aboriginal Christians at the present time. Individual churches and other groups conduct Bible camps, teaching week-ends and other meetings to encourage them to know more about what they believe, and ways in which they can be helped in their Christian life. Nungalinya College in Darwin also has a number of courses which help Aboriginal men and women who are preachers or ordinands to understand more about the Bible, the church to which they belong, worship, and how to live the right way.

The highest priority at the present time is the training of Aborigines to become fully qualified ministers to minister to their own people in their own communities. The Reverend Lazarus Lamilami was the first United Church minister ordained for this work, but he died in Darwin in 1977. The Uniting Church currently has two ministers, the Reverends Philip Mugulnir and Terry Djiniyini, who are full-time, ordained ministers. The Anglican Church only has one such minister. He is the Reverend Michael Gumbuli, who was ordained in 1973 and who ministers at Roper River (Ngukurr).

Writing about the ordination of the Reverend Michael Gumbuli, I said at the time, 'Europeans and Aborigines from all over Arnhem Land came by car and plane to share in the historic occasion. For the first time among many visits to the various communities, I experienced a new sense of freedom and dignity among the Aboriginal people, similar to that which I had known among Africans in Kenya as they approached "uhuru" — freedom and independence. They were all excited about what was happening and kept on talking about it to each other. "We have now our own minister. Our minister is an Aboriginal, one of us. That Michael Gumbuli is Number One fella."'

For practical reasons Michael works as a supervisor during the week. This limits his task as a minister. But as he said just before his ordination, 'After I am ordained, I will go on doing work. By working with men I can witness to them and show them how the Christian life is real to me.'

Aboriginal Christians like Michael Gumbuli have been given the responsibility of ministering to their own people and making the gospel relevant for them. They are able to express the faith in their own way to people whose way of life they understand far better than any non-Aboriginal can. Aborigines in turn minister to the non-

Aborigines who are working in their communities. Having grown up with European teaching they often understand Europeans far better than Europeans understand Aborigines.

The ministry of Aborigines and non-Aborigines in the Church demonstrates the universality of the Christian faith. The ministries by Fijians, Tongans, Aborigines and Europeans with different backgrounds in the Uniting Church in Arnhem Land illustrates this in a small way. International Christian Conferences usually have representives from every country in the world.

Christianity is a universal religion and is for all people. It is certainly not a European western religion. Jesus was a Jew, a Semite, and Christianity started in the Middle East. Christianity rapidly spread throughout the then-known world within a century. Since that time people of every nationality and race have become Christian.

Aborigines have entered into this heritage. Not all Aborigines are Christian but some Christians are Aboriginal. They are maintaining a true and faithful witness, often under difficult circumstances. They are true Christians and at the same time true Aborigines. As Lazarus Lamilami said, 'He can still be an Aboriginal and be a Christian.'

21
We want to be free

The Aborigines of Arnhem Land say, 'We want to be free.' They do not feel free. They are bewildered by the problems which they are facing and are confused by the difficult decisions which they are called upon to make. They feel threatened as they realise that they are being caught between two worlds. They are frightened that they might be the ones who again will suffer most in the conflict of the cultures.

In former days the Aborigines struggled to survive in the face of the inexorable march of the expanding white frontier. They retreated into the bush or quickly dissipated themselves with the vices of the invaders. The missions belatedly saw their plight and smoothed the way for their final demise. But they did not die. They lived and increased in numbers. They were cared for in segregation, being isolated for their protection.

They were still not free. These proud nomads of the northland lived as dependent people, cooped up in communities, living with tribes with whom they had no real affinity. They were confused and they were not happy.

The subsequent massive welfare grants brought to the Aborigines of Arnhem Land many benefits. They were now very much better off. Most of the children could go to school. The general health of the community began to improve dramatically. Child morbidity and mortality started to fall. Larger and more qualified non-Aboriginal staff were able to provide improved facilities, better housing, more employment, and better living standards.

Even though they had all these benefits they still did not feel free. They did not spend their days in close fellowship with the natural

266

world around them searching for their food as in former days. Instead they were being processed to reach the required standards necessary for assimilation into the wider Australian society. They became deeply disturbed. They would say, 'What is happening to our culture? What are you doing with our land? Without our land how can we stand? What is happening to us?' As one of them said, 'If I do not know who I am, I am not.' They were facing a crisis of identity. The future gave no promise that they would be free to be themselves, to be Aboriginal people still.

'We want our freedom', Aborigines are constantly saying. 'We want the best of western culture, but we still want our way of life. We want your motor cars, we want your houses, we want your motor boats. But we still want to be Aborigines. We still have our totems and our ceremonies. We have two ways of looking at life — the Balanda way and our own way.'

The Aborigines of Arnhem Land are caught hanging between the cultures. They want to get as much as they can from non-Aboriginal ways, but they do not want to be Balanda. They want at the same time to retain their former ways and to be true Aborigines. They often find that they cannot have both ways, and the result is traumatic. In trying to get what both offers, they sometimes miss out on both and lose themselves. Alcohol is their only answer in this predicament.

The conflicts and tensions which Aborigines are facing come from a variety of causes. The first obviously has been the disastrous history of race relations in the North in the past. Their futile attempts to fight with spears against guns resulted in their retreat into the unwanted wilderness of Arnhem Land. Even here they had to fight for their lives and their land against pastoralists and buffalo shooters who came overland, and the pearlers and trepangers who came by sea. They had always to be on the defensive, fighting a losing battle.

Another major cause for tension and unrest was their changing life-style. They were now becoming settled and living in communities. They had to become artisans and agriculturists if they wanted to get any money. They constantly had to make a choice. To remain in settlements and gain some of the material goods which life offered there, or to revert to their nomadic way of life and miss out on them. This was the dilemma which they continually had to face.

Further tensions occurred when the Arnhemlanders went to Darwin. Their contact with Western civilisation and technology was limited while they remained in the missions and settlements. Their European mentors had their interests at heart and shielded them from the more sordid aspects of Western society. This was not the case when they themselves moved into Darwin and the other towns of the Top End. Here they quickly became prey to opium, alcohol and prostitution. At this time there was no conflict, just destruction.

During World War II their northern homelands became Australia's front line of defence. They were plunged overnight into the complexities of wartime Western culture. They now had money. They could now get a wide variety of goods. They were able to purchase tobacco and alcohol. They saw the good ways and the bad ways of large numbers of non-mission white people. They could not ever be the same afterwards. But what of their culture back home? What was happening to their ceremonies and their land which had now almost become a battlefield? New pressures appeared. New conflicts became evident. The old culture was under increased threat.

As the years rolled by the Aborigines of Arnhem Land became more accustomed to the advantages of Western life-styles. The store supplanted work in the gardens of the early missions. Guns were more effective than spears for hunting. High-powered motor boats were easier to handle than the old dugout canoes with their Macassan-type sails. More fish could be caught far more quickly with nets than with spears. Visits to relatives and to corroborees were so much quicker by four-wheel drive and aeroplane than by foot. The demand for Western goods increased in tempo. Houses, washing machines, water and electricity reticulation soon became common-place. Camp riots almost took place if the weekly or twice-weekly film show did not eventuate. In this respect Arnhem Land Aborigines were becoming acculturated, their first step in assimilation.

At the same time they kept much of the old way. Although they had no wish to do many things the same as in olden times they still performed their ceremonies. They had to maintain their identity. They had to follow two ways. As one old Aboriginal said, 'That is the way you see it, but not as we see it. We see it in a different way. You are a white man and you see it that way.' They were seeing the material benefits through the same eyes that were seeing the age-old ceremonies of the ancestors. The old ways were under threat, but they were still being maintained. From time to time some of the old customs looked like being lost, but they were revived. It seemed at one stage that they even might lose their land, but they were able to keep this. For as they say so often, 'If I have no land, I have no name.'

Alcohol is another major threat to their culture, to their health and to their very existence. They could not cope with it, as they had

268

no dreamtime law to direct its use. They could not handle it, although they quickly realised its effects. For a short while it can drown their sorrows, make them forget their tensions, and cause them to feel like free men. The trouble is that there is always the morning after. Liquor also threatens their dances. The song leaders do not arrive at the ceremonies because they become drunk along the way. The dances sometimes have to be abandoned.

Education, the presence of large mining towns, the mineral exploration over hundreds of square kilometres of the country, intermarriage, employment away from home are further factors bringing conflict and stress into the lives of the Arnhemlanders. They want the best of what these things offer. They cannot avoid making continual contact. Balanda pressures are numerous, attractive in some ways, and powerful. But they often say, 'We want your goods but we do not want to be Balanda. We are Aborigines.'

The response of the Arnhem Land Aborigines to the threats to their identity and the cross-cultural tensions takes various forms. The first is seen in their retreat to their homelands. This movement had been going on for a number of years, when several of the more far-sighted missionaries encouraged the moves. The concept was given great impetus by the Labor Government in 1973 and has gained in momentum since that time.

The Aborigines who are going back to their homelands say that they are going home. They also say, 'It is not good seeing our tribal land barren without people there.' They can get away from the fights and drunken brawls. They can live with their families and control their children and young people. They can get 'bush tucker' instead of tinned food. They can have their ceremonies and maintain their identity.

They do not return to their former way of life fully, and could not even if they wanted to. The Balanda way of life has become part of theirs and they have to adapt to it. They wear European clothes, are in radio contact with their central communities, and have airstrips and roads. The very sick are evacuated by plane. They have simple houses made with corrugated iron, or they live in tents or bush shelters. They supplement their 'bush tucker' with imported food.

The advantages of the homeland movement are obvious. People are living back where they know that they belong. They live in the country given to them by their ancestors. They do what they want to do at their own pace in their own time. They have a great pride in their camp and keep it clean and tidy. They are conscious of their identity once more.

The homeland movement also has great disadvantages. Children's education poses a very real problem. They try to meet this need by having their own Aboriginal teachers, but there will not be sufficient teachers for a number of years. Children who are left with relatives in the main community centres also face problems.

Health care is also another area of great concern. Health worker training programs will provide limited Aboriginal help. There will always be the need for more intensive specialised care in the main centres or in Darwin. During the Wet roads and airstrips can become completely unserviceable for weeks on end. On these occasions they can get no outside help.

One of the long-term disadvantages of the homeland movement is the fragmentation of Aboriginal people into small, isolated groups throughout many parts of Arnhem Land. This isolation must prevent them from sharing fully in the social and economic development of their own people in other parts of the country. Instead of maintaining their own identity, but integrating with the non-Aboriginal community to mutual advantage, they could become greatly impoverished by their isolation and lack of communication. This situation could easily result in a renewed feeling of inferiority similar to that in which they found themselves several decades earlier.

The homeland movement also does not generate any form of wealth. Some may see that as an advantage. They may think that survival through 'bush tucker', the sale of artifacts and paintings supplemented by social security benefits are sufficient. The danger is that continued dependence at a poverty level according to generally accepted Western standards could make a number of the young people dissatisfied and disgruntled. The final result could be a form of shanty town existence extending from the larger community centres.

A large number of Aborigines on the other hand do not want to return to their homelands and live there permanently. They might go and camp there for a while. But they prefer to live with the comforts and tensions of the Arnhem Land communities.

The Arnhem Land Reserve towns therefore will continue to be important Aboriginal places. Here men and women can get employment on award wages. Children can be educated to a fairly high level, and medical facilities are readily available. And of course they are the homelands for at least one of the clans in each of the places. They also fulfil the important function of providing supplies for the outstations.

Arnhem Land Aborigines living in the towns now have a greater awareness of their civic responsibilities. They have their own Town

Councils and they run their own affairs. They acknowledge immediately that they need the help and expertise of a number of non-Aborigines, who for a number of years will need to provide the skills which they have not yet been able to acquire.

Aboriginal councils administer the civic affairs of the Arnhem Land towns. These councils are certainly not part of the earlier culture. Everyone realises this, but there seems to be no viable alternative. When people agree to live in communities on European lines, then they accept the general way in which Town Councils anywhere operate. This is very necessary as large sums of money, often amounting to over a million dollars a community, is required each year to pay for their activities.

Even though councils have to operate in a European way, they can be run effectively by incorporating some Aboriginal features. For example, council membership may be obtained by clan nomination instead of by open elections. The decision-making process is often made by community as well as the council. As one Aboriginal said, 'In the Aboriginal way, I think that you should have a meeting of the whole community instead of the Town Council meeting. Then the Town Council can work it out afterwards.' Another way of conducting meetings is to raise the questions, allow the clan members to take these back to the community, then bring their decisons to the next or to subsequent meetings. In this way the whole community becomes involved.

Town Councils in Arnhem Land also have their problems. There are frequent clashes between the older, more conservative, people, and those who are younger and more progressive. Clan claims and loyalties can often cloud the main issues and make for controversy and indecision. Pressures brought about by power groups, or even powerful individuals can disrupt the good functioning of meetings. Aborigines, within a very short space of time, have accustomed themselves to the working of councils and are acting very responsibly in the decisions which they are making.

Aboriginal Town Councils are important for the communities which they serve. They also have the function of introducing Aborigines to European-type administration. They can become important training centres for the meeting of Aboriginal and Balanda culture. This had been the aim of the former assimilationist policies. But there is now a major difference. Formerly non-Aborigines required all Aborigines to be assimilated completely. Now Aborigines, on their own terms, managing their own affairs, incorporate and use in their ways those things which they find advantageous. The choice belongs to them, not to Europeans.

271

Town Councils have the responsibility for community services. They are concerned with water and electricity reticulation, sewerage, workshops, roads, community projects, such as fishing, cattle raising, timber milling and so on. Because of this, councils now employ a large number of non-Aborigines, who formerly were employed by the missions or the Government. This raises the important issue whether missions should continue to function in the community as they have done in former years.

Most Aborigines say that they want the help of non-Europeans to work on the various community projects, which they themselves cannot yet do. Some have said, 'We want help in running our communities. We do not like Aboriginal people to be left alone to run the place by themselves. It is too early for us to do this. We do not think that way.' This contrasts sharply with the clear policy of the clan leaders in the homeland communities. Being far less sophisticated, and requiring much less expertise, they say that they do not want non-Aborigines to help them run their affairs. They want to be left alone to manage them themselves.

This then raises important questions for 'missions' and their activities in Aboriginal communities today. 'Missions' has become the accepted word linking the organisation with the past, but operating as church and community centred rather than in its own right. 'Are missions still wanted in Arnhem Land? Are missionaries still wanted? Should missionaries still function, even though they are asked to do so?' These are some of the questions that are being asked at the present time.

Even though the questions are being asked, one thing is quite clear. Aboriginal communities are now run by Aboriginal people. Any function of any mission or missionary or any outside person or organisation must be that of serving rather than that of managing, of advising rather than directing.

The answer to the question put to Aboriginal people about their need for missions and missionaries is quite specific. 'We want the missionaries. They have been with us for a long time. We know the mission. We know its foundation. We want the missionaries to stay.'

In response to this clear statement the United Church in its document 'Free to Decide' stated that 'the mission of the Church among Aboriginal people in Northern Australia today is: (1) to identify with the Aboriginal person and community as broken victims of the dominating Australian society, and help him to move for his freedom ... (2) to proclaim the mercy of God in Christ ... (3) to live and work with Aborigines in their communities in ways which bring new awareness of both problems and possibilities, and which offer them new freedom in shaping their style of life in their way and at their pace, and (4) to help the Aboriginal person and community, caught between two worlds, to know his own identity . . .'

As a result of this policy the Uniting Church in Australia is maintaining a large, continuing presence in the Arnhem Land communities. The Anglican Church on the other hand, in line with its overseas policy over a number of years, is trying to reduce its numbers with the hope of giving Aborigines more freedom in their decision-making processes. Both churches are sensitive to the requests of Aborigines and their great need to advise rather than to direct. They need constantly to avoid continued over-reliance by Aborigines on them, otherwise this could lead to a new form of dependance and bondage. This could also be the case in the non-mission communities in Arnhem Land.

Arnhem Land Aborigines can achieve and maintain an increased sense of freedom, dignity and identity through relevant educational procedures and adequate vocational training. The right kind of education can be a most important tool for freedom just as it can be manipulated for oppression. Bilingual education is the first step in better learning and understanding. Further curricular changes still need to be provided to make the learning processes more meaningful and provide the greatly needed motivation. Similarly vocational training should be geared to work opportunities in both societies. Only then will Aborigines be free to choose what they want to do.

Many Aboriginal parents and children need to have a far greater sense of purpose in schooling. Visitors from Third World countries usually express surprise and dismay at the apparent lack of application of children to their studies. In their countries, the increasing demand for greater skills makes students work very hard. They find Aboriginal children, generally speaking, very different. Perhaps present educational programs do not give the right interest and motivation. It may be that the general situation in the communities hinders children from achieving, or wanting to achieve at school. Community upheavals caused by alcohol have certainly had a devastating effect on children, causing absenteeism and, in some cases, malnutrition. Only by greater diligence in academic work and vocational training will Aborigines be free men in the highly competitive wider Australian society.

The Aboriginal quest for identity, freedom and fulfilment also raises issues of much wider significance.

The first concerns the nature of the Aboriginal people themselves.

273

The question often rightly is asked, 'Who are the Aborigines?' Different groups now identify as Aborigines.

First of all there are the full-bloods, whose tribal structures remain basically intact. They usually live in the reserves. Those living in Arnhem Land have been granted full land rights.

Aborigines working on cattle stations form another large group. Many families have been living on these stations for years. Others have moved backwards and forwards to and from the reserves. The number has decreased in more recent years as the result of the rural recession. In most cases Aborigines living on cattle stations also have retained much of their tribal traditions.

Part-Aborigines living as fringe dwellers in country towns or in the big cities are two other very large groups who identify as Aborigines. They are often vocal regarding Aboriginal rights. They are usually completely detribalised and do not know their tribal origins or customs.

The expectations of these different groups vary greatly acording to their location and background. The need to combat malnutrition in the slums of Redfern is a far cry from the land rights issues of the Northern Territory. Problems concerning housing in the country towns in NSW are very different from the need for non-discrimination in employment opportunities on the cattle stations.

They all unite on one thing. They are Aborigines with a common Aboriginal ancestry. They have all experienced to a greater or lesser degree racial discrimination and intolerance. They all combine in demanding their right to identity, and to live as free people in a country which was once theirs.

There is among all Aboriginal people a rapidly growing awareness of political power. Their rural vote in the recent Northern Territory Legislative Assembly elections was a clear indication of this when they toppled the Leader of the Majority Party, Dr Goff Letts. There is also a very strong desire to be responsible for their own affairs nationally as well as in the communities. The first action of the National Aboriginal Consultative Council (NACC) was to call itself the National Aboriginal Congress (NAC). The Aboriginal delegates made it clear that they did not wish to consult or to advise. They wanted authority to administer.

Aborigines were unsuccessful in the first round, as the NACC remained advisory. They probably will not succeed the second time round in their efforts to get executive powers for the revamped National Aboriginal Conference. The time nevertheless must come when Aborigines themselves have control of their own affairs at every level of the administration. Far too many non-Aborigines and far too few Aborigines are working for the Department of Aboriginal Affairs in Canberra, in the Territory, and on the settlements. The same applies to the missions. Far too many non-Aborigines are working for Aborigines instead of allowing Aborigines to do things themselves, or at least have the clear direction of the work.

An obvious corollary to the above is the lack of initiative and decision-making on a national level. The hope is that the new NAC will provide more positive suggestions. But even then, suggestions and advice are not the same as taking the initiative and making the decisions. Aborigines must be given the opportunity to manage their own affairs and to make their own decisions if they are to be fully free.

At the same time self-determination itself should not be exempt from scrutiny and debate. Governments and missions at various times thought that the various policies of protection, segregation, assimilation were right. They probably were for their times in the nation's history. Integration seems appropriate for us at the present. Aboriginal and non-Aboriginal cultures should be allowed to develop separately, but to be integrated and together to become part of Australian society. The question which many people now ask is, 'Are self-determination or self-management the final answers in the Aboriginal search for identity and freedom?'

The immediate answer of the Aborigines of Arnhem Land is, 'Yes, we think that self-determination is the right way.' There is no doubt that they have a new sense of dignity and confidence. They say, 'We want authority and responsibility. We want to be Aborigines and we want to be free.' To have shared this new mood and this new feeling among Aboriginal people has been an exciting experience.

This said there are still questions unanswered. Self-determination and self-management require some form of integration, whereby the black and white races are free to follow their own cultural needs, but at the same time be linked together, so that the two parts form a composite whole, the one nation of Australia. Are the two separate developing races prepared to accept each other and live in harmony? Will the growing black power movement and the white back-lash be prepared to accept *rapprochement*? Are races able to live in freedom when remaining in such a state of confrontation?

One fundamental issue appears to be insoluble. Any form of self-determination for the Aborigines of Arnhem Land is completely dependent upon massive Government grants. The communities there and in other parts of the Territory are economically completely non-viable. They generate almost no capital or revenue whatever.

Town Councils are able to function only within the parameters of Government funding. If Government funds were removed for any reason, then the community services would collapse immediately. There would be complete chaos.

The Aborigines of Arnhem Land are therefore not free economically. They are still dependent on Government money. They are free to determine what they will do with the money once they have received it. At the same time they have no power to determine how much, because they have none of their own. All comes from the Government of the day. This basic fact could once again militate against them as they continue in their journey to freedom. Once again they could feel that they were still second-rate, dependent people.

Self-determination nevertheless has brought a sense of freedom and purpose to all Aborigines throughout the Northern Territory. They are also aware of another fact. The present Aboriginal reserves occupy about 244 000 square kilometres. This is just under one-fifth of the total area of the Territory of 1 356 000 square kilometres. All the reserves are becoming Aboriginal land. Other unalienated Crown land is subject to claim under the Land Rights Act of 1976, provided Aboriginal ownership can be established. This will mean that Aborigines will have freehold title in perpetuity to at least one-fifth of the Territory. They will be able to control access to and activity on their land, including mining. The result is a kind of black state within a larger white state, which could lead to political conflict and confrontation in the future.

Moreover the Aboriginal control of the right to mine on their land (unless the Government declares that such mining is in the national interest) means that future mining, when existing leases or agreements expire, will be determined by Aborigines. These measures ensure that their land is protected. It may also place the new State of the Northern Territory or whatever it is to be called in considerable jeopardy. With doubts hanging over the viability of Territory pastoral enterprises, the only other major source of revenue comes from mining royalties. If this source of income cannot be guaranteed then the new state may find that it has grave economic problems.

Future uranium royalties could make many Aboriginal clan owners rich people. All Aborigines and the Northern Land Council will also greatly benefit from the receipt of these royalties. This may offset to some extent the dependent state of the communities. It may also lead to Aboriginal investment in mining and further income.

The number of Aborigines living in the Territory is also growing. The 1976 census showed that of the total Territory population of approximately 101 000, about 26 000 were people identifying as Aborigines. Thus about one in four in the Territory is Aboriginal. Projections of European population in the towns are hard to establish. One thing is clear. The Aboriginal population is increasing. The result well could be that the proportion of non-Aborigines to Aborigines will decrease. Thus the possibility of an Aboriginal State some time in the future is not outside the bounds of possibility.

But to return to the present. The Aborigines of the Territory, and especially those in Arnhem Land, stand on the threshold of a new way. They have experienced tragedy and despair for more than a century. Their long, long road to freedom has been marked by sincere but sometimes misguided attempts by others to make them free. They are now in the position for the first time, where they themselves have the opportunity of making themselves free. Their civic freedom may depend on Government money. But there are other things which money cannot buy. There is the freedom of the spirit. They are now able to determine what they want, to live their own life-styles, to adopt or adapt European ways. They are men free to choose, for as they say, 'We want to be free'.

Tables

TABLE I   POPULATION CENSUS, 30 JUNE 1976.
ARNHEM LAND.

Locality	Total Population	Estimated Aboriginal Population
Croker Island	244	215
Goulburn Island	243	210
Oenpelli	508	450
Between Oenpelli & Goulburn Is.	60	60
Maningrida	660	540
Milingimbi	677	625
Arnhem incl. Ramingining	1,027	990
Galiwinku (Elcho Is.)	987	875
Arnhem incl. Lake Evella	422	410
Numbulwar	371	330
Ngukurr	250	235
Angurugu	700	620
Umbakumba	371	335
Yirrkala	647	550
Outer Yirrkala	341	235
Totals	7,508	6,680
Nhulunbuy	3,553	
Alyangula	988	
	12,049	6,680

Approximately fifty per cent of the Aboriginal population is under the age of eighteen years.

278

TABLE 2   MONTHLY RAINFALL (MEDIAN) OF THE
ARNHEM LAND
COMMUNITIES.

Place	Jan	Feb	Mar	Apr	May	Jun	Jul	Aug	Sep	Oct	Nov	Dec
Oenpelli	317	271	260	36	1	0	0	0	0	11	92	202
Croker Is.	342	314	194	90	11	1	0	0	0	0	33	139
Goulburn Is.	249	242	223	57	4	0	0	0	0	2	45	150
Maningrida	253	234	212	42	11	0	0	0	0	?	36	133
Milingimbi	233	216	202	62	17	0	0	0	0	1	36	139
Elcho Is.	302	287	188	95	15	2	0	0	0	1	26	154
Yirrkala	194	213	225	180	66	21	7	2	1	0	11	106
Groote Eylandt	213	229	274	114	18	2	0	0	0	15	83	124
Roper River	139	134	122	15	0	0	0	0	0	1	27	95

TABLE 3   ARNHEM LAND: ANNUAL TEMPERATURES,
RAINFALL AND RAINDAYS.

Place	Temperatures (C)		Rainfall (mm)		Raindays (No)
	Max. (mean)	Min. (mean)	mean	median	mean
Oenpelli	33.9	21.8	1360	1295	92
Croker Is.	30.4	24.0	1343	1380	89
Goulburn Is.	31.1	24.0	1148	1122	75
Maningrida	31.6	21.5	1141	1128	82
Milingimbi	31.7	22.6	1143	1080	79
Elcho Is.	32.1	22.9	1329	1328	93
Yirrkala	30.5	23.1	1315	1293	90
Groote Eylandt	32.4	19.7	1277	1251	80
Roper River	34.2	20.8	752	729	49

Chapter bibliography

The following Chapter Bibliography is a select reference list only. Books referred to in one chapter are often used in other chapters. The Chapter Bibliography should be used in conjunction with the General Bibliography.

CHAPTERS 1 and 2

Alligator Rivers Region Environmental Fact Finding Study. A Review Report, Darwin, 1973. Printed Report, Canberra, 1977. (Also supplementary reports.)

Australian Bureau of Statistics. Northern Territory, Census of Population and Housing, 30th June 1976.

Bauer, F. H., *Historical Geography of White Settlement in Part of Northern Australia, Part 2. The Katherine-Darwin Region.* CSIRO Divisional Report No 64/1. Canberra, 1964.

Breeden, S. and K., *Australia's North: A Natural History of Australia: 3.* Sydney, 1975.

Department of Science, Australia, Bureau of Meteorology. Reports.

Harmer, Jenny, *North Australian Plants, Part 1, Wildflowers of the Northern Territory Top End.* Darwin, (undated).

Learmonth, N. and A., *Regional Landscapes of Australia: Form, Function and Change.* Sydney, 1971.

Sharp, A., *The Discovery of Australia.* Oxford, 1963.

Slater, Peter, *A Field Guide to Australian Birds. Non-Passerines.* Adelaide, 1970.

_____ *A Field Guide to Australian Birds. Passerines.* Adelaide, 1974.

CHAPTER 3

Abbie, A. A., *The Original Australians*. Adelaide, 1969. (Revised 1976).

Blainey, Geoffrey, *Triumph of the Nomads*. Melbourne, 1975.

Capell, A., *A New Approach to Australian Linguistics*. Sydney, 1962.

Dixon, R.M.W. (ed.), *The Grammatical Categories of Australian Languages*. AIAS, Canberra, 1976.

Elkin, A.P., *The Australian Aborigines*. Sydney, 1938/1964.

Gale, Fay, *Woman's Role in Aboriginal Society*. AIAS, Canberra, 1974.

Kearney, G.E. (and others), *The Psychology of Aboriginal Australians*. Sydney, 1973.

Kirk, R.L. and Thorne, A.G., *The Origin of the Australians*. AIAS, Canberra, 1976.

Maddock, Kenneth, *The Australian Aborigines*. Melbourne, 1974.

Mulvaney, D.J., *The Prehistory of Australia*. London, 1969.

_____ (ed.), *Australian Archaeology*. AIAS, Canberra, 1972.

_____ and Golson, J. (eds.), *Aboriginal Man and Environment in Australia*. Canberra, 1971.

Oates, L.F., *The 1973 Supplement to a Revised Linguistic Survey of Australia*. Armidale, 1975.

_____ and W.J., *A Revised Linguistic Survey of Australia*. AIAS, Canberra, 1970.

Peterson, Nicolas (ed.), *Tribes and Boundaries in Australia*. AIAS, Canberra, 1976.

Spencer, Sir W. Baldwin., *Native Tribes of the Northern Territory of Australia*. London, 1914.

Tindale, N.B., *Aboriginal Tribes of Australia*. California, 1974.

_____ Map of Tribal Boundaries in Aboriginal Australia. AIAS, Canberra, 1976.

White, Carmel, "Early Stone Axes in Arnhem Land". *Antiquity* 41, (1967) pp. 149-52.

_____ "Prehistory of the Kakadu people". *Mankind* 6, pp. 426-31.

CHAPTERS 4 and 5

Berndt, C.H., *Women's Changing Ceremonies in North Australia*. Paris, 1950.

Berndt, R.M., *Kunapipi: A Study of an Aboriginal religious cult*. Melbourne, 1951.

_____ *Djanggawul*, London, 1952.

_____ (ed.), *Aboriginal Australian Art*. Sydney, 1964.

Berndt, R.M., and C.H., *The First Australians*. Sydney, 1952, (revised 1967).

_____ *Arnhem Land: its history and its people*. Melbourne, 1954.

_____ *The World of the First Australians*. Sydney, 1964.

_____ *Aboriginal Man in Australia: essays in honour of Emeritus Professor A.P. Elkin*. Sydney, 1965.

Edwards, Robert, *The Preservation of Australia's Aboriginal Heritage*. AIAS, Canberra, 1975.

Elkin, A.P., *Aboriginal Men of High Degree*. Sydney, 1945.

Harney, W.E. and Elkin, A.P., *Songs of the Songmen*. Melbourne, 1949.

Hasluck, P., *Black Australians*. Melbourne, 1942.

Hiatt, L.R., *Kinship and Conflict*. Canberra, 1965.

McCarthy, F.D., *Australian Aboriginal Rock Art*. Sydney, 1958.

Mountford, C.P. (ed.), Records of the American-Australian Scientific Expedition to Arnhem Land. (4 vols.) Melbourne, 1960-4.

Rose, F.G.G., *Classification of kin, structure and marriage among the Groote Eylandt Aborigines*. Berlin, 1960.

Thomson, D.F., *Economic Structure and Ceremonial Exchange Cycle in Arnhem Land*. Melbourne, 1949.

Turner, H., *Tradition and Transformation*. AIAS, Canberra, 1974.

Warner, W.L., *A Black Civilization: a social study of an Australian tribe*. (3rd ed.) New York, 1964.

CHAPTER 6

Cole, Keith, *Totems and Tamarinds*. Darwin, 1973.

Macknight, C.C. (ed.), *The Farthest Coast: a selection of writings relating to the northern coast of Australia*. Melbourne, 1969.

_____ *The Voyage to Marege: Macassan trepangers in northern Australia*. Melbourne, 1976.

Macknight, C.C., and Gray, W.J., *Aboriginal Stone Pictures in Eastern Arnhem Land*. AIAS, Canberra, 1970.

Searcy, A., *In Northern Seas*. Adelaide, 1905.

_____ *In Australian Tropics*. London, 1907.

Spillett, P.G., *Forsaken Settlement: An illustrated history of the settlement of Victoria, Port Essington, North Australia, 1838-1849*. Melbourne, 1972.

Warner, W.L., 'Malay influence on the Aboriginal cultures of north-eastern Arnhem Land'. *Oceania*, Vol. 2(1932), pp. 476-95.

Worsley, P.M., 'Early Asian contacts with Australia'. *Past and Present* (1955), pp.1-11.

CHAPTER 7

Beaglehole, J.C., *The Exploration of the Pacific*. London, 1966.

Cadell, Francis, *Exploration of the Northern Territory*. Adelaide, 1868.

Flinders, Matthew, *A Voyage to Terra Australis* ... (2 vols.) London, 1814.

Howard, D.D., 'The English Activities in the North Coast of Australia in the First Half of the Nineteenth Century'. *'Proceedings of the Royal Geographical Society of Australasia (S.A. Branch)*, Vol. 33 (1933).

King, Phillip Parker, *Narrative of a Survey of the Intertropical and Western Coasts of Australia, Performed between the Years 1818 and 1822*. (2 vols.) London, 1827.

Leichhardt, Ludwig, *Journal of an overland expedition from Moreton Bay to Port Essington ... during the years 1844-45*. Adelaide, 1868.

Lockwood, Douglas, *The Front Door, Darwin, 1869-1969*. Adelaide, 1968.

Stokes, John Lort, *Discoveries in Australia*. (2 vols.) London, 1846.

Threadgill, B., *South Australian Land Exploration: 1856 to 1880*. (2 parts). Adelaide, 1922.

Stuart, J.McD. 'Diary of Mr John McDouall Stuart's explorations from Adelaide across the continent of Australia, 1861-2. *Journal of Royal Geographical Society of London*, Vol. 33.

CHAPTER 8 and 9

Bleakley, J.W. *The Aborigines of Australia*. Brisbane, 1961.

_____ 1928 Report 'The Aboriginals and Half-Castes of Central Australia and North Australia'. CPP No 21, 1929.

Duguid, Charles, *No Dying Race*. Adelaide, 1963.

Foxcroft, E.J.B., *Australian Native Policy*. Melbourne, 1941.

Long, J.P.M., *Aboriginal Settlements*. Canberra, 1970.

McEwen, J., 'The Northern Territory of Australia: Commonwealth Government's Policy with respect to Aboriginals'. Canberra, 1939.

Price, A.G., *The History and Problems of the Northern Territory of Australia*. Adelaide, 1930.

Roberts, S.H., *History of Australian Land Settlement (1788-1920)*. Melbourne, 1924.

Rowley, C.D., *The Destruction of Aboriginal Society*. Canberra, 1974 reprint.

Sharp, I.G., and Tatz, C.M. (eds.), *Aborigines in the Economy*. Brisbane, 1966.

Spencer, Sir W. Baldwin, 'Preliminary Report on the Aboriginals of the Northern Territory'. Melbourne, 1913.

Thomson, Donald, 'Interim General Report of Parliamentary Expedition to Arnhem Land, Northern Territory of Australia, 1935-36'. (Roneoed.) Melbourne, 1936.

____ Report on Expedition to Arnhem Land, 1936-7. Canberra, 1939.

Welfare Branch (Division), Department of the Northern Territory. Annual Reports, Other reports and papers.

CHAPTERS 10 and 11

Chaseling, W., *Yulengor: nomads of Arnhem Land*. London, 1957.

Church Missionary Society Records. Sydney.

Cole, Keith, *A History of the CMS Roper River Mission 1908-1968*. Melbourne, 1969.

____ *A History of the Church Missionary Society of Australia*.

____ *Groote Eylandt Mission*, Melbourne, 1971.

____ *Groote Eylandt Pioneer*. Melbourne, 1971.

____ *Groote Eylandt*. Darwin, 1975.

____ *A History of Oenpelli*. Darwin, 1975.

Ellemore, A.F., *Warrawi Jubilee, 1916-1966*. Darwin, 1966.

Herbert, Xavier, *Capricornia*. Sydney, 1937.

Lamilami, Lazarus, *Lamilami Speaks*. Sydney, 1974.

Langford-Smith, K., *Sky Pilot in Arnhem Land*. Sydney, 1935.

McKenzie, Maisie, *Mission to Arnhem Land*. Adelaide, 1976.

Methodist Overseas Mission, Records in the Mitchell Library, Sydney.

National Missionary Council, Records in Australian Council of Churches Office, Sydney.

Nungalinya College, Records. Darwin.

United Church in North Australia, *Free to Decide. Report of Commission of Enquiry, Arnhem Land*. Darwin, 1974.

Wells, A.E. *Milingimbi*. Sydney, 1963.

Wilkins, G.H. *Undiscovered Australia*. London, 1928.

CHAPTER 12

Aboriginal Affairs, Department of, Annual Reports, Various Reports, Non-confidential documents.

Cavanagh, J.L., 'Selected Policy Statements on Aboriginal Affairs, 1973-74'. DAA, Canberra, 1974.

McMahon, W., 'Statement of Objectives'. Canberra, 1972.

National Aboriginal Consultative Committee, Report of Committee of Inquiry. DAA, 1976.

Stanner, W.E.H. *After the Dreaming*. Sydney, 1968.

CHAPTER 13

Aboriginal Land Rights (Northern Territory) Act, 1976.

'Aboriginal Lands Rights Commission', First (Woodward) Report, July, 1973.

'Aboriginal Land Rights Commission', Second (Woodward) Report. April, 1974.

House of Representatives. Weekly Hansard, No 23, 1976. 16-18 November 1976.

Senate, Weekly Hansard, No 25, 1976, 6-10 December 1976.

'Land Rights News, a Newsletter for Aborigines and their friends'. Nos 1-12, July 1976 — June 1977.

'Report from the Select Committee on grievances of Yirrkala Aborigines, Arnhem Land Reserve'. Canberra, 1963.

CHAPTER 14

Groote Eylandt Mining Co Pty Ltd, Reports.

Nabalco Reports.

Ranger Uranium Environmental Inquiry. First (Fox) Report, 1976. Second (Fox) Report, 1977.

CHAPTER 15

Beckhenham, P.W., *The Education of the Australian Aborigine*. Melbourne, 1948.

Berndt, Ronald M., 'Traditional Australian Aboriginal Life and the Native School'. Reprinted from *The Western Australian Teachers' Journal*, 1965.

Commonwealth Office of Education, Annual Reports, 1950-56.

Department of Education, Northern Territory Division, Reports.

Duke, C. and Sommerlad, E., *Design for Diversity: Further education for tribal Aborigines in the north*. Canberra. 1976.

Eedle, James, 'Selected Papers, 1975-6'. Darwin, (undated).

Edwards, N.R., 'Native Education in the Northern Territory of Australia'. (Typed.) Sydney, (undated).

Flynn, K., 'Brief History of Native Education in the Northern Territory'. (Typed.) 1960.

Groves, W.C., 'Preliminary Outline of Proposals for Education and Welfare of Natives of Northern Territory Force' and 'Report on Education and Welfare of Natives of Northern Territory Force'. Canberra, 1944.

Hart, A.M., *Their earlier years; Educational Experiences in their own words*. Adelaide, 1977.

Miller, E.P. *Manual Training Facilities for the Special Schools of the Northern Territory*. Darwin, 1964.

'A Review of N.T. Residential Colleges, 1977'. (Randall Report.)

Watts, B.H. and Gallacher, J.D., 'Report on investigation and the Curriculum and Teaching Methods used in Aboriginal Schools in the Northern Territory'. Darwin, 1964.

_____ *Access to Education*. Canberra, 1976.

Bilingual Education.

'Bilingual Education in the Northern Territory.' Reprint of three articles from *Education News*, 1975.

O'Grady, G., Hale, K., *Recommendations concerning Bilingual Education in the Northern Territory*. Darwin, 1974.

Watts, B.H., McGrath, W.J. and Tand, J.L., *Bilingual Education in Schools in Aboriginal Communities in the Northern Territory*. Darwin, 1973.

Film, 'Not to lose you, my language'.

First Annual Report on the Bilingual Education Programme in Schools in the Northern Territory. Darwin, 1973.

Second Progress Report on the Bilingual Education Program in Schools in the Northern Territory. Darwin, 1974.

CHAPTER 16

Department of Aboriginal Affairs, Reports and papers dealing with employment.

The Environmental Conditions of Aborigines and Torres Strait Islanders and the Preservation of their Sacred Sites. AIAS, Canberra, 1976.

Stevens, F.S., *Equal Wages for Aborigines*. Sydney, 1968.

CHAPTER 17

'Aborigines and the Law', National Seminar Centre for Research into Aboriginal Affairs at Monash University, July, 1974.

'A National Aboriginal Legal Service: Government Proposals'. *Law Institute Journal*, 47 (1973).

Australian Law Reform Commission 1977, Interim Reports 1 and 2.

Australian Law Reports.

Elkin, E.P. 'Aboriginal Evidence and Justice in North Australia', *Oceania*, Vol. 17 (1947).

Goldring, J. 'White Laws, Black People', *Australian Quarterly*, Vol. 45, No 3 (1973), pp. 5-18.

Kriewaldt, M.C., 'The application of the Criminal Law to the Aborigines of the Northern Territory of Australia'. *University of W.A. Law Review*. 1960.

Nettheim, Garth (ed.), *Aborigines, Human Rights and the Law*. Sydney, 1974.

_____ *Out Lawed, Queensland's Aborigines and Islanders and the Rule of Law*. Sydney, 1973.

Strehlow, T.G.H., 'Notes on Native Evidence and its Value'. *Oceania*, Vol. 6 (1936), pp.323-35.

CHAPTER 18

'Aboriginal Health Worker Training Programme in the Northern Territory'. A report of the work carried out by the Education and training task force: 22 November 1976 to 30 June 1977.

Baddeley, J., 'History of Health Services in the Northern Territory'. (Typed.) Darwin, (undated).

Department of Health, Reports.

Eastwell, H., 'The Traditional Healer in Modern Arnhem Land'. *Medical Journal of Australia*, 1973. 2:1011-1017.

Forster, Leslie, 'Family Health in Tribal Aborigines'. *Medical Journal of Australia*. Special Supplement, 1975, 2:27-32.

Soong, F.S., 'Health Education as a means of improving Aboriginal Health.' *Medical Journal of Australia*. Special Supplement, 1975, 1:4-8.

Wood, Beverley, (ed.) *Tucker in Australia*. Melbourne, 1977.

CHAPTER 19

'Alcohol Problems of Aboriginals: Northern Territory Aspects.' Canberra, 1976.

Beckett, J., 'Aborigines, Alcohol and Assimilation' in *Aborigines Now,* ed. M. Reay. Sydney, 1964.

Report of the Board of Inquiry appointed to inquire concerning the liquor laws of the Northern Territory. Canberra, 1973.

Sansom, Basil, *Aborigines and Alcohol: a Fringe Camp Example.* Darwin, 1977.

Nungalinya College, The Grog-Breakers. Practical suggestions for ending the present wave of drunkenness in Aboriginal communities. Darwin, 1977.

Films

'Just One'; 'Shall we drink'; 'To your health'; 'Cheers'.

General bibliography

These references should be used together with the Chapter Bibliographies.

Anderson, D.S., (and others), *Communities and Colleges*. Canberra, 1976.
Australian Encyclopedia. Sydney, 1965.
Australian Institute of Aboriginal Studies,
  Bibliographies.
  Newsletter.
  Reports.
Bates, D., *The Passing of the Aborigines*. London, 1941.
Clark, M., *A Short History of Australia*. New York, 1963.
Clark, M., (ed.) *Sources of Australian History*. Sydney, 1957.
Commonwealth Parliamentary Papers.
Crowley, F., *A New History of Australia*.
Department of the Interior, Reports.
Department of Labour and National Service, Reports.
Department of Territories, Reports.
Drysdale, Ingrid and Durack, Mary, *The End of Dreaming*. Adelaide, 1974.
Duke, C., and Sommerlad, Elizabeth, *Design for Diversity*. Canberra, 1976.
Franklin, M.A., *Black and White Australians*. Melbourne, 1976.
Gale, G.F., and Brookman, Alison, *Race Relations in Australia — The Aborigines*. Sydney, 1975.

Hansard, Parliamentary debates.
Historical Records of Australia.
Journals, *Antiquity*
  Hemisphere
  Mankind
  Oceania
  Past and Present
  Practical Anthropology
  South-Western Journal of Anthropology
King-Boyes, M., *Patterns of Aboriginal Culture: Then and Now*. Sydney, 1977.
Lockwood, D., *I, the Aboriginal*. Adelaide, 1962.
Northern Land Council, Non-confidential records.
Northern Territory, Annual Reports.
  _____ Proceedings of the Legislative Assembly.
Northern Territory News.
Northern Territory Newsletter.
Report from the Select Committee on Voting Rights of Aboriginals. 1961.
Reynolds, Henry, *Aborigines and Settlers 1788-1939*. Melbourne, 1972.
Rowley, C.D., *Outcasts in White Australia*. Canberra, 1970.
  _____ *The Remote Aborigines*. Canberra, 1970.
Shaw, A.G.L., *The Story of Australia*. London, 1967.
South Australian Parliamentary Debates.
South Australian Parliamentary Papers.
Stone, S.H., *Aborigines in White Australia*. Melbourne, 1974.
Tatz, C.M., 'Aboriginal Administration of the Northern Territory of Australia'. (Thesis) ANU, 1964.

Index

293

Sansom, Dr Basil 241–43
Searcy, Alfred 57
Select Committee on Education 181
Select Committee on the Grievances of
  the Yirrkala Aborigines 151,
  163–64
Senate Select Committee on Aborigines
  and Torres Strait Islanders
  1976 195
Senate Standing Committee on the
  Social Environment 139
Sexual relationships 39–41
Sharwood, Judge 212
Shepherdson, Ella 114
Shepherdson, Rev. Harold 113–14,
  145
Singapore trade 55, 68
Smallpox 223–24
Smyth, Captain Henry 70
Snake Bay 240
Social Service benefits 202–4
Social Welfare Ordinance
  1964–67 100
Soils 9–11
Somerville Cottage Homes 132
Somerville, Margaret 130–32
Soong, Dr F. S. 235
Sorcery 50–52
South Alligator River 63
South Australian Act no. 1024,
  1910 79, 83
South Australian Government
  administration 76–77, 79–82, 121,
  209, 223–24
Spears 31
Spencer, Professor W. Baldwin 83–85,
  122, 226
Spillett, Peter G. 72
Spirits 37, 51, 258
Springfield station 81
Stanner, Professor W. E. H. 145
Starke, Mr Justice 211–13
State Grants (Aboriginal Assistance)
  Act 1977 158
Stevens, Dr Frank 195–96
Stevens, Mrs G. D. 176
Stirling, Captain James 70
Stokes, Captain John Lort 74–75
Stokes, Judith 43–45
Strehlow, T. G. H. 213
Stretton, W. G. 83, 226
Stuart Highway 76

Stuart, John McDouall 76
Subincision 39
Sulawesi 24, 55
Summer Institute of Linguistics
  (SIL) 204
Survey of Educational Buildings on
  Aboriginal Communities 188
Swiss Aluminium Australia Ltd 168

Taboos 37, 39, 40, 49
Tasman, Abel Janszoon 64
Tasmanian Aborigines 20
Tatz, Dr Colin 99–100, 199
Territory Parks and Wildlife
  Conservation Ordinance 1976 160
Theology 256–59
Thomson, Dr Donald 89
Thunderman dreaming 171
Timor 55, 69
Tiwi tribe 69
Tobacco 33, 61, 109
Toohey, Mr Justice 160
Topography 8–10
Tor Rock 9, 47
Totems 4, 36, 42–45, 52–53, 150, 206,
  258
Town Councils 100, 110, 117, 138,
  143, 247, 270–71
Trade 34, 61
Traeger pedal radio 228
Traynor, F. 210
Tuberculosis 227, 231
Tuberculosis Act 1945 227
Tukiar 88, 210–12
Turtle Hunters' dreaming 171

Ubar ceremony 46
Umbakumba mission 56–57, 108, 110,
  166, 239–40
United Bible Societies 262
United Church in North Australia
  (UCNA) 116–19, 251–65
Uniting Church of Australia 116–19,
  273
Universal Declaration of Human
  Rights 209
Uranium mining 4, 160–61, 172–78

Viner, Robert Ian 157–59, 204–5, 219
Voting 100, 134

Walang tribe 26, 45
Ward, Mr Justice Richard C. 160

297

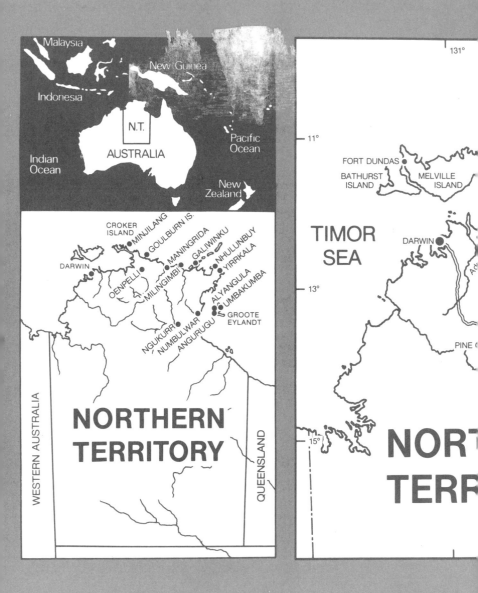

Malaysia

New Guinea

Indonesia

N.T.

Pacific
Ocean

AUSTRALIA

Indian
Ocean

New
Zealand

CROKER
ISLAND

MINJILANG

GOULBURN IS.

DARWIN

OENPELLI

MANINGRIDA

MILINGIMBI

GALIWINKU

NHULUNBUY

YIRRKALA

ALYANGULA

UMBAKUMBA

NGUKURR

NUMBULWAR

ANGURUGU

GROOTE
EYLANDT

WESTERN AUSTRALIA

**NORTHERN
TERRITORY**

QUEENSLAND

131°

11°

FORT DUNDAS

BATHURST
ISLAND

MELVILLE
ISLAND

TIMOR
SEA

DARWIN

Ad

13°

PINE C

15°

NOR

TERR